House Church

SIMPLE, STRATEGIC, SCRIPTURAL

New Testament Reformation Fellowship
Atlanta, Georgia
www.NTRF.org

House Church

SIMPLE, STRATEGIC, SCRIPTURAL

EDITED BY
STEVE ATKERSON

CONTRIBUTORS

BRIAN ANDERSON

BERESFORD JOB

STEVE & SANDRA
ATKERSON

JONATHAN
LINDVALL

STEPHEN DAVID

TIM MELVIN

MIKE INDEST

DAN WALKER

Cover Design by
Navigation Advertising
www.navertise.com

New Testament Reformation Fellowship
Atlanta, Georgia
www.NTRF.org

Steve Atkerson, editor
House Churches: Simple, Strategic, Scriptural
© 2008 by New Testament Reformation Fellowship
ISBN 978-0-9729082-2-1

Published by the New Testament Reformation Fellowship
2752 Evans Dale Circle, Atlanta, GA 30340
www.NTRF.org
Printed in thte United States of America
Cover design by Navigation Advertising

To Sandra, the love of my life.

TABLE OF CONTENTS

INTRODUCTION

A wine bottle is the twenty-first century, dynamic equivalent to a first century wineskin. "No one," Jesus said, "pours new wine into old wineskins. If he does, the wine will burst the skins, and both the wine and the wineskins will be ruined. No, he pours new wine into new wineskins" (Mk 2:22). New wine gives off gas as it ferments. A new wineskin can expand to handle these gases, but an old one cannot. A burst wineskin is not only itself ruined, but its precious contents are lost, spilled to the ground.

Comparing the new wine to new life in Christ, the wineskin could represent the outward, organized expressions of our faith, what we do as God's people when we come together (ecclesiology). A study of church practice is thus much like a study of bottles (or wineskins). Jesus' point in His wineskin illustration was that some behavior is simply inappropriate. So too, some ways of doing church may be inappropriate — harmful even — to the new wine of our lives in Christ.

Wine connoisseurs prefer to enjoy their wine in special wine glasses. The wine in the glass is held up to the light, examined, swirled around, smelled, and finally, tasted. Why is it that wine coinsurers don't pour their wine into the type of cheap plastic cups found in motel rooms? Nothing would change about the wine, yet their enjoyment of it would be diminished. The container makes a difference. Similarly, if we were airy wraiths who floated though life unaffected by our surroundings, where and how we meet as God's people might not matter greatly. Since we are not airy wraths, such things do impact our lives together in Christ, and our individual walks with Christ.

Thus, both the wine and the wineskin, both the precept and the pattern, are important. Without dispute the wineskin exists for the sake of the wine, but without the proper skin the wine spills to the ground and is wasted. It is a false dichotomy to hold to either one without the other. Attention to both is needed.

Readily found in the trash are empty bottles — even those in perfect condition. Yet there is no mystery why they were thrown away. After the liquid is gone, the bottle is considered worthless. Bottles clearly exist for the sake of whatever they contain. Yet each discarded bottle once served a very important purpose: to deliver its contents safely to the end user.

This book is thus about wineskins. What really matters, of course, is the wine itself, not the skin. We are writing to those who already have the new wine. Those who do not have the new wine of life in Jesus may as well throw their theories on church practice into the trash. However, if a church genuinely does have new life in Christ, then a careful study of wineskins is critical to insure that the wine is enjoyed to its fullest.

Suppose the maker of a soft drink attempted to ship the beverage to the consumer packaged inside a plastic cup with an open top. The cola would never make it to the customer. Suppose you tried to drink your morning coffee out of a paper sack. The sack would soon leak. You would both lose your coffee and ruin the sack (and your clothes!). A careful study of containers is necessary so that a suitable vessel is chosen for each job. Without the appropriate vessel, there would be nothing for the consumer to enjoy.

We are persuaded that the best container for the wine of the New Covenant is found in the practice of the early church. Who knew better than the original apostles how best to set up and order churches? The traditions that we advocate are those of the apostles, as found exclusively on the pages of the New Testament. Today's church has not just added to those traditions, it is often doing the exact *opposite*. In our opinion, this is much like drinking wine from a plastic motel room cup.

In *The Innovator's Dilemma*, Harvard scholar and business expert Chris Gonsalves argued that successful new products offer features that customers value, typically because they are cheaper, simpler, smaller or more convenient to use. House churches are cheaper, simpler, smaller and revolutionary. They are, to use Gonsalves' word, "disruptive" to the *status quo*. House churches can be strategic to the disruption of the gates of Hell. House churches can be a strategically disruptive force to the slumbering portions of the church. God, in His providence, has shown us some areas of church practice that we believe have been neglected by the church at large. We are persuaded that a return to the ways of the original apostles could bring a tremendous blessing to the Bride of Christ. Those of us who participated in the writing of this book have enjoyed these blessings for years, and desire very much to see all who belong to Jesus feast at the banquet along with us.

Most importantly, house churches are scriptural. We advocate orthodox, historic, classic Christianity poured into the wineskin of New Testament church practice as established by the apostles and revealed on the pages of the Bible. The traditions of the apostles encompass far more than merely meeting in homes. House churches are just one facet of a multifaceted diamond. Our goal is to be Christ honoring and thoroughly biblical in every area concerning our church life. In the pages that follow, we do argue strongly from Scripture for living-room sized churches, but also for the Lord's Supper as a full meal, church leaders as servants (rather than lords), government by consensus, the right and responsibility of the brothers to make decisions corporately, no clergy-laity distinction, the importance of special teaching times and participatory church meetings. As should be evident from the above, our advocacy of home-based, relational, family-styled church does not mean that we think careful attention to order and organization to be unimportant.

We respectfully present this book to the church universal for consideration. It is the result of both years of study and daily practical experience. This entire study of the church is only a stepping stone to put us in a better position of being all Christ wants us to be as His body of people. May the Lord be pleased to grant all His people an ever deeper knowledge of Himself and His Bride, and greater effectiveness in our service to Him.

Stephen E. Atkerson
March, 2008
Atlanta

Part I
CHURCH MEETINGS

1

APOSTOLIC TRADITIONS — OBSOLETE?

Suppose a newly formed, first century congregation in Alexandria, Egypt, wrote a letter to the twelve apostles in Jerusalem. Imagine that this church consisted of Jewish believers who had heard the gospel on a visit to Jerusalem. Now back home in Egypt, they didn't know how to function as a New Covenant body of believers. So, in their letter was a series of questions about church life:

Dear Apostles . . .

Why is it that we meet together as Jesus' people?

What should we do in our church meetings?

How often should we come together?

Does it matter where we gather?

Should we build a temple, like in Jerusalem, or at least a synagogue building?

What type of church government should we have?

What should we look for in church leaders?

Do we even need leaders?

What is the purpose of the Lord's Supper?

How often should we eat it? (Annually, like Passover?)

Should we eat the Lord's Supper as a true meal or a symbolic ritual?

How do you suppose the Twelve would have answered? Would they have written that each church was free to do whatever it wanted to do? That each fellowship must independently pray and follow the Holy Spirit's leading? That each congregation should be unique and different, free from apostolic influence? Or conversely, might they have replied with very specific instructions for church life? With a particular way of doing things? With a definite agenda? With unmistakable congregational guidelines?

This same issue has faced believers for the past two thousand years. How, exactly, should today's church view New Testament patterns of church practice? As obsolete? Is the practice of the early church merely optional, or is it imperative for us? Are the traditions of the apostles just interesting history or should they constitute some kind of normative church practice?

Apostolic Traditions: Obsolete?

The church's problem has been compounded because the New Testament has almost *nothing* to say by way of direct command concerning church matters. Consequently, it has been common for believers to dismiss New Testament patterns for church practice as optional. For instance, Fee and Stuart, in *How To Read The Bible For All Its Worth*, state: "Our assumption, along with many others, is that unless Scripture explicitly tells us we must do something, what is merely narrated or described can never function in a normative way."[1] No one, for example, would advocate following Jephthah's tragic example in Judges 11:29ff. The question for us is whether or not Scripture explicitly tells us that we must copy the patterns for church practice described in the New Testament.

Most churches still do follow *some* New Testament patterns. Our question is: *Why not follow all of them?* This book argues for consistency. The apostles had a definite and very particular way in which they organized churches. We are convinced that they intended for all congregations to follow these same apostolic traditions, for as long as the church exists.

There are certain things that all true churches focus on, regardless of whether Methodist, Presbyterian, Baptist, Pentecostal, Anglican, or whatever. Oxford University professor of ecclesiastical history, Stanley Greensdale, stated that "the church exists to promote the worship of God, the inner life of the spirit, the evangelization of the world and the molding of society according to the will of God."[2] Our proposal is that the apostles knew the best context in which to achieve these objectives, and purposely patterned such for us in the churches they established.

Holding To Apostolic Traditions Is Logical

In 1 Corinthians 4:16-17, we read that Paul planned to send Timothy to Corinth. Timothy was to remind the Corinthians of Paul's life-style so that they could imitate him. The immediate context concerns Paul's faithfulness in service and his humility as an apostle. Thus Paul wrote, "I urge you to imitate me. For this reason I am sending to you Timothy, my son whom I love, who is faithful in the Lord. He will remind you of my way of life in Christ Jesus, which agrees with what I teach everywhere in every church."

Notice the uniformity of practice reflected in Paul's words. His way of life in Christ was consistent with what he taught everywhere in every church. There was integrity. There were life-style traditions that grew out of Paul's teachings. His belief determined his behavior. His doctrine naturally determined his duty. In similar fashion, *the apostles'*

16

beliefs about the function of the church would surely have affected the way they organized churches (form follows function). Though the direct import of 1 Corinthians 4 is far afield from church practice, to imitate the apostles' ways regarding church life would also seem to be a wise choice for any fellowship.

If anyone truly understood the purpose of the church, surely it was the original apostles. They were hand picked and personally trained by Jesus for three years. After His resurrection, our Lord appeared to them over a forty day period (Ac 1:3). Finally, Jesus sent the Holy Spirit to teach them things He had not taught them before (Jn 14-16). Thus, whatever Jesus had taught His apostles about the church was naturally reflected in the way they subsequently set up and organized churches.

In Titus 1:5, a passage that deals directly with church practice, Paul wrote, "The reason I left you in Crete was that you might straighten out what was left unfinished." Titus 1 concerns the appointment of qualified elders in every city. It is evident from this passage that the apostles did indeed have a definite way they wanted certain things done regarding the church. It was not left up to each individual assembly to find its own way of doing things. There was obviously some kind of order, pattern, or tradition that was followed in organizing the churches. Similarly, in 1 Corinthians 11:34 (a passage about the practice of the Lord's Supper, another church life topic), Paul wrote, "The rest I will *set in order* when I come" (KJV, italics mine).

Southern Baptist theologian J. L. Dagg astutely wrote in 1858 that the apostles "have taught us by example how to organize and govern churches. We have no right to reject their instruction and captiously insist that nothing but positive command shall bind us. Instead of choosing to walk in a way of our own devising, we should take pleasure to walk in the footsteps of those holy men from whom we have received the word of life . . . respect for the Spirit by which they were led should induce us to prefer their modes of organization and government to such as our inferior wisdom might suggest."[3]

HOLDING TO APOSTOLIC TRADITIONS IS PRAISEWORTHY

In 1 Corinthians 10:31-11:1, Paul again urged the Corinthians, "Follow my example, as I follow the example of Christ." The immediate context concerns seeking the good of others so as to glorify God and bring them to salvation (10:31 - 11:1). The word "follow" (1Co 11:1) is from *mimatai,* the basis for "mimic." Paul wanted the Corinthian believers to imitate him in that regard. Apparently they were doing well in imitating him in other matters also, since Paul stated in the very next verse, "I praise you because you remember me in everything, and hold firmly to the traditions, just as I delivered them to you" (11:2, NASV).

What is a tradition? The regular Greek word for "teaching" is *didaskalia* (the basis for "didactic"), but significantly that is not the word used here. Instead, *paradosis* (tradition) is used. Gordon Fee pointed out that although *paradosis* was a technical term in Judaism for oral transmission of religious instruction, in this context in almost certainly does not refer to teachings, but rather to religious traditions regarding worship.[4] The Greek word fundamentally means, "that which is passed on."[5] That which was passed on could have been anything: custom, teaching, or even a person (in the sense of a betrayal or arrest).[6] This same Greek word (in verb form) is used in 1 Corinthians 11:23 with regard to the theology and practice of the Lord's Supper (that it was passed on). In English usage, a tradition is generally thought of as a custom or a certain way of doing things. It is an inherited pattern of thought or action. A popular definition might be, "things people *do* on a regular basis." A tradition is thus something that is passed on or handed down (either by example or explicit teaching). Here in 1 Corinthians 11, we see an apostle praising a church for holding to his traditions regarding worship.

Consider the word "everything" as Paul used it in 1 Corinthians 11:2. It means "all that exists," or at least, "all that pertains to the subject." When Paul wrote "everything" (1Co 11:2), what subjects did he have in mind? His use of the word "everything" certainly suggests that Paul's intended application was larger than just the exhortation found in 1 Corinthians 10:31-11:1 (evangelism). Might "everything" have also included church order? Indeed it did. Paul's praise in 11:2 signals the beginning of a new topic: head coverings (11:3-16). This new subject is clearly in the realm of church practice. (It is beyond the scope of this chapter to deal with the correct application of this passage on head coverings, but whatever was appropriate for the church then is still true for us today).

What do the words "just as" (11:2) indicate about the extent of their compliance with Paul's traditions? They adhered to every iota; it was sort of a photocopy effect! They were not willy-nilly about it. Paul praised them for holding to his traditions exactly as he had passed them on to them. The apostles evidently designed for churches to precisely mimic at least *some* of the traditions they established (here, head coverings). Yet the word "traditions" (11:2) is in the plural. Paul apparently had in mind more than the one tradition of head coverings.[7] Should we shut up our observance to this one tradition only, or should we follow *all* the patterns for church organization that can be observed on the pages of the New Testament?

Mosaic legislation was paradigmatic in nature. It was case law. Only a few, sample, legal examples were recorded by Moses. The believer was expected to apply those case studies to other areas of life not specifically mentioned. For instance, the corners of fields were to be left unharvested for the poor to gather and eat. Nothing was said about olive groves. Does this mean that a wheat farmer alone was burdened with feeding the poor, but that the man with an olive grove could harvest every last olive? Certainly not. Every farmer, regardless of the crop, was to leave a similar portion of his harvest to meet the needs of the poor. Similarly, we argue that adherence to apostolic tradition is paradigmatic in nature. If we observe that the apostles were pleased when churches followed specific traditions (such as regarding head coverings), then we are expected to apply that example to other patterns we see modeled by the apostles in their establishment of churches.

An interesting paradox can be observed about tradition. The same word (*paradosis*) used by Paul in 1 Corinthians 11:2 was also used by Jesus in Matthew 15:1-3. Jesus said to the Pharisees, "Why do you break the command of God for the sake of your tradition?" Jesus blasted the tradition of the Pharisees, but Paul blessed the Corinthians for following the traditions of an apostle. Pharisaic tradition broke the command of God. Apostolic tradition, however, is consistent with the commands of Jesus. Holding to the traditions of the apostles is thus praiseworthy, as proven by Paul's praise for the Corinthians (11:2). We must be careful not to develop our own church traditions that might actually inhibit our ability to obey the commands of our Lord. Care must also be taken not to develop traditions that replace the original traditions of the apostles.

HOLDING TO APOSTOLIC TRADITIONS IS TO BE Universal

Paul quieted those inclined to be contentious about head coverings by appealing to the universal practice of all the other churches: "If anyone wants to be contentious about this, we have no other practice — nor do the churches of God" (1Co 11:16). This final statement was designed to win over the contentious people and settle any argument. The point is that Paul expected all the churches to be doing the same thing. Just to realize that one was different was argument enough to silence opposition. Obviously, prior emphasis had been given to certain practices that were *supposed to be done the same way, everywhere.*

Thus, 1 Corinthians 11:16 indicates a uniformity of practice in all New Testament churches.

In 1 Corinthians 14:33b-34 (another passage about church practice), Paul mentioned something else that was to be true universally: "As in *all the congregations* of the saints, women should remain silent in the *churches*" (italics mine). Regardless of the correct application of this verse, notice how Paul again appealed to a universal pattern that existed in all the churches as a basis for obedience.

Finally, note how Paul chided the Corinthians in 1 Corinthians 14:36, "Did the word of God originate with you? Or are you the only people it has reached?" The obvious answer to both questions is *no*. This further indicates a uniformity of practice among New Testament churches. The Corinthians were tempted to do something differently from what all the other churches were doing. Evidently all the churches were expected to follow the same patterns in their church meetings. These two questions were designed to keep the Corinthians in line with the practice of all the other churches. Holding to apostolic traditions (New Testament church patterns) was to be universal in the first century and, we argue, today as well.

Chinese house church pioneer Watchman Nee, in *The Church And The Work: Rethinking The Work*, wrote, "Acts is the 'genesis' of the church's history, and the Church in the time of Paul is the 'genesis' of the Spirit's work . . . We must return to 'the beginning.' Only what God has set forth as our example in the beginning is the eternal Will of God. It is the Divine standard and our pattern for all time . . . God has revealed His Will, not only by giving orders, but by having certain things done in His church, so that in the ages to come others might simply look at the pattern and know His will."[8]

HOLDING TO APOSTOLIC TRADITIONS BRINGS GOD'S PEACEFUL PRESENCE

"Rejoice in the Lord always, I will say it again: Rejoice! Let your gentleness be evident to all. The Lord is near. Do not be anxious about anything, but in everything, by prayer and petition, with thanksgiving, present your requests to God. And the peace of God, which transcends all understanding, will guard your hearts and your minds in Christ Jesus" (Phlp 4:4-7). The main point of Philippians 4:4-7 is that by rejoicing in the Lord we can gain God's peace, regardless of circumstances.

In the next paragraph (Php 4:8-9), the church at Philippi was given the recipe for how to have the God of Peace be with them. By extension, this can be true for our churches as well. Paul wrote, "Finally, brothers, whatever is true, whatever is noble, whatever is right, whatever is pure, whatever is lovely, whatever is admirable - if anything is excellent or praiseworthy - think about such things. Whatever you have learned or received or heard from me, or seen in me - put into practice. And the God of peace will be with you."

The Philippians were instructed to put into practice *whatever* they learned, received, heard from Paul, or saw in Paul (Phlp 4:9). The primary application in context concerned imitating Christ's humility, putting others first, and rejoicing in the Lord. By extension, could this *whatever* not also include the way we see in the New Testament that Paul organized churches? It is clear from Scripture how the apostles set up the early church. To bypass apostolic tradition in this area may be to also bypass some of God's blessing. Could it be that those fellowships which also follow the apostle's *church* practice may enjoy even more of God's peaceful presence?

HOLDING TO APOSTOLIC TRADITIONS IS COMMANDED

In 2 Thessalonians 2:15, the Thessalonian church was instructed to "stand firm and hold to the traditions which you were taught, whether by word of mouth or by letter from us" (NASV). Here, the Thessalonians were specifically commanded to hold to the traditions (*paradosis*) of the apostles, whether received orally or in writing. The Twelve are not here today to teach us in person, by word of mouth, what to do. However, we do have letters that record their traditions (the New Testament). The overall context of 2 Thessalonians 2 refers to end-time events, not church practice. Yet the word "traditions" (2:15) is in the plural; the author had more in view than merely his traditional teaching about the second coming. Would it not also apply in principle to his traditions regarding church order, as patterned in the New Testament?

Interestingly, rather than "traditions," the NIV renders this "teachings." This may be because a tradition (*paradosis*) can include a teaching (*didaskalia*), and the immediate context concerned the apostles' oral tradition about end-times (2Th 2:1-12). However, the KJV, ASV, RSV, and NASV all translate it as "traditions," which is also a valid translation of *paradosis*. The import of the various "traditions" passages such as this must be grappled with. Many believers think that while apostolic traditions may be interesting, following them is never commanded. Yet what does 2 Thessalonians 2:15 indicate? Is adherence to apostolic traditions actually commanded or merely suggested? Significantly, it is clearly commanded. It is not just apostolic teachings to which we are to adhere, but also apostolic traditions (as revealed exclusively on the pages of Scripture). We are to follow the traditions of the apostles, not only in their theology, but also in their practice.

A similar attitude toward traditions is expressed in 2 Thessalonians 3:6-7a, "Keep away from every brother who is idle and does not live according to the tradition you received from us. For you yourselves know how you ought to follow our example." The specific context here refers to gainful employment versus being idle and lazy. In context, this tradition refers to a practice more so than a doctrine. The apostles clearly wanted the churches to follow their traditions (of both theology and practice). Should we limit those Biblical traditions that we follow *only* to eschatology and work habits?

Roger Williams, founder of Rhode Island and of the first Baptist church in the Americas (1600s), is another example of a Christian leader who believed that churches should strive to follow as near as possible New Testament church forms and ordinances.[9] This belief led Williams to found the Rhode Island colony on the New Testament pattern of a separation between church and state.

Consistency

What can be concluded about God's interest in your church adhering to New Testament patterns for church practice? It seems to us that whatever was normative church practice for all the churches in the New Testament should be normative practice for churches today. Perhaps these patterns of church practice are part of what gave the early church the dynamic that today's church has been missing for so long.

If the Bible directly commands something, then we obviously ought to follow that command. The fact is that the Bible commands adherence to the *traditions* of the apostles (2Th 2:15). The real question thus is not, "Must we do things the way they were done in the New Testament?" Rather, the question is: "Why would we want to do things any other way?!"

What are some obvious, biblical, apostolic traditions for church practice that should still be followed by the church today? (Remember as you read over these that there is general consensus in scholarly circles, regardless of denomination, as to how the early church functioned).

1 *The Lord's Supper celebrated as a full fellowship meal (1Co 11:17-34), partaken of weekly (Ac 20:7, 1Co 11:17-22), as the main reason for gathering each week (Ac 20:7, 1Co 11:33).*

2 *Participatory church meetings (1Co 14:26, 37, Heb 10:24-25), with mutual edification, encouragement and fellowship as the*

goals of the assembly (Ac 2:42, 1Co 14:3-5, 12, 26, Heb 10:24-25).

3   Church government by consensus: elder led more so than elder ruled churches (Lk 22:24-27, 1Pe 5:1-4). Further, church elder-ship is to be male, plural, non-hierarchical, homegrown, servant leadership (1Ti 3:1-7).

4. Home sized churches, i.e., smaller congregations (Ro 16:5, Col 4:15, Phlm 2), that are one in attitude with all other believers and congregations. There is nothing magic about meeting in a home per se; it's what happens there that matters, and it happens best in a smaller church. The New Testament norm is many micro churches rather than a few mega churches.

5. Meeting regularly on the Lord's Day (Mt 28:1-7, Ac 20:7, 1Co 16:1-4, Re 1:9-11), the first day of the week, in honor of Jesus' resurrection.

6. Children present with their parents in the church meeting (Mt 19:13-15, Lk 2:41-50, Ac 21:5, Ep 6:1-3, Col 4:16). Thus, churches that strengthen and unite families, not further divide them.

7. A community-based church that can easily experience daily fel-lowship (Ac 2:42-47).

8. Church reproduction and equipping through the ministry of itin-erant church workers such as apostles, pastor-teachers, or evan-gelists (Ep 4:11-13). Such ministers may well have large ministry meetings that support, but do not supplant, the regular, partici-patory meetings of the local church.

9. Regular ministry meetings specifically devoted to the in-depth teaching of the scriptures (Ac 2:42, 15:32, 20:7, Ro 12:7, 1Ti 5:17).

What we argue for here is consistency. Most churches already follow some of these patterns, but not all. Again we wonder *why not?* The burden of explanation ought to fall on those who deviate from the New Testament pattern, not on those who desire to follow it. This con-sistency is especially important since the apostles evidently expected for all churches to follow their traditions just as they were handed down (1Co 11:2).

Apostolic Traditions: Obsolete?

Lifelessness. Critical to any outworking of church life is first having an inner life to work out! Jesus came that we might have life, and have it abundantly (Jn 10:10). A wine bottle is nearly worthless without wine in it. Similarly, technically correct church practice without the wine of the Spirit is a hollow shell. It is dry, seasoned wood, all stacked up, with no fire. Jesus is the Vine, we are the branches. Apart from Jesus we can no nothing (Jn 15:5). It is folly to give attention to outward perfection while neglecting that which is vital — a daily walk with the Risen Lord. Jesus is the reality; apostolic church practice is the application of that reality.

License. A temptation for those who truly possess the inner reality of life in Jesus is to treat its outward expression as a matter of liberty. Having the greater (the wine), they feel that they themselves are competent to decide in lesser matters (the wineskin). They believe they have a license from the Spirit to do with the outward form whatever they please. To be bound by the ways of the apostles is seen as mindless aping. Once a person is truly centered in Christ, he is supposedly free to make his own applications. However, no less a spiritual authority than Jesus Himself warned that pouring wine into the wrong container could lead to the loss of the wine (Mt 9:17). Do we really know better than the apostles how to organize churches? Specifically with reference to church practice, Paul admonished, "If anyone thinks he is a prophet or spiritually gifted, let him acknowledge that what I am writing to you is the Lord's command" (1Co 14:37).

Occasionally believers will overreacted to the stifling bureaucracy of some conventional churches, and become anarchists. In their idealism, they become anti-organizational. They feel that the visible and physical inevitably work against the invisible and spiritual. This is a false dichotomy. It is similar in error to those who claimed that Jesus could not be sinless since he was born of flesh, or that if sinless He could not actually have been incarnate. The New Testament church was quite organized, and faithfulness to our Lord's requirements will necessitate our churches being organized as well.

Legalism. Are there justified exceptions to following New Testament patterns? Yes. Just as the Sabbath was made for man, and not man for the Sabbath (Mk 2:27), so too people are more important than rigid adherence to New Testament patterns. In qualifying these exceptions, London house church pastor Beresford Job cautions, "We must make sure that we don't let deviations from the norm, done because of extenuating circumstances, actually become the norm. Take water baptism for example. Although its actual mode isn't anywhere commanded, we know from the way the early church did it (apostolic tradition again) that it was done upon conversion by immersion. (Immersion is also what the actual word *baptizo* means). In order for it to be based on the New Testament pattern, a person's baptism should be after his profession of faith by full submersion under water. But suppose a bedridden quadriplegic comes to the Lord. Baptism by immersion would clearly be out of the question. To come up with another, more appropriate, mode of baptism would arguably be quite permissible. Although technically out of step with the example of Scripture, it would still be fully submitted in intention and spirit. Yet none of what I have just said could possibly apply to the baptism of an able bodied person — the normal mode would have to be employed in order for things to be as the Lord wants."

Church renewal advocate Darryl Erkel has appropriately pointed out the "danger of making distinctive New Testament patterns a form of legalism wherein we begin to look down or distance ourselves from our fellow brothers because they don't quite do it the way that we think it should be done. We should always be careful to not give the impression to others that their church is false or that God can't use their church because they're not following apostolic patterns as closely as we are. That is nothing but sheer pride. On the other hand, we ought to look for opportunities to respectfully and tactfully demonstrate that there is a better way — one which is more conducive to the spiritual growth of God's people — for the function of the New Testament church is best carried out by the New Testament form of the church!"

If the Bible is silent about something — if there is neither command nor pattern to follow — then we have the freedom to do whatever suits us (following the leading of the Holy Spirit). We do not advocate a negative hermeneutic, insisting that if a practice is not found in the Bible, then we can't do it. Rather, we promote a normative hermeneutic, insisting that we should hold to those practices that clearly were normative for the early church. Matters of silence are matters of freedom.

The Roman world is gone forever. There is a big difference between holding to apostolic tradition versus mindlessly copying everything seen in the New Testament (wearing sandals and togas, writing on parchment, studying by oil lamps, etc.). The key is to focus in on New Testament church practice. We must also beware of making patterns out of things that are not patterns in the New Testament. For instance, the Christian communalism of Acts 4 was a one time event for a single church. It is an option for believers of any age, but it is neither a command nor a scriptural pattern.

Apostolic Traditions: Obsolete?

- God directs by biblical pattern (tradition) as well as by biblical precept (teaching).
- The patterns for church practice found in the New Testament are generally to be followed by the church of all ages.
- Apostolic tradition (as found only in the Bible) is perfectly consistent with apostolic teaching.
- The most important traditions for New Testament life church are the celebration of the Lord's Supper weekly as a full fellowship meal (1Co 11), regular participatory church meetings (1Co 14), church government by consensus (elder led more so than elder ruled, Lk 22:24ff), and living room sized churches (Ro 16:5).
- Following New Testament patterns does not mean blindly attempting to recreate Roman culture (like wearing togas, writing on parchment, lighting by oil lamps, etc.).   The issue here is church practice.   There should be obvious reasons behind the practices being followed.
- Following New Testament patterns does not mean every church will be exactly alike.   Certainly there will be similarity in the basics, but there is also freedom within the boundaries of the form.
- Biblical house churches are not nearly so program or building oriented as are many conventional churches.   Because of this, some have mistakenly concluded that biblically-based house churches are unorganized.   Faithfulness to our Lord and His Word necessarily results in a church that follows God's complete pattern for His church.   Home churches may not be institutional, but they are to be organized.   Following the traditions laid down by the apostles means that house churches are to have definite leaders, regular and orderly meetings, solid theology proper, active church discipline, and weekly Lord's Supper celebrations.
- Without Christ at the center of things, these patterns become legalism and death, a hollow form, an empty shell (Jn 15:5).   We need the proper wine skin, but more importantly we need the wine.   Both have their place.   Either one without the other is problematic (Lk 5:36-38).

Remember the earlier quote by Professors Fee and Stuart that what is merely narrated or described can never function in a normative way?   In the second edition of their book, they changed their statement somewhat.   It now reads, *"Unless Scripture explicitly tells us we must do something, what is only narrated or described does not function in a normative way — unless it can be demonstrated on other grounds*

that the author intended it to function in this way."[10] We have attempted to demonstrate that the apostles did indeed design for churches
to follow the patterns they laid down for church order.

Why is that the majority of church leaders have not adopted the
practice of the early church? Is it because they have studied the passages presented here and rejected our applications? Our own experience has been that very little attention is paid in seminary to the role that
apostolic traditions should play. We suspect that many pastors have
simply adopted the historical traditions inherited from their denomination. Many churches today are firmly entrenched in cultural church
traditions that were developed after the close of the apostolic era. In
such cases, there is danger of nullifying the inspired tradition of the
apostles for the sake of more modern tradition (Mt 15:1-3).

We resonate with the sentiments of Jim Elliot, missionary and martyr, who wrote, "The pivot point hangs on whether or not God has revealed a universal pattern for the church in the New Testament. If He
has not, then anything will do so long as it works. But I am convinced
that nothing so dear to the heart of Christ as His Bride should be left
without explicit instructions as to her corporate conduct. I am further
convinced that the 20th century has in no way simulated this pattern in
its method of 'churching' a community . . . it is incumbent upon me, if
God has a pattern for the church, to find and establish that pattern, at all
costs."[11]

— Steve Atkerson

NOTES

[1] Gordon Fee & Douglas Stuart, *How To Read The Bible For All Its
Worth,* 1st ed. (Grand Rapids, MI: Zondervan, 1982), 97.

[2] Stanley Lawrence Greensdale, "Early Christian Church,"
Encyclopaedia Britannica, ed. Warren Preece, Vol. 7 (Chicago:
William Benton, Publisher, 1973), 844.

[3] J.L. Dagg, *Manual of Theology: A Treatise on Church Order*
(Harrisonburg, VA: Gano Books, 1990*)*, 84-86.

[4] Gordon Fee, *New International Commentary on the New Testament, The First Epistle to The Corinthians* (Grand Rapids, MI:
Wm. B. Eerdmans Publishing Co., 1987), 499.

[5] Fritz Rienecker, Linguistic Key to the Greek New Testament (Grand
Rapids, MI: Zondervan Publishing House, 1980), 423.

[6] Bauer, Arndt, Gingrich & Danker, A Greek-English Lexicon of the
New Testament (Chicago: University of Chicago Press, 1979),
615.

[7] Fee, 500.

Apostolic Traditions: Obsolete?

[8] Watchman Nee, *The Normal Christian Church Life* (Colorado Springs, CO: International Students Press, 1969), 8-9.

[9] Edwin Gaustad, *Liberty of Conscience: Roger Williams In America* (Grand Rapids, MI: Wm. B. Eerdmans Publishing Co.), 106.

[10] Fee & Stuart, 2nd Ed., 106.

[11] Elizabeth Elliot, *Shadow of The Almighty: Life and Testimony of Jim Elliot* (San Francisco, CA: Harper & Row, 1989), 138-139.

DISCUSSION QUESTIONS

1. Suppose it were possible to write to the original apostles, asking them about church life. Do you suppose they would answer back that they expected you to follow their examples regarding church practice, or would they have encouraged you to follow a way of your own devising? Explain.

2. How can the axiom *form follows function* be applied to the way that the apostles first set up and organized churches?

3. What passages in the New Testament indicate whether there was a basic uniformity of practice in all New Testament churches or whether each was unique and different?

4. Jesus criticized the Pharisees for holding to their traditions (Mt 15), but Paul praised the Corinthians for holding to his traditions (1Co 11). Why the difference?

5. Why is it important to make a distinction between apostolic tradition, as found within the New Testament, and the later tradition of the church fathers, as found in history? Which should be given preference? Why?

6. Mosaic law was paradigmatic in nature. How would the paradigmatic principle apply to commands in the New Testament to follow specific apostolic traditions (2Th 2:15, 3:6)?

7. How might Philippians 4:9 apply today with respect to the way that Paul organized churches?

8. What gave the apostles authority to establish patterns that all churches are obliged to follow? Jn 13:20, 15:20, Ac 1:1-3, 2:42.

9. What is the difference between holding to apostolic traditions and mindlessly copying everything seen in the New Testament (wearing sandals, writing on parchment, studying by oil lamps, dressing in togas, etc.)?

10. Jesus washed His disciples' feet and the Jerusalem church practiced communalism. How can we determine what is and is not intended to be an apostolic tradition?

11. What are some of the apostolic traditions for church practice that are often neglected today?

12. What should we make of the fact that there is general scholarly consensus regarding the actual practice of the early church?

13. How, exactly, should today's church view New Testament patterns of church practice? Are the traditions of the apostles just interesting history or should they constitute some kind of normative church practice?

14. Some think it folly to try to recreate the "primitive" first-century church, since it was far from perfect. God expected His church to mature, to grow up, beyond the infancy state, they say. As much as anything, early believers are seen as examples of how *not* to function as a church. Besides, it is argued, it is impossible to behave exactly like the first-century church since we no longer have the original apostles with us. How would you respond to this argument?

15. Why is historical church tradition often given preference over New Testament historical tradition?

16. Does the church you fellowship with give careful attention to New Testament patterns, ignore them almost totally, or select cafeteria style which apostolic examples will be followed? How do you feel about this?

Note: NTRF also offers a teacher's resource to help lead a discussion of New Testament church life. Request *The Practice of The Early Church: A Theological Workbook (Leader's Guide)* from www.NTRF.org.

How Sweet And Awful Is The Place

How sweet and awful is the place
With Christ within the doors,
While everlasting love displays
The choicest of her stores!

Here ev'ry bowel of our God
With soft compassion rolls;
Here peace and pardon bought with blood
Is food for dying souls.

While all our hearts and all our songs
Join to admire the feast,
Each of us cry, with thankful tongues,
Lord, why was I a guest?

Why was I made to hear Thy voice,
And enter while there's room;
When thousands make a wretched choice,
And rather starve than come?

'Twas the same love that spread the feast
That sweetly forced us in
Else we had still refused to taste,
And perished in our sin.

Pity the nations, O our God!
Constrain the earth to come;
Send Thy victorious Word abroad,
And bring the strangers home.

We long to see Thy churches full,
That all the chosen race
May with one voice, and heart, and soul,
Sing Thy redeeming grace.

— Isaac Watts, 1707

2

THE LORD'S SUPPER — FEAST OR FAMINE?

The meal is potluck, or as we jokingly say, "pot-providence." Everyone brings food to share with everyone else. When the weather is nice, all the food is placed on a long folding table outside. A chest full of ice sits beside the drink table. Kids run wildly around. They are having so much fun that they must be rounded up by parents and encouraged to eat. After a prayer of thanksgiving is offered, people line up, talking and laughing as they load their plates with food. In the middle of all the food sits a single loaf of bread next to a large container of the fruit of the vine. Each believer partakes of the bread and juice/wine while going through the serving line.

The smaller kids are encouraged to occupy one of the few places at a table to eat. (They sure can be messy!). Chairs for adults (there are not enough for everyone) are clustered in circles, mainly occupied by the women, who eat while discussing home schooling, child training, sewing, an upcoming church social, the new church we hope to start, etc. Most of the men stand to eat, balancing their plates on top of their cups, grouped into small clusters and solving the world's problems or pondering some interesting topic of theology. The atmosphere is not unlike that of a wedding banquet. It is a great time of fellowship, encouragement, edification, friendship, caring, catching-up, praying, exhorting, and maturing. The reason for the event? In case you did not recognize it, this is the Lord's Supper, New Testament style!

Foreign though it may seem to the contemporary church, the first-century church enjoyed the Lord's Supper as a banquet that foreshadowed the Marriage Supper of the Lamb. It was not until after the close of the New Testament era that the Lord's Supper was altered from its pristine form. If this was indeed the practice of the early church, should we not follow their example?

ITS FORM AND FOCUS: A FEAST & THE FUTURE

The very first Lord's Supper is also called the Last Supper, because it was the last meal Jesus shared with his disciples before His crucifixion. The occasion for the meal was the Passover. At this Passover Feast, Jesus and His disciples reclined at a table that would have been heaped with food (Ex 12, De 16). Jewish tradition tells us that this meal typically lasted for hours. During the course of the meal ("*while they were eating,*" Mt 26:26), Jesus took a loaf of bread and compared it to his body. He had *already* taken up a cup and had them all drink from it. Later, "*after* the supper" (Lk 22:20), Jesus took the cup again and compared it to his blood, which was soon to be poured out for our sins. Thus, the bread and wine of the Lord's Supper were introduced in the context of a full meal, specifically, the Passover feast.

Would the Twelve have somehow concluded that the newly instituted Lord's Supper was *not* to be a true meal? Or would they naturally have assumed it to be a feast similar to the Passover?

According to one Greek scholar, "The Passover celebrated two events, the deliverance from Egypt and the anticipated coming Messianic deliverance."[1] Soon after that Last Supper, Jesus became the ultimate sacrificial Passover Lamb, suffering on the cross to deliver His people from their sins. Jesus keenly desired to eat that last Passover with His disciples, saying that He would "not eat it again until it finds fulfillment in the kingdom of God" (Lk 22:16). Note that Jesus looked forward to a time when He could eat the Passover again in the kingdom of God. Many believe that the "fulfillment" (Lk 22:16) of this was later written about by John in Revelation 19:7-9. There, John recorded an angel declaring, "Blessed are those who are invited to the wedding supper of the Lamb!" Thus, the Last Supper and all Lord's Suppers look forward to a fulfillment in the wedding supper of the Lamb. What better way to typify a banquet than with a banquet? Celebrating the Lord's Supper weekly as a full fellowship meal is like rehearsal dinner before a wedding. No less an authority than the *Encyclopaedia Britannica* declared that "EARLY CHRISTIANITY REGARDED THIS INSTITUTION AS A MANDATE . . . LEARNING TO KNOW, EVEN IN THIS PRESENT LIFE, THE JOYS OF THE HEAVENLY BANQUET THAT WAS TO COME IN THE KINGDOM OF GOD . . . the past, the present, and the future came together in the Eucharist."[2]

His future wedding banquet was much on our Lord's mind that particular Passover evening. Jesus first mentioned it at the beginning of the Passover feast ("I will not eat it again until it finds fulfillment in the kingdom of God," Lk 22:16). He mentioned it again when passing the cup, saying, "I will not drink again of the fruit of the vine until the kingdom of God comes" (Lk 22:18). Then, after the supper, He referred to the banquet yet again, saying, "I confer on you a kingdom . . . so that you may eat and drink at my table in my kingdom " (Lk 22:29-30). R.P. Martin, Professor of New Testament at Fuller Theological Seminary, wrote that there are "eschatological overtones" to the Lord's Supper "with a forward look to the advent in glory."[3]

Whereas modern Gentiles associate heaven with clouds and harps, first century Jews thought of heaven as a time of feasting at Messiah's table. This idea of eating and drinking at the Messiah's table was common imagery in Jewish thought during the first century. For instance, a Jewish leader once said to Jesus, "Blessed is the man who will eat at the feast in the kingdom of God" (Lk 14:15). Jesus Himself said that "many will come from the east and the west, and will take their places at the feast with Abraham, Isaac and Jacob in the kingdom of heaven" (Mt 8:11). This picture of heaven as dining in God's presence may have developed from the Sinai experience. The elders of Israel went with Moses up to the top of the mountain where "they saw God, and they ate and drank" (Ex 24:11). Significantly, Moses noted that "God did not raise his hand against these leaders of the Israelites."

This eating that is associated with the coming of Christ's kingdom may also be reflected in the model prayer suggested by Jesus in Luke 11. In reference to the kingdom, Jesus taught us to pray, "Thy kingdom come" (11:2, KJV). The very next request is "Give us each day our daily bread" (11:3, NIV). However, the Greek underlying Luke 11:3 is difficult to translate. Literally, it reads something akin to, "the bread of us belonging to the coming day give us today." Thus the NASV marginal note reads, "bread for the coming day." Linking together both 11:2 and 11:3, Jesus may well have been teaching us to ask that the bread of the coming Messianic banquet be given to us today. That is, "Let your kingdom come — Let the feast begin today!" Athanasius explained it as "the bread of the world to come."[4]

Obviously, major changes came with the transition from Old Covenant to New, and from the Passover Feast to the Lord's Supper. The Passover was an annual event. The Lord's Supper was celebrated weekly. Passover regulations necessitated lamb and bitter herbs. No such dietary requirements bind the Lord's Supper — indeed, the Lord Jesus is our Passover Lamb! Jesus added the fruit of the vine as an essential part of the Supper. Moses said nothing about wine for the Passover. Yet little of what Jesus had to say about such foundational changes was recorded in the Gospels. It was left to His apostles to more fully explain and model Jesus' teachings, and this they did in the epistles. The writings of the Apostles are, in essence, commentaries on the teachings of Jesus as found in the Gospel accounts. Among the changes from Passover to Lord's Supper, some might argue that Jesus orally instructed the apostles to do away with the meal, keeping only a token sip and bread crumb. Since Jesus said that He would not eat of it again until its future consummation, could it not be argued that the church also should wait for Jesus to return before eating it again? The answer to this would be found in the subsequent practice and teachings of the apostles.

The most extensive treatment of the Lord's Supper is found in chapters ten and eleven of 1 Corinthians. The deep divisions of the Corinthian believers resulted in their Lord's Supper meetings doing more harm than good (11:17-18). They were partaking of the Supper in an "unworthy manner" (11:27). The wealthier people among them, perhaps not wanting to eat with the lower social classes, evidently came to the gathering so early and remained there so long that some became drunk. Making matters worse, by the time that the working-class believers arrived, delayed perhaps by employment constraints, all the food had been consumed. The poor went home hungry (11:21-22). Some of the Corinthians failed to recognize the Lord's Supper as a sacred, covenant meal (11:23-32). (Chinese believers today call it the "Holy Meal"). It is the sign of the New Covenant.

The abuses were so serious that what was supposed to be the *Lord's* Supper had instead become their *own* supper (11:21, NASV). If merely eating their own supper were the entire objective, then private dining at home would do. Thus Paul asked, "Don't you have homes to eat and drink in?" Their sinful selfishness absolutely betrayed the very essence of what the Lord's Supper is all about.

From the nature of their abuse, it is evident that the Corinthian church regularly partook of the Lord's Supper as a full meal. In contrast, very few people in modern churches would ever come to a typical Lord's Supper service expecting to have physical hunger satisfied. Nor could they possibly get drunk from drinking a thimble-sized cup of wine. Keep in mind that Paul wrote to the Corinthian church some twenty years after Jesus turned His Last Supper into our Lord's Supper. Just as the Last Supper was a full meal, so too the Corinthians understood the Lord's Supper to be a true meal. Where would they have gotten the idea of celebrating the Lord's Supper as a true banquet if not from the apostles themselves?

Some have suggested that Jesus, the apostles, and the early church did indeed celebrate the Lord's Supper as a full meal, but that its abuses in Corinth caused Paul to put an end to it. For instance, the original commentary found in the Geneva Bible of 1599 states, "The Apostle thinketh it good to take away the love feasts, for their abuse, although they had been a long time, and with commendation used in Churches, and were appointed and instituted by the Apostles."[5] To this we wonder, can one apostle single-handedly overturn something that was established by the Lord Himself and practiced by all the other apostles and churches? Indeed, would he even if he could?

The inspired solution to the Corinthian abuse of the Supper was not that the church cease eating it as a full meal. Instead, Paul wrote, "when you come together to eat, wait for each other." Only those so famished or undisciplined or selfish that they could not wait for the others are instructed to "eat at home" (1Co 11:34). C.K. Barrett cautioned, "On the surface this seems to imply that ordinary non-cultic eating and drinking should be done at home . . . But Paul's point is that, if the rich wish to eat and drink on their own, enjoying better food than their poorer brothers, they should do this at home; if they cannot wait for others (verse 33), if they must indulge to excess, they can at least keep the church's common meal free from practices that can only bring discredit upon it . . . Paul simply means that those who are so hungry that they cannot wait for their brothers should satisfy their hunger before they leave home, in order that decency and order may prevail in the assembly."[6]

Additionally, the word behind "supper" (1Co 11:20), *deipnon*, fundamentally means "dinner, the main meal toward evening, a banquet." Arguably, it never refers to anything less than a full meal, such as an appetizer, snack or *hors d'oeuvres*. What is the possibility that the authors of the New Testament would use *deipnon* to refer to the Lord's "Supper" if it were not supposed to be a full meal? The Lord's Supper has numerous forward looking aspects to it. As a full meal, it prefigures the feast of the coming kingdom, the marriage supper of the Lamb.

The opinion of most Bible scholars is clearly weighted toward the conclusion that the Lord's Supper was originally eaten as a full meal. For example, British New Testament scholar Donald Guthrie stated that the apostle Paul "sets the Lord's supper in the context of the fellowship meal."[7]

Gordon Fee, Professor Emeritus of Regent College, pointed out "the nearly universal phenomenon of cultic meals as a part of worship in antiquity" and "the fact that in the early church the Lord's Supper was most likely eaten as, or in conjunction with, such a meal." Fee further noted that, "from the beginning the *Last* Supper was for Christians not an annual Christian Passover, but a regularly repeated meal in 'honor of the Lord,' hence the *Lord's* Supper."[8]

G. W. Grogan, principle of the Bible Training Institute in Glasgow, writing for the *New Bible Dictionary*, observed that "St. Paul's account (in 1 Cor. 11:17-37) of the administration of the Eucharist shows it set in the context of a fellowship supper . . . The separation of the meal or Agape from the Eucharist lies outside the times of the NT."[9]

In his commentary on 1 Corinthians, C. K. Barrett made the observation that "the Lord's Supper was still at Corinth an ordinary meal to which acts of symbolical significance were attached, rather than a purely symbolical meal."[10]

Williston Walker, professor of ecclesiastical history at Yale, noted that "Services were held on Sunday, and probably on other days. These had consisted from the Apostles' time of two kinds: meetings for reading the Scriptures, preaching, song and prayer; and a common evening meal with which the Lord's Supper was conjoined."[11]

Dr. John Gooch, editor at the United Methodist Publishing House in Nashville, Tennessee, wrote, "In the first century, the Lord's Supper included not only the bread and the cup but an entire meal."[12]

J.J. Pelikan, Sterling Professor of Religious Studies at Yale, concluded, "often, if not always, it was celebrated in the setting of a common meal."[13]

ITS FUNCTIONS: 1) REMINDING JESUS

Partaking of the bread and cup as an integral part of the meal originally served several important functions. One of these was to remind Jesus of His promise to return. Reminding God of His covenant promises is a thoroughly scriptural concept. In the covenant God made with Noah, He promised never to destroy the earth by flood again, signified by the rainbow. That sign is certainly designed to remind *us* of God's promise, but God also declared, "whenever the rainbow appears in the clouds, *I will see it and remember the everlasting covenant* between God and all living creatures of every kind on the earth" (Ge 9:16, italics mine).

Later in redemptive history, as part of His covenant with Abraham, God promised to bring the Israelites out of their coming Egyptian bondage. Accordingly, at the appointed time, "God heard their groaning and *He remembered his covenant* with Abraham, with Isaac and with Jacob. So God looked on the Israelites and was concerned about them" (Ex 2:24-25, italics mine).

During the Babylonian captivity, Ezekiel records that God promised Jerusalem, "*I will remember the covenant* I made with you" (Eze 16:60, italics mine).

The Lord's Supper is the sign of the new covenant. As Jesus took the cup He said, "This is my blood of the covenant, which is poured out for many for the forgiveness of sins" (Mt 26:28). As with any covenant sign, it is to serve as a reminder of the promises of the covenant. Thus Jesus said that we are to partake of the bread "in remembrance of Me" (Lk 22:19). The Greek word translated "remembrance," *anamnesis*, means "reminder." Literally translated, Jesus said, "do this unto my reminder."

The question before us is whether that reminder is to be primarily for Jesus' benefit or ours. German theologian Joachim Jeremias understood Jesus to use *anamnesis* in the sense of a reminder for God, "The Lord's Supper would thus be an enacted prayer."[14] In *The Eucharistic Words of Jesus*, it is argued that the Greek underlying the word "until" (1Co 11:26, *achri hou*) is not simply a temporal reference, but functions as a kind of final clause. That is, the meal's function is as a constant reminder to God to bring about the Parousia.[15]

The words "of me" in Luke 22:19 are translated from the single Greek word, *emou*, which grammatically denotes possession (suggesting that the reminder actually belongs to Jesus). More than a mere personal pronoun, it is a possessive pronoun. Thus, the church is to partake of the bread of the Lord's Supper specifically to remind Jesus of His promise to return and eat the Supper again with us, in person (Lk 22:16, 18). Understood in this light, it is designed to be like a prayer asking Jesus to return ("Thy kingdom come," Lk 11:2). Just as the rainbow reminds God of His covenant with Noah, just like the groaning reminded God of His covenant with Abraham, so too partaking of the bread of the Lord's Supper was designed to remind Jesus of His promise to return.

Paul, in 1 Corinthians 11:26, confirms this idea by stating that the church, in eating the Lord's Supper, does actually "proclaim the Lord's death until He comes." To whom do we proclaim His death, and why? Arguably, it is proclaimed it to the Lord Himself, as a reminder for Him to return. It is significant that the Greek behind "until" is *achri hou*. As it is used here, it grammatically can denote a goal or an objective.[16] According to the English usage, I may say that I use an umbrella "until" it stops raining, merely denoting a time frame. (Using the umbrella has nothing to do with making it stop raining). However, this is not how the Greek behind "until" is used in 1 Corinthians 11:26. Instead, Paul was instructing the church to partake of the bread and cup as a means of proclaiming the Lord's death (as a reminder) with the goal of ("until") persuading Him to come back! Thus, in proclaiming His death through the loaf and cup, the Supper looked forward to and anticipated His return.

The Lord's Supper — Feast or Famine?

This concept of seeking to persuade the Lord to return is not unlike the plea of the martyrs of Revelation 6 who called out, "How long, Sovereign Lord, holy and true, until you judge the inhabitants of the earth and avenge our blood?" (Re 6:10). And what did Peter have in mind when he wrote that his readers should look forward to the day of God and "speed its coming" (2Pe 3:12)? If it were futile to seek to persuade Jesus to return, then why did He instruct us to pray, "Thy kingdom come, Thy will be done?" (Mt 6:10). It is interesting that the earliest believers (in *Didache* x. 6) used *maran atha* ("Our Lord, come") as a prayer in connection with the Lord's Supper, "a context at once eucharistic and eschatological."[17] With regard to the use of the word *maranatha* in 1 Corinthians 16:22, Dr. R.P. Martin writes, "*Maranatha* in 1 Cor. 16:22 may very well be placed in a eucharistic setting so that the conclusion of the letter ends with the invocation 'Our Lord, come!' and prepares the scene for the celebration of the meal after the letter has been read to the congregation."[18]

ITS FUNCTIONS: 2) CREATING UNITY

All this emphasis on the Supper as a true meal does not mean that we should jettison the loaf and cup, representative of the body and blood of our Lord. To the contrary, they remain a vital part of the Supper (1Co 11:23-26). The bread and the wine serve as representations of the body and blood of our Lord. His propitiatory death on the cross is the very foundation of the Lord's Supper.

Just as the form of the Lord's Supper is important (a full fellowship meal that prefigured the wedding banquet of the Lamb), also important are the form of the bread and cup. Mention is made in Scripture of *the* cup of thanksgiving (singular) and of only *one* loaf: "Because there is one loaf, we who are many, are one body, for we all partake of the one loaf" (1Co 10:16-17). The one loaf not only pictures our unity in Christ, but according to 1 Corinthians 10:17 even *creates* unity! Notice carefully the wording of the inspired text. "Because" there is one loaf, therefore we are one body, "for" we all partake of the one loaf (1Co 10:17). Partaking of a pile of broken cracker crumbs and multiple cups of juice is a picture of disunity, division, and individuality. At the very least, it completely misses the imagery of unity. One scholar wrote that Lord's Supper was "intended as means of fostering the unity of the church . . ."[19]

Some in Corinth were guilty of partaking of the Lord's Supper in an "unworthy manner" (1Co 11:27). The wealthy refused to eat the Supper with the poor. Thus, the rich arrived at the place of meeting so early that when the poor got there later, some of the rich had become drunk and all the food had been eaten. The poor went home hungry. These shameful class divisions cut at the heart of the unity the Lord's Supper is designed to achieve. The Corinthian abuses were so bad that it had ceased being the Lord's Supper and had instead become their "own" supper (1Co 11:21, NASV). This failure of the rich to recognize the body of the Lord in their poorer brethren resulted in divine judgment: many of them were sick, and a number had even died (1Co 11:27-32). Paul's solution to the harmful meetings? "So then, my brothers, when you come together to eat, wait for each other" (1Co 11:33). Anyone so hungry he could not wait was instructed to "eat at home" (1Co 11:34). Part of the reason the Corinthians were not unified is precisely because they failed to eat the Lord's Supper *together*, as an actual meal, centered around the one cup and loaf.

ITS FUNCTIONS: 3) FELLOWSHIP

In speaking to the church at Laodicea, our resurrected Lord offered to come in and eat (*deipneo*) with anyone who heard His voice and opened the door, a picture of fellowship and communion (Re 3:20). The idea that fellowship and acceptance is epitomized by eating together was derived not only from the Hebrew culture of Jesus' day, but also from the earliest Hebrew Scriptures. Exodus 18:12 reveals that Jethro, Moses, Aaron, and all the elders of Israel came to eat bread in the presence of God. More divine dining occurred at the cutting of the Sinai covenant, when Moses, Aaron, Nadab, Abihu and the seventy elders of Israel when up on Mount Sinai where they "saw God, and they ate and drank" (Ex 24:9-11). It is significant that "God did not raise his hand against these leaders" (Ex 24:11a). They were accepted by Him, as evidenced in the holy meal they ate in His presence.

This "fellowship in feasting" theme is continued on in the book of Acts, where we learn that the early church devoted themselves to "fellowship in the breaking of bread" (2:42, literal translation). In many English versions, in Acts 2:42 there is an "and" between "teaching" and "fellowship," and between "bread" and "prayer," but not between "fellowship" and "bread." In the Greek, the words "fellowship" and "breaking of bread" are linked together as simultaneous activities. They had fellowship with one another *as* they broke bread together. Luke further informs us that this eating was done with "glad and sincere hearts" (2:46). Sounds inviting, doesn't it?

Many commentaries associate the phrase "breaking of bread" throughout the books of Acts with the Lord's Supper. This is because Luke, who wrote Acts, recorded in his gospel that Jesus took bread and "broke it" at the last supper (Lk 22:19). If this conclusion is accurate, then the early church enjoyed the Lord's Supper as a time of fellowship and gladness, just like one would enjoy at a wedding banquet. It was also the opinion of F.F. Bruce that in Acts 2, the fellowship enjoyed was expressed practically in the breaking of bread. Bruce further held that the phrase "breaking of bread" denotes "something more than the ordinary partaking of food together: the regular observance of the Lord's Supper is no doubt indicated . . . this observance appears to have formed the part of an ordinary meal."[20]

In contrast, many modern churches partake of the Lord's Supper with more of a funeral atmosphere. An organ softly plays reflective music. Every head is bowed, every eye is closed, as people quietly and introspectively search their souls for unconfessed sin. The cup and loaf are laid out on a small table, covered over by a white cloth, almost like a corpse would be during a funeral. Deacons somberly, like pall bearers, pass out the elements. Is this really in keeping with the tradition of the apostles concerning the Supper? Remember that it was the unworthy *manner* that Paul criticized (1Co 11:27), not the unworthy *people*. That unworthy manner consisted in drunkenness at the table of the Lord, in not eating together, and in the poor going home hungry and humiliated. Indeed, every person ought to examine himself before arriving for the meal, to be sure he is not guilty of the same gross sin that the Corinthians were guilty of: failing to recognize the body of the Lord in his fellow believers (1Co 11:28-29). Once we have each judged ourselves, we can come to the meal without fear of judgment and enjoy the fellowship of Lord's Supper as the true wedding banquet it is intended to be.

Its Frequency: Weekly

How often did the New Testament church partake of the Supper? Early believers ate the Lord's Supper weekly, and it was the main purpose for their coming together each Lord's Day. Again quoting the *Encyclopaedia Britannica*, the Lord's Supper is "the central rite of Christian worship" and "has been an indispensable component of the Christian service since the earliest days of the church"[21]

The first evidence for this is grammatical. The technical term, "Lord's Day" is from a unique phrase in the Greek, *kuriakon hemeran*, which literally reads, "the day belonging to the Lord." The words "belonging to the Lord" are from *kuriakos*, which occurs in the New Testament only in Revelation 1:10 and in 1 Corinthians 11:20, where Paul uses it to refer to the "Lord's Supper" or the "Supper belonging to the Lord" (*kuriakon deipnon*). The connection between these two uses must not be missed. If the purpose of the weekly church meeting is to observe the Lord's Supper, it only makes sense that this *supper* belonging to the Lord would be eaten on the *day* belonging to the Lord (the first day of the week). John's revelation (Re 1:10) evidently thus occurred on the first day of the week, the day in which Jesus rose from the dead and the day on which the early church met to eat the Supper belonging to the Lord. The resurrection, the day, and the supper go together as a package deal.

Second, the only reason ever given in the New Testament for the regular purpose of a church meeting is to eat the Lord's Supper. In Acts 20:7, Luke informs us that, "On the first day of the week we came together to break bread." The words "to break bread" in Acts 20:7 reflect what is known as a telic infinitive. It denotes a purpose or objective. Their meeting was a meating!

Another place that the New Testament states the purpose for a church gathering is 1 Corinthians 11:17-22. Their "meetings" (11:17) were doing more harm than good because when they came "together as a church" (11:18a) they had deep divisions. Thus Paul wrote, "when you come together, it is not the Lord's Supper you eat" (11:20). From this it is obvious that the primary reason for their church meetings was to eat the Lord's Supper. Sadly, their abuses of the Supper were so gross that it had ceased being the Lord's Supper, but officially they were gathering each week to celebrate the Supper.

The third and last location of a reference to the reason for an assembly is found in 1 Corinthians 11:33, "When you come together to eat, wait for each other." As before, it shows that the reason they came together was to "eat." Lest this appear to be making much out of little, it must be realized that no other reason is ever given in the Scriptures as to the purpose of a regular, weekly church meeting.

The fellowship and encouragement that each member enjoys in such a gathering is tremendous. It is the Christian equivalent of the neighborhood pub. It is the true happy meal or happy hour. It is a time that God uses to create unity in a body of believers. This aspect of the church's meeting should not be rushed or replaced. Certainly it is appropriate to also have a "1 Corinthians 14 phase" of the gathering (an interactive time of teaching, worship, singing, testimony, prayer, etc.), but not at the expense of the weekly Lord's Supper.

The Lord's Supper — Feast or Famine?

PRACTICAL CONSIDERATIONS

Practicing the Lord's Supper as a full meal today can be a means of great blessing to the church. Here are some practical considerations concerning its implementation.

Attitude. Be sure the church understands that the Lord's Supper is the main purpose for the weekly gathering. It is neither optional nor secondary to some type of "worship service." Even if all a church does on a given Sunday is celebrate the Lord's Supper, it has fulfilled one of its primary reasons for having a meeting that week.

Food. If at all possible, make the meal one that is shared and purpose to eat whatever is brought. This makes the administration of the food much easier. Trust God's sovereignty! Over-planning the meal can take a lot of the fun out and make it burdensome. The one thing that should be pre-planned is who supplies the one loaf and the fruit of the vine. (In our church, the family that is hosting the meeting always supplies these things.)

Giving. Since celebrating the meal is a New Testament pattern and something important to the life of a properly functioning church, time and money spent by individual families on food to bring is truly a part of their giving unto the Lord. Rather than merely dropping an offering in a plate each week, go to the food store and buy the best food you can afford. Bring it to the Supper as a sacrificial offering!

Clean Up. To facilitate clean up, you may want to consider using paper plates and napkins along with plastic forks and cups. Also, since folks sometimes carelessly throw away their utensils along with the rest of their trash, it is better to accidentally throw away a plastic fork than a metal one! To help avoid spills the host family supplies wicker plate holders, which can be reused and don't usually need to be washed.

Logistics. In warm weather it may be appropriate to eat outside. Spilled food and drink is inevitable, and clean up is much easier. A large folding table can be placed where necessary and stored away after the meeting. In cold weather, when eating indoors is necessary, consider covering any nicely upholstered furniture with a layer of plastic and then cloth. Since children make the most mess, reserve any available seating at a table for them and insist they use it!

One Cup and Loaf. Some have found that taking the cup and loaf prior to the meal separates it from the meal too much as a separate act. It is as if the Lord's Supper is the cup and loaf, and everything else is just lunch. To overcome this false dichotomy, try placing the cup and loaf on the table with the rest of the food of the Lord's Supper. The cup and loaf can be pointed out in advance of the meeting and mentioned in the prayer prior to the meal, but then placed on the buffet table with everything else. This way, believers can partake of it as they pass through the serving line.

Should the loaf be unleavened and the fruit of the vine alcoholic? The Jews ate unleavened bread in the Passover meal to symbolize the quickness with which God brought them out of Egypt. Jesus used unleavened bread in the original Last Supper. Nothing is said in the New Testament, however, about Gentile churches using unleavened bread in the Lord's Supper. Though sometimes in the New Testament yeast is associated with evil (1Co 5:6-8), it is also used to represent God's kingdom (Mt 13:33)! As we see it, this is a matter of freedom. Regarding wine, it is clear from 1 Corinthians 11 that wine was used in the Lord's Supper, because some had become drunk. No clear theological reason is ever given in Scripture, however, for using wine (but consider Ge 27:28, Isa 25:6-9, and Ro 14:21). As with the unleavened bread, it would seem to be a matter of freedom for each church to decide.

Unbelievers. Should unbelievers be allowed to partake of the Lord's Supper? The Lord's Supper, as a sacred, covenant meal, has significance only to believers. To nonbelievers, it is merely food for the belly. It is implied from 1 Corinthians 14:23-25 that unbelievers will occasionally attend church meetings. Unbelievers get hungry just like believers do, so invite them to eat too. Love them to Jesus! The danger in taking the Lord's Supper in an unworthy manner applies only to believers (1Co 11:27-32).

Regarding the one cup and loaf, if an unbelieving child desires to drink the grape juice just because he likes grape juice, that is fine. However, if the parents purposely give it to an unbelieving child as a religious act, then that might be a violation of what the Lord's Supper is all about. It would be closely akin to the concept of infant baptism.

Ordained Clergy. Some believe that only an ordained clergyman can officiate at the Lord's table. The New Testament makes no so such requirement.

Conclusion

Now that the New Testament form of the Supper has been duly established, the next question facing believers today concerns our Lord's intent for modern churches. Does Jesus desire for His people to celebrate the Lord's Supper in the same way it was eaten in the New Testament? Or could it be a matter of indifference to Him? Do we have the freedom to deviate from the Supper's original form as a true banquet? We think not. Why would anyone want to depart from the way Christ and His apostles practiced the Lord's Supper? The apostles clearly were pleased when churches held to their traditions (1Co 11:2) and even commanded that they do so (2Th 2:15). We have no authorization to deviate from it.

There is general agreement within the scholarly circles of all denominations regarding the fact that the early church celebrated the Lord's Supper as a full meal. The controversy arises over the call to return to the New Testament example. The church of history has at points, and for a time, deviated from the New Testament pattern. For instance, for well over a millennia, believer's baptism by immersion was essentially unheard of within Christendom. Yet since the time of the Reformation this long neglected apostolic tradition has again taken root and is now widely practiced. Similarly, Charismatic and Pentecostal churches would say that many of the gifts of the Spirit were neglected for nearly two thousand years, until the Azusa Street Revival. We feel that the church is missing a tremendous blessing in neglecting the practice of the early church regarding the Lord's Supper.

In summary, the Lord's Supper is the primary purpose for which the church is to gather each Lord's Day. Eaten as a full meal, the Supper typifies the wedding supper of the Lamb and is thus forward looking. It is to be partaken of as a feast, in a joyful, wedding atmosphere rather than in a somber, funeral atmosphere. A major benefit of the Supper as a banquet is the fellowship and encouragement each member experiences. Within the context of this full meal, there is to be one cup and one loaf from which all partake. One whole loaf is to be used, not only to symbolize the unity of a body of believers, but also because God will use it to create unity within a body of believers. They are also symbolic of Jesus' body and blood and serve to remind Jesus of His promise to return and eat of the meal again with His church. Amen. Come quickly, Lord Jesus!

— Steve Atkerson

Addendum: At the back of the book is a practical article, How Many Are Coming for Supper? Helpful Hints for Hosting the Lord's Supper.

NOTES

[1] Fritz Reinecker & Cleon Rogers, *Linguistic Key to the Greek New Testament* (Grand Rapids, MI: Zondervan, 1980), 207.

[2] Jaroslav Jan Pelikan, "Eucharist," *Encyclopaedia Britannica*, ed. Warren Preece, Vol. 8 (Chicago: William Benton, Publisher, 1973), 807-808.

[3] R. P. Martin, "The Lord's Supper," *The New Bible Dictionary*, ed. J. D. Douglas (Wheaton, IL: Tyndale House Publishers, 1982), 709.

[4] Frederick Godet, *Commentary on Luke* (Grand Rapids, MI: Kregel Publications, 1981), 314.

[5] *1599 Geneva Bible* (White Hall, WV: Telle Lege Press, 2006), 1180.

[6] C. K. Barrett, *Black's New Testament Commentary, The Fist Epistle to The Corinthians* (Peabody, MA: Hendrickson Publishers, 1968), 263 & 277.

[7] Donald Guthrie, *New Testament Theology* (Downers Grove, IL: Inter-Varsity Press, 1981), 758.

[8] Gordon Fee, *New International Commentary on the New Testament, The First Epistle to The Corinthians* (Grand Rapids, MI: Wm. B. Eerdmans Publishing Co., 1987), 532, 555.

[9] G. W. Grogan, "Love Feast," *The New Bible Dictionary*, ed. J. D. Douglas (Wheaton, IL: Tyndale House Publishers, 1982), 712.

[10] Barrett, 276.

[11] Williston Walker, *A History of The Christian Church*, 3rd Ed. (New York, NY: Charles Scribner's Sons, 1970), 38.

[12] John Gooch, *Christian History & Biography,* Issue 37 (Carol Stream, IL: Christianity Today) 3.

[13] Pelikan, 808.

[14] Colin Brown, *New International Dictionary of New Testament Theology*, Vol. III (Grand Rapids, MI: Zondervan, 1981) 244.

[15] Joachim Jeremias, *The Eucharistic Words of Jesus* (New York, NY: Charles Scribner's Sons, 1966), 252-254.

[16] Reinecker, 34.

[17] Barrett, 397.

[18] Martin, 709.

19 Pelikan, 807.

[20] F. F. Bruce, *Acts of The Apostles* (Grand Rapids, MI: Wm. B. Eerdmans Publishing Co., 1981) 79.

[21] Pelikan, 807.

The Lord's Supper — Feast or Famine?

1. What are some Old Testament examples of God remembering His covenant promises? How might this impact our understanding of the "remembrance" aspect of the Lord's Supper (Lk 22:19)?

2. What scriptural evidence is there that the first century Jews envisioned heaven as a time of feasting in the Messiah's presence?

3. Jesus said that the Lord's Supper would find fulfillment in the kingdom of God (Lk 22:16). How and when might this be fulfillment take place?

4. The last supper occurred in the context of the Passover feast. Would the twelve apostles have somehow deduced that future Lord Suppers were not also to be feasts? Explain.

5. What is the scholarly consensus as to how the early church celebrated the Lord's Supper? Why does this consensus matter?

6. If Acts 2:42-47 refers to the Lord's Supper, how would you describe the mood of these meals? Why?

7. What is the only reason ever given in the New Testament as to why the early church came together each Lord's Day?

8. What theological reason was given by Paul for using a single loaf in the Lord's Supper?

9. In 1 Corinthians 11:17-22, what indicates that the Lord's Supper was eaten as an actual meal?

10. What was the biblical solution to the Corinthian abuse of the Lord's Supper?

11. Why does the word "until" in 1 Corinthians 11:26 indicate purpose and not merely duration?

12. What "unworthy manner" made some in Corinth guilty of sinning against the body and blood of the Lord (1Co 11:27)? How should this effect us today?

13. What evidence is there as to the frequency with which the early church ate the Lord's Supper?

14. What was the original form of the Lord's Supper (token ritual or actual meal)? Explain.

15. Was the original focus of the Lord's Supper past looking or forward looking? How so?

16. What were the original functions of the Lord's Supper?

17. Since Jesus said that He would not eat of it again until its future consummation, could it not be argued that the church also should wait for Jesus to return before eating it again? Why?
18. How can the Lord's Supper be celebrated like a wedding banquet when the threat of death is made (1 Co 11) and 1 Corinthians 10 speaks of eating with demons (even more frightening!)?
19. What were the original frequency, form, focus (past or future) and functions of the Lord's Supper?
20. How can the cup and loaf be integrated into the meal so that they are not seen as separate from the rest of the feast?
21. What bearing should the practice of the early church have on how the contemporary church celebrates the Lord's Supper?
22. What blessings is a church missing by not celebrating the Lord's Supper as an actual holy meal?

Note: NTRF also offers a teacher's resource to help lead a discussion of New Testament church life. Request *The Practice of The Early Church: A Theological Workbook (Leader's Guide)* from www.NTRF.org.

The first song begins promptly at 10:30 Sunday morning. Prior to that, folks are hugging and greeting each other, bringing food or children inside the house, getting a cup of coffee from the kitchen, or standing around talking. That first song is the cue for everyone to assemble in the living room so that the more formal time of the meeting can begin. There are usually about ten families and two singles present. Counting children, there are around fifty people. Some are usually late in arriving. There are typically enough chairs for the adults, and the children sit on the floor near their parents. Young children color or play quietly with toys during the entire meeting. People are dressed casually and comfortably.

The musicians (banjo, djembe, two guitars and a mandolin) do not try to be worship leaders. Their goal is simply to facilitate and support the group's singing. As many or as few songs are sung as are requested by those present. Spontaneous prayer is often offered between songs, sometimes leading to longer times of conversational prayer. There is no bulletin or order of service, though everything is done in a fitting and orderly way. Only one person at a time may speak. The prime directive is that anything said or done must be designed to build up, edify, encourage or strengthen the whole church.

Sometimes several brothers teach. Other weeks no one brings a word of instruction. Those burdened to instruct prepare prior to the meeting, but rarely is anyone officially scheduled to teach. Interspersed between the songs and teachings, testimonies are shared of God's provision, of lessons learned, of prayers answered, of encouraging events, etc. Sometimes there are periods of silence. Frequently a visiting Christian worker will report on his ministry and of God's work in other places.

It is not a show or performance. There is neither moderator nor emcee. Unless there is a problem to resolve, a visitor would not even know who the leaders were. There is not an official ending time for the meeting. Often it lasts one and a half to two hours. Either everyone who desires to sing or speak has done so, or the kids are at the end of their endurance, or corporate hunger motivates a conclusion. Generally, the meeting closes with prayer. Afterwards, folks stay and fellowship as long as they desire. The meeting usually transitions into the Lord's Supper, a full meal that everyone enjoys.

Participatory Meetings

The church meeting described above is not fictional. Such meetings take place every Lord's Day, all over the world. They even occur in such unlikely places as England, America, Canada, Australia and New Zealand! They are modeled after the church meetings described in the New Testament. Modern believers are so accustomed to attending church in special sanctuaries with stained glass, steeples, pipe organs, pews, pulpits, choirs, bulletins, and worship leaders that it is assumed Scripture dictates such trappings. The reality is that New Testament church meetings were vastly different from what typically is practiced today.

SCRIPTURAL ARGUMENTS FOR PARTICIPATORY MEETINGS

Participatory church meetings are indeed scriptural. For example, Paul asked the Corinthians, "What then shall we say, brothers? When you come together, everyone has a hymn, or a word of instruction, a revelation, a tongue, or an interpretation. All of these must be done for the strengthening of the church" (1Co 14:26).

Had Scripture used the words "only one" instead of "everyone," which would be more descriptive of most modern church services? It is clear from the text that those original church meetings were much different from what often goes on today. There was interaction, spontaneity and participation. In a sense there really wasn't an audience because all the brothers were potential cast members (depending on the gifting and leading of the Spirit).

The generally spontaneous and participatory nature of early church meetings is also evident in the regulations concerning those who spoke in tongues: "If anyone speaks in a tongue, two — or at the most three, should speak, one at a time, and someone must interpret. If there is no interpreter, the speaker should keep quiet in the church and speak to himself and God" (1Co 14: 27-28).

Were these speakers in unknown tongues scheduled in advance to speak? Not likely, given the supernatural nature of the gift. That the meetings were participatory is evident from the fact that up to three people could speak in tongues and that there was the need for an interpreter to be present.

Further indication of the participatory nature of their gatherings is seen in the guidelines given for prophets in 1 Corinthians 14:29-32. We are informed that "Two or three prophets should speak, and the others should weigh carefully what is said" (14:29). The spontaneous nature of their participation also comes out in 14:30-31a, "If a revelation comes to someone who is sitting down, the first speaker should stop. For you can all prophesy in turn." Clearly, some of the prophets came to church not planning to say anything, but then received a revelation while sitting there and listening.

One of the most controversial paragraphs in the New Testament occurs in 1 Corinthians 14:33b-35, regarding the silence of women in the meeting. No matter how one interprets this passage, there would have been no need for Paul to have written it unless first century church meetings were participatory. The would be little reason for Paul to write this to modern churches, since in general no one is allowed to speak except the pastoral staff. It is implied in 14:35 that people were asking questions of the speakers during the church meeting: "If they want to inquire about something, they should ask their own husbands at home." Even if Paul only meant that women were not to be the ones doing the questioning, it still remained that the men were free to so. The point to be gleaned is that a church meeting is not supposed to be a one man show. There are to be edifying contributions and encouraging input by those who gather.

Almost every New Testament letter is an "occasional document," so-called because it was written in response to some local problem. Evidently some in Corinth wanted to conduct their meetings differently than this passage requires. Some aspect of the church meetings in Corinth was probably amiss. This much is obvious from the nature of the two questions asked of them: "Did the word of God originate with you? Or are you the only people it has reached?" (1Co 14:36).

The word of God clearly had not originated with the Corinthians, and they most certainly were not the only people it had reached. These questions were thus designed to convince the Corinthian believers that they had neither right nor authorization to conduct their meetings in any other way than what is prescribed by the apostles. As such, whatever applied to the Corinthian church applies to us as well. The inspired correction served to regulate orderly participation at church gatherings, not prohibit it. Paul wrote, "Be eager to prophesy, and do not forbid speaking in tongues. But everything should be done in a fitting and orderly way" (14:39-40).

Holding church meetings in this generally spontaneous, participatory manner is in fact declared to be imperative. According to 1 Corinthians 14:37, "If anybody thinks he is a prophet or spiritually gifted, let him acknowledge that what I am writing to you is the Lord's command." Thus, 1 Corinthians 14 is not merely *descriptive* of primitive church meetings. Rather, it is *prescriptive* of the way our Lord expects meetings of the whole church to be conducted. Not every gathering of believers need be participatory — only to the regular Lord's Day gatherings of the whole church. Other types of meetings, which may not be participatory, are also appropriate (evangelistic crusades, worship services, seminars, etc.). Caution should be taken that larger meetings, where a select few exercise their ministry gifts, do not become substitutes for the weekly, participatory Lord's Day gathering of the local church.

When we understand the historical context of the early church, it is not surprising that the meetings of the first-century church would have been participatory. The first believers in most areas of the Roman Empire were Jewish. They were accustomed to gathering in the typical synagogue format, which was, at least to some degree, open to participation from those in attendance. An examination of the book of Acts will reveal that the apostles could never have evangelized the way they did unless the synagogues allowed input from individuals with the congregation (13:14-15, 14:1, 17:1-2, 17:10, 18:4, 19:8). The apostles apparently were always permitted to speak in the meetings of the synagogue. Had first century synagogue meetings been anything like most twenty-first century church worship services, Paul and his companions would have had to find another way to reach the Jews with the gospel!

There are other biblical indicators as well. In Acts 20:7, we discover that Paul "kept on talking" ("preached," KJV) to the church at Troas until midnight. The Greek word translated "talking" is *dialegomia,* which primarily means "consider and discuss, argue." In fact, our English word "dialogue" is derived from it. That meeting in Troas was likely participatory. As one who had known Jesus in person, Paul surely did most of the talking, but the way he taught was not necessarily uninterrupted monolog.

There is still more. The author of Hebrews urged his readers to "not give up meeting together, as some are in the habit of doing, but let us encourage one another" (10:25). Early believers encouraged one another when they gathered. Clearly, they met together in order to do this. Such encouragement, of course, requires interaction. Additionally, believers are instructed in Hebrews 10:24 to meet in order to stimulate each other to love and good deeds. This too requires interaction. How much "one anothering" really goes on in a modern worship service?

The over-arching purpose for anything done in a church gathering was, according to Paul, for the "strengthening of the church" (14:26). The Greek word used here, *oikodome,* means "building up" or "edification" (NASV). Thayer pointed out in his lexicon that it is the action of one who promotes another's growth in Christianity. Thus, any comments made in a church meeting should be calculated to encourage, build up, strengthen or edify the other believers present. If not, it is inappropriate and should not be spoken. Any teaching brought must be both true and uplifting. Even questions must be designed to ultimately strengthen the whole assembly. All songs need to be edifying. Every testimony is required to build up the church. As Peter said, "If anyone speaks, he should do it as speaking the very words of God" (1Pe 4:11). In keeping with this, Paul encouraged prophecy over the public speaking in tongues. This is because everyone who prophesied in a church meeting spoke to others for their "strengthening, encouragement and comfort" (1Co 14:3) with the result that the church was "edified" (14:5). The Corinthians were instructed to "try to excel in gifts that build up the church" (14:12). All of this points to the participatory nature of early church gatherings (participatory in the sense that any brother could potentially address the assembly).

One final observation: today's church gatherings are commonly referred to as worship services. This title suggests that the reason for regular Christian gatherings is to worship God. Yet the New Testament never refers to a church meeting as a worship service. As we have already seen, Scripture indicates that the early church gathered primarily for the purpose of mutual edification and strengthening.

Don't misunderstand me. Corporate worship can certainly contribute to the strengthening of the church. Worship, however, is not the only activity that can edify. The problem lies partially in naming the meeting a worship service. First, church meetings are to be open to meaningful audience input, not a service where everything is done for them. Second, such a title suggests that worship is the only appropriate activity that is to occur. Other modes of edification are seen as less important. People are led to expect emotional feelings such as are associated with cathedral architecture, candles, hushed sanctuaries, stained glass windows, awe-inspiring music, and the presentation of a program that is in essence a performance. With such unbiblical expectations, a truly biblical 1 Corinthians 14 meeting will seem strange, uncomfortable, or even disconcerting.

So where does worship fit? Jesus told the woman at the well, "A time is coming when you will worship the Father neither on this mountain nor in Jerusalem" (Jn 4:21-24). In saying this, He made it clear that the new covenant worship would have nothing to do with any particular location. It transcends 11:00 a.m. on a Sunday morning and should not be localized in any church sanctuary.

Participatory Meetings

There are primarily two Greek words in the New Testament for worship. The first is *proskuneo* and refers to an attitude of adoring awe toward God. It is humility toward the Father. It is reverence, appreciation, fear and wonder.

This attitude of inner devotion is very practically worked out in the second New Testament word for worship (*latreia*), which refers to a life-style of obedience and service. Worship is thus *both* an attitude and an action. As Francis Scott Key penned in a hymn: "And since words can never measure, let my life show forth Thy praise." Thus, while our participation in the weekly church meeting is undeniably an act of worship, so is going to work honestly, the discipline of our children, loving our families, etc. Our daily lives are to be a continual act of worship.

The Sunday gathering is for the benefit of the people present. It is not God who needs strengthening because He is not weak. The Lord doesn't need to be encouraged since He is neither tired nor discouraged. Jesus is not lacking in anything, but His people certainly are. Thus the primary purpose of a church meeting is to equip God's people to go out to worship and serve Him another week (Heb 10:24-25). It is to motivate the elect to deeper worship and obedience.

LOGICAL ARGUMENTS FOR PARTICIPATORY MEETINGS

It is a simple fact of history that the early church met in the homes of its members. No special church buildings were constructed during the New Testament era, nor during the following two hundred years. This necessarily meant that their gatherings were smaller rather than larger. Such smaller settings would have essentially eliminated the possibility that those pristine meetings might consist of an eloquent sermon delivered to a massed crowd of hushed listeners.

After Christianity was made the official religion of the Roman Empire, pagan temples were turned, by government decree, into church buildings. Believers were herded out of their home meetings and into large basilicas. Such huge gatherings naturally were more of a show or service. Interactive teaching became nonexistent, and instruction was monologue oration. Questions from the audience were not allowed. Spontaneity was lost. Individual participation was squelched. The "one another" aspect of an assembly became impossible. Informality gave way to formality. Church leaders began to wear special costumes. Worship aids were introduced: incense, icons, hand gestures, etc. It continues even today, to a lesser or greater degree. In short, the New Testament way was jettisoned for a way of man's own devising.

Which type of church meeting best meets the needs of God's people? Certainly much good comes from the weekly proclamation of God's Word by those church leaders who have come to be known as preachers or pastor-teachers. The worshipful and inspirational singing of the great hymns of the faith is also beneficial. Yet scripturally, there is supposed to be more to a church meeting than merely attending a service.

Allowing any of the brothers who so desire to participate verbally in the meeting lends for a greater working of the Spirit as the various ministry gifts begin to function. Not allowing them to function causes atrophy and even apathy. According to what Paul wrote, God may burden several brothers, independent of each other, to bring a teaching. Learning is increased as appropriate questions are asked of a speaker. Additional applications and illustrations can be offered to a word of instruction by the body at large. New believers learn how to think biblically with the mind of Christ as more mature believers are observed reasoning together. Maturity rates skyrocket. The brothers begin to own the meeting, take responsibility for what goes on and become active participants rather than passive spectators.

SCHOLARLY TESTIMONY FOR PARTICIPATORY MEETINGS

That New Testament church gatherings were completely open and participatory, with no one leading from the front, is agreed upon by researchers. For instance, Dr. Henry Sefton, in *A Lion Handbook - The History of Christianity*, stated, "Worship in the house-church had been of an intimate kind in which all present had taken an active part . . . (this) changed from being 'a corporate action of the whole church' into 'a service said by the clergy to which the laity listened.'"[1]

Ernest Scott, in *The Nature of the Early Church*, writes, "The exercise of the spiritual gifts was thus the characteristic element in the primitive worship. Those gifts might vary in their nature and degree according to the capacity of each individual, but thy were bestowed on all and room was allowed in the service for the participation of all who were present . . . Every member was expected to contribute something of his own to the common worship."[2]

In the Mid America Baptist Theological Journal, Dr. J. Milikin stated that in early Christian congregations "there was apparently a free expression of the Spirit. In the public assembly one person might have a psalm, another a teaching, another a revelation, another a tongue, another an interpretation."[3]

Participatory Meetings

Dr. John Drane, in *Introducing the New Testament*, wrote, "In the earliest days . . . their worship was spontaneous. This seems to have been regarded as the ideal, for when Paul describes how a church meeting should proceed he depicts a Spirit-led participation by many, if not all . . . There was the fact that anyone had the freedom to participate in such worship. In the ideal situation, when everyone was inspired by the Holy Spirit, this was the perfect expression of Christian freedom."[4]

A. M. Renwick, writing in *The Story of the Church*, said, "The very essence of church organization and Christian life and worship . . . was simplicity . . . Their worship was free and spontaneous under the guidance of the Holy Spirit, and had not yet become inflexible through the use of manuals of devotion."[5]

PRACTICAL CONSIDERATIONS

One aspect of New Testament meetings that is still practiced today is the singing. The Ephesian church was instructed to "speak to one another with psalms, hymns, and spiritual songs. Sing and make music in your heart to the Lord" (Ep 5:19). Similarly, the Colossians were exhorted to "let the word of Christ dwell in you richly as you teach and admonish one another with all wisdom, and as you sing psalms, hymns, and spiritual songs with gratitude in your hearts to God" (Col 3:16). Perhaps not so familiar to modern believers, however, is the "one another" (Ep 5:19, Col 3:16) emphasis of the singing. According to 1 Corinthians 14:26, everyone of the brothers had the opportunity to bring a hymn. No mention is made anywhere in the New Testament of a minister of music or worship leader controlling the singing. It is certainly a blessing to have gifted musicians who can assist the congregation in worship and singing. However, to be true to the New Testament prescription, musicians must be careful not to perform like those on stage in a show. The brothers of the church must be given the freedom and responsibility of requesting which songs are sung, and when.

On a related note (pun intended!), some Christians are adamantly against the use of musical instruments in church meetings. However, the Greek word for "hymn" (1Co 14:26) is translated from *psalmos* and which fundamentally means, "songs accompanied by a stringed instrument." Since instruments are not forbidden, and since there is no known pattern of specifically not using them, this arguably is an issue where each church has liberty to determine its own practice.

Another feature of early church meetings that is still practiced today is the teaching of God's Word. Our Lord instructed the apostles to make disciples of all nations, teaching them to obey everything He had commanded (Mt 28:20). Accordingly, we learn from Acts 2:42 that the Jerusalem church devoted themselves to the apostles' teaching. Further, teaching is listed as a spiritual gift in both Romans 12:7 and 1 Corinthians 12:28. Moreover, one of the requirements of an elder is that he be able to teach (1Ti 3:2). Elders who work hard at teaching are worthy of double honor (financial support, 1Ti 5:17-18). In 1 Corinthians 14, however, teaching is tossed in with the other activities in an almost cavalier way. The teacher is not given the prominence that one sees in today's typical church meeting. Every one of the brothers in good standing with the church was to be given the opportunity to contribute a word of instruction (14:26).

All this, taken together, demands of us an appreciation for the importance of those called to teaching ministries, yet we should also allow opportunity for any brother to teach in our regular 1 Corinthians 14 gatherings. Practically, it would also suggest each teaching during the 1 Corinthians 14 style of meeting be shorter, rather than longer, in order to allow the opportunity for others who might desire to teach.

Amazingly, pastors and elders are not even mentioned in 1 Corinthians 14. This may be because pastors did not dominate these types of gatherings with their teachings. This is not to say that elders did not teach in the meetings, but it is clear from 1 Corinthians 14 that non-elders also had the opportunity to do so. Thus, the author of Hebrews made the general statement that "by this time you ought to be teachers" (5:12). That he did not have the leaders in mind is evident from his salutation ("greet all your leaders," 13:24), revealing that he did not even expect the elders to read the letter! Still, just because the opportunity *exists* for someone to teach, it does not necessarily follow that they *should* teach. The elders must remind the church of James' warning that "not many of you should presume to be teachers, my brothers, because you know that we who teach will be judged more strictly" (3:1). James' caution makes sense in light of the intimate, participatory meetings that characterized the early church.

This freedom for any brother to teach is precisely when the elders are needed most. If a brother brings an erroneous teaching or application, the elders must gently correct the error. Timothy, an apostolic worker stationed temporarily at Ephesus, was to "command certain men not to teach false doctrines any longer" (1Ti 1:3). Scripture also tells us that one qualification for an elder is that he must "hold firmly to the trustworthy message as it has been taught, so that he can encourage others by sound doctrine and refute those who oppose it" (Tit 1:9). Similarly, Titus was told to "encourage and rebuke with all authority. Do not let anyone despise you" (Tit 2:15). The aged apostle John warned about a known deceiver: "do not take him into your house" (2Jn 1:10). (One can easily see how John's instructions could have been applied to house churches with participatory meetings.)

Obviously, some brothers are far more qualified to teach than are others. An aged, godly man, gifted to teach, who loves the Lord, and who has studied the Bible and served people all his life, is going to have profound insights to share with the church. Especially in the presence of such men, the rest should be "quick to listen, slow to speak" (Jam 1:19). Special times should be devoted to allow such a man the opportunity of expounding God's Word. However, these teaching meetings should be considered worker's meetings or apostolic meetings or ministry meetings, not 1 Corinthians 14 church meetings. There is a time and a place for both. Rather than a lot of participation by one person, a Lord's Day church meeting is to be characterized by a little input from a lot of people.

Charismatic and Pentecostal churches are quite familiar with revelations, tongues, and interpretations. Churches that practice such gifts should be sure the guidelines of 1 Corinthians 14:26-32 are followed closely. Uninterpreted tongues are not to be allowed. There is a limit on the number of those who do speak in tongues. Only one person at a time should speak. Prophecies must be judged, and anyone who desires to prophesy needs to realize in advance that his words will be weighed carefully. Doubtless some that passes for prophecy and tongues is bogus. Dealing with this area can be messy and frustrating since the overly-emotional and unstable often imagine they have such gifts. Perhaps that is why the Thessalonians had to be told, "do not treat prophecies with contempt. Test everything. Hold on to the good. Avoid every kind of evil" (1Th 5:20-22). In the midst of all these supernatural utterances, there must be order: "The spirits of the prophets are subject to the control of the prophets. God is not a God of disorder but of peace" (1Co 14:33a). Elders play a key role in helping everything that goes on in the meeting to be done in a "fitting and orderly way" (1Co 14:40).

Some churches believe that charismatic gifts ended in the first century, or have no one present who is so gifted. Even so, the principle of participatory meetings remains. Brothers should still be free to spontaneously bring teachings, request or introduce songs, share testimonies, offer prayer, question speakers, etc. Yet despite their theological suspicions, it should give pause to read that Scripture clearly instructs, "do not forbid to speak in tongues" (1Co 14:39). Perhaps tongues have indeed ceased, but maybe not. Are we really so sure of our theology that we are willing to directly contradict a biblical command?

Another practical consideration for participatory meetings concerns the idea of a moderator or master of ceremonies. Notice that none is mentioned in 1 Corinthians 14. As a church matures in experiencing participatory gatherings, the need for someone to moderate the meeting will diminish. Ideally, a visitor to a properly functioning church would not even know who its leaders were unless there were a problem that requires correction.

A warning shot across the bow was fired by the inspired writer in 1 Corinthians 14:38. After stating that these orderly, participatory meetings are the "Lord's command" (14:37), he then cautioned that anyone who disregards what was written would be ignored. Though unclear as to exactly what this meant, some type of penalty was threatened. A price would be paid for disregarding the Lord's command for church meetings.

PROBLEMS TO EXPECT

The authors of this book have many combined years of practical experience with participatory meetings. We have observed that there are some typical problems to be expected. We detail these below in the hope that those just beginning to experiment with participatory meetings can avoid some of the more common pitfalls.

Pew Potatoes. Most church folks, after years of attending services, are conditioned to sit silently, as if watching TV. It takes encouragement and patience to over come this. Meaningful participation will seem awkward to people at first. Continual prompting and encouraging by the leadership during the week may be necessary until people "break the sound barrier." The leaders can prompt interaction by asking, "Is there a testimony the Lord would have you to bring? Is there a song that would edify the church? Is there some subject or passage of Scripture to teach on?"

If a string were stretched across a stream at water level, various things would become attached to it as the day passed, things that otherwise would have floated on past. Similarly, thinking all week long about what to bring to the meeting helps greatly. If no one brought food for the *agape* love feast, there would not be much of a feast. Similarly, if no one comes to the meeting prepared to contribute, there will not be much of a meeting! Men, do your wives spend more time preparing for church (by cooking food for the *agape* feast) than you do (in considering something to say in the meeting)?

Unedifying Remarks. Sometimes after folks do start talking, they get a little too casual. They begin to chat about things that really don't edify the assembly. Just because it is an open meeting does not mean people can say anything they want to say. Leaders need to remind the church that anything said in the meeting must be designed to build up the body and to encourage everyone. Church meetings are also not to be therapy sessions for the wounded, with everything focused on one person and his needs. Though such people do need counseling, it is generally to be done at a time other than the corporate assembly.

False Teachings. The lure of an participatory meeting may be strong enough to draw in those with aberrant theology who are looking for a place to promote their unique doctrine. Following the biblical pattern of participatory meetings must not become an occasion for false teachings to flourish! The prevention and correction of error is precisely one reason elders are needed. Elders must be men who are mature and grounded in the faith. They must detect and refute error when they hear it, giving it no quarter. No teaching should be allowed in the meeting that is contrary to historic Christian orthodoxy.

Pooled Ignorance. Rather than study a subject in advance to bring a teaching, some folks will come to the meeting totally unprepared and simply plop a question out before the gathered church for an answer. This is the opposite of bringing a teaching. It is sort of an anti-teaching. Leaders should discourage people from asking such questions to the church out of ignorance. Such questions only draw attention to the person asking the question and are not designed to edify the church. It is too self oriented. It is asked to meet a personal need. Moreover, since it is unlikely that anyone will have recently studied the topic under question, pooled ignorance will likely abound as everyone offers their opinions. There simply is no substitute for the careful, systematic, in-depth study of Scripture in private and in advance of the meeting, and there is no excuse for not so doing.

Over-Scheduled Meetings. Those used to church bulletins will want to arrange such things as teaching, music and prayer in advance. Beware of quenching the Spirit! It is clear from 1 Corinthians 14 that New Testament church meetings were generally spontaneous.

Disruptive Visitors. There are many kinds of disruptive visitors. Uninformed guests can easily hijack a meeting by unedifying remarks. Self-centered people will try to take dominate the meeting. The mentally unstable will speak loudly and often, to the chagrin of the assembly. Critics may attack what the church does or believes in the meeting. Heretics will view the participatory meetings as a chance to promote their errant theology. Leaders are needed in such cases to restore order with wisdom and patience. Visitors should be prompted *in advance* of the divine guidelines found in 1 Corinthians 14. An ounce of prevention is worth a pound of cure! (See the sample prospective visitor's letter at the end). It may be appropriate to invite the critic to air his opinions later, after the meeting is over, during the fellowship of the Lord's Supper or in private with the elders.

Population Control. Meetings that are either too big or too small create their own set of hindrances to participatory gatherings. Too few people can seem dull. Too many people present will intimidate the shy and work against open sharing.

Worship Leaders. Musicians are to facilitate the church's singing and worship, not control it. Beware of worship leaders who would take over the meeting and make it into a show.

Punctuality. Relation-based churches are notoriously bad about starting late. If it is announced that a meeting will begin at a certain time, then the leaders need to be sure that it does start at that time. It is a matter of courtesy and respect for the value of other people's time. Arriving on time also shows respect. Consistently being late for a meeting is often a sign of passive aggression. At the very least it is rude and inconsiderate.

The Master of Ceremonies. Some leaders will tend to want to emcee the meetings, as if they were television talk show hosts. Perhaps such prompting will be necessary in the infancy of a church, but in maturity this will not be needed. Further, there is nothing wrong with silence occasionally. Trust the Holy Spirit to guide the assembly. Ideally, a visitor in a 1 Corinthians 14 meeting should not be able to tell who the elders are in the church. Unless there is a problem, the elders should just blend in with everyone else! Admittedly, lack of participation on the part of the members can be a problem, so elders may need to lead out more in such cases to encourage input from others.

Children. The New Testament pattern seems to indicate that children were present in the meeting with their parents. For example, Paul intended some of his letters to be read aloud to the entire church (see Col 4:16). Based on Ephesians 6:1-3, children were present in the Ephesian church meetings or they would not have been present to hear Paul's instructions to them when the letter was read. (Compare also Mt 19:13-15, Lk 2:41-50, Ac 21:5.)

However, a very young child who begins crying loudly in the meeting should be removed from the meeting by a parent until he is quieted. Older children must be taught to sit still or play silently on the floor so as not to disrupt the meeting. Some parents will be oblivious to this need and in such cases the leadership must speak to the parents in private to enlist their cooperation in controlling their children.

False expectations. People will invariably come to the 1 Corinthians 14 gatherings with preconceived notions of what the meeting should be like. Some, for instance, will want a moving worship service, or to sing only the great hymns of the faith. Others will exclusively associate praise songs with heartfelt worship, or expect dramatic healings to take place, or want a high powered Bible lecture, or some emotional presentation of the gospel. When their expectations are not met, disappointment and discontentment are the result. Church leaders need to be aware of this and take steps to help people to have biblical expectations of the meetings and to have the same goals that our Lord does.

Some Objections

Some overseers voice vigorous objection to this type of church meeting. With good reason they fear that chaos and anarchy could break out. Remember, however, that while there is order in a cemetery, there is no life there. It is much better to have life and risk a little disorder! Keeping order is one of the duties of an elder. Church leaders are also responsible for training the saints so that they are equipped to contribute meaningfully to such a meeting and to judge error for themselves. Further, the Holy Spirit must be trusted to work in the life of a church. If the Scriptures truly reveal God's desire for participatory meetings, then God will also see to it that the meetings will be successful in the long run.

In commenting on the contrast between early church meetings and modern church meetings, Gordon Fee observed, "By and large the history of the church points to the fact that in worship we do not greatly trust the diversity of the body. Edification must always be the rule, and that carries with it orderliness so that all may learn and all be encouraged. But it is no great credit to the historical church that in opting for 'order' it also opted for a silencing of the ministry of the many."[6]

Frankly, some pastors will oppose the guidelines of 1 Corinthians 14 precisely because enacting them will result in a lack of focus on the pastor. Sadly, a small percentage of pastors are on ego trips, or have their need for self affirmation fulfilled by being the star player in a service. This is a blind-spot that must be overcome.

Impedance to the commands of 1 Corinthians 14 can also occur if believers become so intoxicated with their newly found freedom that they essentially run off into anarchy or gnosticism. They become overly wary of agendas. To them, anyone with leadership skills is somehow self-willed or evil. Yet it is obvious that Paul, a godly leader, had a godly agenda for the churches to which he ministered. Balance is a key consideration. We need to be about the Lord's agenda of helping His churches come into compliance with everything the Lord commanded!

Many people have read 1 Corinthians 14 and judged their churches to be in complete compliance merely because the congregation participates through responsive readings, genuflecting, partaking of the wafer and wine of the Lord's Supper, singing hymns, giving tithes and offerings, etc. Part of the problem is that all of this is planned out, it is not spontaneous, the structure is the same every week, and the entire order of worship is laid out in the bulletin. There may be limited audience participation, but there is no real liberty. Is any one of the brothers free to pick a hymn? To bring a teaching? To raise his hand and ask a question? Is there spontaneity?

CONCLUSION: AFFIRMATIONS & DENIALS

What conclusions can be drawn about the way God desires the weekly, Lord's Day church meeting to be conducted? We deny that:

1. *"Worship services" were held by the New Testament church.*
2. *Huge assemblies of Christians meeting for weekly worship is a New Testament pattern.*
3. *Church meetings need to be led from the front by a worship leader.*
4. *Bulletins are necessary or even slightly beneficial to a church meeting.*
5. *Only one person can teach in the meeting.*
6. *Teachers should be scheduled in advance.*
7. *Ritual and ceremony were part of New Testament church meetings.*
8. *Special aids to worship are important, such as incense, costumes, icons, statues, stained glass, or ornate cathedral-like buildings.*
9. *Performance-like shows are legitimate substitutes for the New Testament prescription of interaction.*

On the positive side, we affirm that:

1. *The regular weekly church meeting is to be participatory and spontaneous.*
2. *Anything said or done must be designed to strengthen (edify) the whole church.*
3. *Only one person at a time is to address the assembly.*

Participatory Meetings

4. Everything is to be done in a fitting and orderly way.
5. One of an elder's roles in such meetings is to keep it "on track" and true to the prime directive that all things be done unto edifying.
6. This type of participatory meeting is not optional, is not just interesting history, is not just quaint information. Such meetings are the "Lord's command" (1Co 14:37).

— Steve Atkerson

NOTES

[1] Henry Sefton, *A Lion Handbook - The History of Christianity* (Oxford, UK: Lion Publishing, 1988) 151.

[2] Ernest Scott, *The Nature Of The Early Church* (New York, NY: Charles Scribner's Sons, 1941), 79.

[3] Jimmy Milikin, "Disorder Concerning Public Worship," *Mid America Baptist Theological Journal* (Memphis, TN: Mid-America Baptist Seminary Press, 1983), 125.

[4] John Drane, *Introducing the New Testament* (Oxford, UK: Lion Publishing, 1999), 402.

[5] A. M. Renwick, *The Story of the Church* (Downers Grove, IL: Inter-Varsity Press 1958), 22-23.

[6] Gordon Fee, NICNT, *The First Epistle To The Corinthians* (Grand Rapids, MI: Wm. B. Eerdmans Publishing Co., 1987), 698.

DISCUSSION QUESTIONS

1. Suppose 1 Corinthians 14:26 contained the words "only one" rather than "everyone." Which would be more descriptive of modern worship services? How so?

2. Suppose 1 Corinthians 14:26 is actually a criticism of what the Corinthian church was doing (allegedly chaotic meetings), was the inspired solution a prohibition of participatory meetings or a regulation of it? Explain.

3. What role did music and ministers of music play in the early church meetings?

4. Taken as a whole, what are the various indicators throughout 1 Corinthians 14 that combine to show the participatory nature of early church meetings?

5. What are some of the guiding principles for participatory church meetings, based on 1 Corinthians 14 and Hebrews 10:24-25?

6. Why is it so important that everything said and done in the church meeting be edifying?

7. How can the participatory nature of a church meeting be reconciled with the need for the in-depth exposition of God's Word by gifted teachers?

8. What does 1 Corinthians 14:37 indicate about whether the guidelines of 1 Corinthians 14 are merely descriptive or actually prescriptive?

9. Many churches have no one gifted in the more obviously supernatural "charismatic" gifts. Why would the absence of such gifts not nullify the Lord's command (1Co 14:37) that church meetings be participatory?

10. What other contributions to a church meeting can be made, based on Acts 2:42, 14:26-28 and 1 Timothy 4:13?

11. What setting would better facilitate a participatory church meeting, a smaller congregation in a living room setting, or a huge congregation meeting in a canvernous worship center? Why?

12. What role should an elder play in an participatory meeting?

13. What risk does a church without an elder take when meeting for a time of participative encouragement (1Co 14)?

14. What evidence is there that children remained in the church meeting with their parents?

Participatory Meetings

15. Having a open format could conceivably attract heretics who would seek to advance their novel views. How should this be prepared for and handled?

16. What should be done if, week after week, few people contribute anything of significance in the participatory meeting?

17. Where does the New Testament reveal that the purpose of a church meeting is to conduct a worship service? Explain.

18. In what ways does the church you currently attend conform to, or deviate from, the New Testament standard?

Note: NTRF also offers a teacher's resource to help lead a discussion of New Testament church life. Request *The Practice of The Early Church: A Theological Workbook (Leader's Guide)* from www.NTRF.org.

A LETTER TO PROSPECTIVE VISITORS

We are honored that you have expressed an interest in visiting one of our church meetings. We have made a conscious effort to seek to follow the traditions of the original apostles in our church practice. Thus, even though we are quite traditional in the New Testament sense, what we do is rather unconventional by contemporary standards. Anyhow, the following will give you a good idea of what to expect. Our hope is that you will feel comfortable and encouraged when meeting with us.

We meet in the morning, in the city of Oz. For location and directions, please call Bob & Jane Smith at (000)-000-0000 or Bill & Sue Jones at (000)-000-0000.

1. Following the pattern of the New Testament, the church comes together regularly on the first day of each week. This is known in Scripture as the Lord's Day, the day Jesus conquered death and rose from the grave. We do not, however, see it as any type of sabbath day. Every day is a holy day under the New Covenant (Heb 4, Col 2:16-17, Ga 4:8 - 11).

2. The doors of the host's home open at 10 a.m. and the singing starts promptly one half hour later. Thus you can see that there is a 30 minute window for folks to come in, get settled, visit, get coffee, etc. Please try to park on the same side of the street on which the home is located. This will make it less likely that our cars will choke up the neighborhood street.

3. Our dress code is casual and comfortable. Nobody wears a tie. Ladies wear anything from comfortable dresses to pants to modest shorts. Children usually end up playing outside after the meeting and therefore wear play clothes and shoes. Getting dirty after church is not uncommon for the kids.

4. Inquiring minds will want to know that our church holds to the historic doctrines of the Christian faith, the Doctrine of Grace, New Covenant Theology (www.ids.org), biblical inerrancy (www.churchcouncil.org), and the Danver's Statement on Biblical Manhood and Womanhood (www.cbmw.org). You can find out more about New Testament church life at www.ntrf.org.

5. The meeting itself is spontaneous and participatory (no bulletin!) following the pattern outlined in 1 Corinthians 14:25ff. Nothing is preplanned except the starting time of the first song (10:30 a.m.). Sometimes we sing many songs, sometimes we sing a few songs, depending on how many are requested. On one Sunday three brothers may teach, while on other weeks no one will teach. Sometimes we pray a

long time, sometimes very little. All the brothers can participate verbally, but anything said must be designed to edify the whole church (1Co 14:26). Only one person at a time is allowed to address the assembly, since everything is to be done in a fitting and orderly way. All teaching and prophecies are liable to public cross examination and judgment by those who are present. Further, there is neither moderator nor emcee *per se*. In fact, unless there is a problem to correct, you will not even know who our leaders are. Ladies do not speak out publicly in the 1 Corinthians 14 meeting (look up 1 Corinthians 14:33-35 and you'll see what this is based on). In contrast, they do speak quite a bit during the fellowship of the Lord's Supper.

6. The children stay with us in the meeting, though if a really young child gets noisy one of his parents will take him out until he calms down. If you have young children you may wish to bring along something to keep them happy, such as a drawing pad and crayons or *quiet* toys. The kids usually sit on the floor close to their parents. We believe it is the parents' job, not the church's, to teach their children about Jesus. Thus, we purposely have no Sunday school nor children's church.

7. The Lord's Supper is an integral part of our gathering. Actually, it is the primary reason we come together each week. We celebrate it as a full meal as is clearly described in 1 Corinthians 11b. Everyone brings something to share with the whole church. We believe it is to be a true meal to typify the wedding banquet of the Lamb (Re 19). It's a great time of fellowship and encouragement and very much like a wedding party rather than a funeral. In the middle of all the food you will notice the one cup (one pitcher, actually) and the one loaf, representing the body and blood of our Lord. In fact, we believe that the Lord's Supper is designed to remind Jesus of His promise to return and partake of the meal again with His people.

8. In short, we believe that the patterns for church life evident in the New Testament are not merely descriptive, but are actually prescriptive (2Th 2:15, 1Co 11:2). Thus, we believe in home-based and sized fellowships, elder-led more so than elder-ruled churches, the ministry of itinerant workers, participatory meetings, and that the Lord's Supper and the Agape Feast are synonymous weekly events. You may find it helpful to read through 1 Corinthians 11:17-34 and 1 Corinthians 14:26-40 before coming.

9. For us, true church life occurs every day, as we see each other during the week, all week long. To facilitate this, we place a high priority on living as close together as is practical. So, the Lord's Day activities

described above are a limited expression of our weekly fellowship. To evaluate us based solely on what you observe in a Sunday meeting would be an incomplete analysis!

10. In a perfect situation, church is to be about community, not commuting. To fellowship with the saints only on Sundays is to do yourself a disservice. If you can't move into our area, we would like to help you eventually start (or find) a church in your own neighborhood, once you get the vision for New Testament church life.

In summary, our churches are committed to meeting and living out as simple as possible a reading and understanding of what the New Testament church gave us for a pattern. We know we don't have it all figured out yet. We are a work in progress. We tend to take issues one at a time and attempt to come to a biblically-based consensus before moving on. Everybody counts and ideally nobody gets run over or discounted. This means we sometimes move pretty slow, but with a high degree of peace and unity. For that we have been blessed and are grateful.

See you on the Lord's Day!

THE NEW TESTAMENT WAY OF MEETING

How is it then, brethren? When ye come together, everyone of you hath a psalm, hath a doctrine, hath a tongue, hath a revelation, hath an interpretation. Let all things be done unto edifying.

If any man speak in an unknown tongue, let it be by two or at the most by three, and that by course, and let one interpret. But if there be no interpreter, let him keep silence in the church; and let him speak to himself, and to God.

Let the prophets speak two or three, and let the other judge. If anything be revealed to another that sitteth by, let the first hold his peace. For ye may all prophesy one by one, that all may learn, and all may be comforted. And the spirits of the prophets are subject to the prophets. For God is not the author of confusion, but of peace, as in all the churches of the saints.

Let your women keep silence in the churches: for it is not permitted unto them to speak; but they are commanded to be under obedience, as also saith the law. And if they will learn anything, let them ask their husbands at home: for it is a shame for a woman to speak in the church. What! Came the word of God out from you? Or came it to you only?

If any man think himself to be a prophet, or spiritual, let him acknowledge that the things that I write unto you are the commandments of the Lord. But if any man be ignorant, let him be ignorant.

Wherefore, brethren, covet to prophesy, and forbid not to speak with tongues. Let all things be done decently, and in order.

— 1 Corinthians 14:26-40 (KJV)

The Modern Way Of Meeting

How is it then, brethren? When ye come together, the pastor hath a doctrine, and the minister of music hath psalms. Let all things be done unto worship.

If anyone besides the pastor hath a doctrine, let him not speak; let him hold his peace. Let him sit in the pew, and face the back of the neck of the person which sitteth ahead of him.

Let the people keep silence in the churches: for it is not permitted unto them to speak; but they are commanded to be under obedience, as also saith church tradition. But if they will learn anything, let them ask their pastor after the service, for it is a shame for a layman to speak in the church. For the pastor, he hath a seminary degree, and the layman, he hath not so lofty a degree.

If any man desire to remain a church member in good standing, let him acknowledge that what I write to you is the command of the denominational headquarters. But if any man ignore this, he shall be promptly escorted out the door by the ushers.

Wherefore brothers, covet not to speak in the church. Let all things be done decently and in the order in which it hath been written in the church bulletin.

— Rusty Entrekin

"We are a society with a common religious feeling, unity of discipline, a common bond of hope. We meet in gatherings and congregations to approach God in prayer, massing our forces to surround Him . . . We meet to read the divine Scriptures . . . Our presidents are elders of proved character . . .

Even if there is a treasury of a sort, it is not made up of money paid in initiation fees, as if religion were a matter of contract. Every man once a month brings some modest contribution – or whenever he wishes, and only if he does wish, and if he can; for nobody is compelled; it is a voluntary offering . . . to feed the poor and to bury them, for boys and girls who lack property and parents, and then for slaves grown old . . .

So we, who are united in mind and soul, have no hesitation about sharing property. All is common among us – except our wives. At that point we dissolve our partnership . . .

Our dinner shows its idea in its name; it is called by the Greek name for love . . . We do not take our places at table until we have first partaken of prayer to God. Only so much is eaten as satisfies hunger. After water for the hands come the lights; and then each, from what he knows of the Holy Scriptures, or from his own heart, is called before the rest to sing to God.

Prayer in like manner ends the banquet . . ."

(*Roman Civilization Source Book II: The Empire*, p. 588)

Tertullian lived around A.D. 200

4
CONGREGATIONAL CONSENSUS

Why do you suppose that Jesus chose the word church to describe His followers? "Church" is the English translation of the original Greek term *ekklesia*. Outside the context of the New Testament, *ekklesia* was a secular word that carried strong political connotations. There were other Greek words Jesus could have used to describe His followers and their gatherings, words that carried *religious* and *nonpolitical* connotations. As we will see, one of the reasons He chose the word *ekklesia* to describe His followers is because He wanted them to make corporate decisions that affected all of them as a group. How did Jesus intend for the church to be governed? Let's begin by looking more closely at how the true meaning of the modern word church has been all but lost.

THE MODERN CHURCH AND THE ANCIENT *EKKLESIA*

Webster's New Collegiate Dictionary states that the English word church can be used to refer to either a meeting of God's people or to the special building in which they meet.[1] In contrast, the Greek word *ekklesia* never refers to a building or place of worship, and it can refer to *much more* than just a meeting, assembly, or gathering. Our understanding of God's church will be much impoverished if we fail to factor in the dynamics of the original Greek word used by Jesus. With so much emphasis today on the separation of church and state, the last thing people associate church with is government. Yet, this was exactly the original meaning of *ekklesia*.

During the time of Jesus, the word *ekklesia* was used almost without exception to refer to a political assembly that was regularly convened for the purpose of making decisions. According to Thayer's lexicon it was "an assembly of the people convened at the public place of council for the purpose of deliberation."[2] Bauer's lexicon defines *ekklesia* as an "assembly of a regularly summoned political body."[3] Dr. Lothan Coenen, writing for *The New International Dictionary of New Testament Theology*, noted that *ekklesia* was "clearly characterized as a political phenomenon, repeated according to certain rules and within a certain framework. It was the assembly of full citizens, functionally rooted in the constitution of the democracy, an assembly in which fundamental political and judicial decisions were taken . . . the word *ekklesia*, throughout the Greek and Hellenistic areas, always retained its reference to the assembly of the polis." In the secular *ekklesia*, every citizen had "the right to speak and to propose matters for discussion."[4] (Women were not allowed to speak at all in the secular Greek *ekklesia*).[5]

This secular usage can be illustrated from within the Bible as well, in Acts 19:23-41. These Acts 19 occurrences of *ekklesia* (translated "assembly," "legal assembly," and "assembly" in 19:32, 39, 41) referred to a meeting of craftsmen who had been called together by Demetrius into the town theater to decide what to do about Paul, though there was so much confusion the majority did not know why they had been summoned. This is an example of *ekklesia* used to refer to a regularly summoned political body (in this case, silver craftsmen and those in related trades). They convened (as a sort of trade union) to decide what to do about a damaged reputation and lost business. As it turned out, they overstepped their jurisdiction in wanting to deal with Paul, so the city clerk suggested that the matter be settled by the "legal" *ekklesia* (rather than by the trade union *ekklesia,* Ac 19:37-39*)*.

Jesus' Use Of *Ekklesia*

In light of all this, why did Jesus (in Mt 16:13-20; 18:15-20) choose such a politically "loaded" word as *ekklesia* to describe His people and their meetings? Perhaps Jesus intended His people, Christians, to be function together with the a purpose somehow parallel to that of the political government. Jesus designed that believers propose matters for discussion, decide things together, make joint decisions, and experience the consensus process. Had Jesus merely wanted to describe a gathering with no such political connotation, he could have used *sunagogé, thiasos* or *eranos*. Significantly, however, He chose *ekklesia*.

God's people have a decision-making mandate. A church is fundamentally a body of Kingdom citizens who are authorized (and expected) to weigh issues, make decisions, and pass judgments. Though decision making will not occur at most church meetings (there aren't usually issues to resolve), an understanding that the church corporately has the authority and obligation to settle things is important. Churches whose meetings focus solely on praise music and teaching, never grappling corporately with problems and resolving issues, may be failing to fulfill their full purpose as an *ekklesia*.

There are many examples in the New Testament of God's people making decisions as a body. That Jesus expected decision making from the *ekklesia* is seen in Matthew 16:13-20. After promising to build His *ekklesia* on the rock of Peter's revealed confession, Jesus immediately spoke of the keys of the kingdom of heaven and of binding and loosing. Keys represent the ability to open and to close something, kingdom is a political term, and binding and loosing involves the authority to make decisions. Then, in Matthew 18:15-20, Jesus said that the *ekklesia* (18:17) is obligated to render a verdict regarding a brother's alleged sin, and once again, binding and loosing authority is conferred upon the *ekklesia*.

In Acts 1:15-26, Peter charged the Jerusalem church as a whole with finding a replacement for Judas. Later, the apostles looked to the church corporately to pick men to administer the church's welfare system (Ac 6:1-6). Acts 14:23 (marginal translation) indicates that some churches elected their own elders. During the circumcision controversy, the church of Antioch decided to send to Jerusalem for arbitration, and then the whole church in Jerusalem was in on the resolution of the conflict (Ac 15:4, 12, 22). Finally, in 1 Corinthians 14:29-30 it was made clear that judgment was to be passed on prophetic revelation when "the whole *ekklesia* comes together" (14:23).

It is important to note that the church, in its decision making role, should be judicial rather than legislative. The church's job is not to create law – only God can rightly do that. This is one point where the *ekklesia* of God's people is different in function from the *ekklesia* of the old Greek city-states. Our responsibility as believers within Christ's *ekklesia* is to correctly apply and enforce the law of Christ as contained in the New Covenant. Church members are to be like citizen-judiciaries who meet together to deliberate and decide issues, or to render judgments (when necessary). This form of government works tolerably well in a house church where people love each other enough to work through their disagreements. It is virtually impossible to operate this way in a larger institutional church setting.

APPLICATION

Not all occurrences of the word *ekklesia* in the New Testament involve decision making. The word *ekklesia* is actually used six different ways in the New Testament. Yet its most fundamental usage remains that of a group of people gathered for the purpose of making decisions. In this sense, the *ekklesia* is not merely the coming together of God's people. It is also what *occurs* when God's people come together. The church is authorized by the Lord to make decisions about the correct application of Scripture. It is expected to enforce the law of Christ (within the family of God) and to deal with issues as they arise. This is a *part* of what is to occur in open, participatory church meetings.

Problems must not be swept under the rug. Questions of correct conduct must be resolved. There will not be issues to resolve every week (or even most weeks), but God's people must ever bear in mind their obligation to function as an *ekklesia* when necessary.

In its human organization, the church is not supposed to be a pyramid with power concentrated at the top in either one man or a few. Decisions are not to be made behind closed doors and then handed down from on high for the church to follow. The church is rather like the senate or a congress that deliberates upon, and decides, issues as an assembly. The church's leaders are to facilitate this process and to serve the church by providing needed teaching and advice, but they are not the church's lords.

There are limits to what a local church, as a decision-making body, should decide. Certain topics are out of bounds, are off-limits, are category errors. For instance, no local church has license to redefine the historic Christian faith. Some things are simply not open for debate. Each *ekklesia* is to operate within the bounds of orthodoxy. The elders are to rule out of bounds the consideration of harmful and heretical ideas (1Ti 1:3). This is because the church at large today, and throughout time past, already has consensus on certain fundamental interpretations of Scripture (such as which writings make up the Bible, the bodily resurrection of Jesus, the Gospel message, the Trinity, the future bodily return of Jesus, etc.). The Holy Spirit has not failed in His mission of guiding the elect into all truth (Jn 16:13).

Consensus or Majority Rule?

What we are essentially arguing for is congregational rule. Because the *ekklesia* is to deliberate as an assembly upon issues that arise, what if there is disagreement and the members split on an issue? Are decisions made by *consensus* or *majority vote*? Let's first consider what is implied in those two options.

The word "consensus" means general agreement, representative trend or opinion. It is related to the word "consent" or "consensual." In contrast, majority rule can be a 51% dictatorship for the 49% who didn't agree, and this certainly works against unity. Consensus, however, seeks to build unity. Would God have His church make decisions based on consensus or majority rule? Consider the following biblical texts as you and I reach a consensus on this issue:

"How good and pleasant it is when brothers live together in unity" (Ps 133:1).

"I appeal to you, brothers, in the name of our Lord Jesus Christ, that all of you agree with one another so that there may be no divisions among you and that you may be perfectly united in mind and thought" (1Co 1:10).

"Consequently, you are . . . members of God's household, built on the foundation of the apostles and the prophets, with Christ Jesus himself as the chief cornerstone. In him the whole building is joined together and rises to become a holy temple in the Lord. And in him you too are being built together to become a dwelling in which God lives by his Spirit" (Ep 2:19-22).

"Make every effort to keep the unity of the Spirit through the bond of peace. There is one body and one Spirit - just as you were called to one hope when you were called - one Lord, one faith, one baptism; one God and Father of all, who is over all and through all and in all" (Ep 4:3-6).

"If you have any encouragement from being united with Christ, if any comfort from his love, if any fellowship with the Spirit, if any tenderness and compassion, then make my joy complete by being like-minded, having the same love, being one in spirit and purpose" (Php 2:1-2).

"Therefore, as God's chosen people, holy and dearly loved, clothe yourselves with compassion, kindness, humility, gentleness and patience. Bear with each other and forgive whatever grievances you may have against one another. Forgive as the Lord forgave you. And over all these virtues put on love, which binds them all together in perfect unity" (Col 3:12-15).

Most of the process of building consensus will not occur during a church meeting. Instead, it will go on during the fellowship of the Lord's Supper, in midweek visits, over lunch, via casual phone conversations, by e-mail, etc. Of course sometimes various brothers, and especially leaders, may bring teachings that are relevant to the issue under consideration. The majority of the deliberation, however, will take place one on one, brother to brother. Bringing the church members into agreement with one another takes time, patience, humility and gentleness.

God's Provision

It is important to remember that the process a church goes through in achieving consensus is often just as important as the consensus that is finally achieved. Consensus governing takes time, commitment, mutual-edification, and a lot of brotherly love. It truly *can* work in a small, house-sized church. We must love each other enough to put up with each other! The concept behind consensus might be called government by unity, oneness, harmony, or mutual agreement. Do we really trust in the Holy Spirit to work in our lives and churches?

Lest government by consensus seem too utopian, consider what the Lord has done to help His people achieve unity. First, our Lord Himself prayed for His church "that they may be one as we are one . . . My prayer is . . . that all of them may be one, Father, just as you are in me and I am in you . . . May they be brought into complete unity to let the world know that you sent me and have loved them even as you have loved me" (Jn 17:11, 20-23). Since Jesus prayed this for us, unity is certainly achievable.

Another provision God made for our unity lies in the Lord's Supper. According to 1 Corinthians 10:17, "Because there is one loaf, we, who are many, are one body, for we all partake of the one loaf." Evidently, properly partaking of the one loaf during the Lord's Supper not only pictures unity, it can even create it!

Finally, as already mentioned above, Christ gave various ministry and leadership gifts to the church (such as apostles, prophets, evangelists, and pastor-teachers) for a purpose: "until we all reach unity in the faith and in the knowledge of the Son of God and become mature, attaining to the whole measure of the fullness of Christ" (Ep 4:11-13). One reason Christ give the church such leaders is to help the church achieve consensus.

What About Elders?

Where and how do elders factor into church government by corporate consensus? Elders are critical to the long-term survival of a church. Elders guide, model, persuade, teach, feed, council, protect, warn, advise, rebuke and correct.

The church as a whole may be compared to a senate, with the authority to make decisions and render judgments that are binding on its members. A church elder is just a fellow senator, but one who is on a special senate committee whose purpose is to study issues, make recommendations, teach, inform, or prompt. Normally, the elder is not to make decisions on behalf of the church. He does not usually preempt the consensus process. All elders are senator-servants to the whole senate (church). However, the senate will occasionally find itself in grid-lock, unable to resolve an issue. In such rare cases, the elders serve as predetermined arbitrators, or tie breakers. With these unusual instances those in opposition are to "submit" to the elder's leadership and wisdom (Heb 13:17).

In Hebrews 13:17, believers are encouraged to "obey" church leaders. How does this square with congregational rule? The common word for obey is used with reference to children obeying their parents and slaves their masters (Ep 6:1, 5). It is significant that the Greek behind obey in Hebrews 13:17 is not the usual word. Instead, *peitho* is used, which Bauer's lexicon fundamentally defines as persuade or convince.[6] (Other examples of *peitho* can be found in Luke 16:31, Acts 17:4, 21:14). Paul McReynolds' literal interlinear renders *peitho* in Hebrews 13:17 as "persuade." Used in Hebrews 13:17 in the middle/passive form, it carries the idea of, "let yourselves be persuaded by" your leaders. Certainly, when someone is persuaded of something, he will act on it, or "obey" it (Ro 2:8, Ga 5:7, Ja 3:3). The expositor Vine notes that *peitho* means, "to persuade, to win over to, to listen to, to obey. The obedience suggested is not by submission to authority, but resulting from persuasion"[7] The point to be observed is that mindless obedience is not what is pictured in Hebrews 13:17.

This same verse also instructs believers to "submit" to their church leaders. As with "obey," the common Greek word for "submit" is not used. Instead, *hupeiko* was chosen by the author, a word that still does mean to give in, to yield, but after a fight. It was used of combatants. The idea behind *hupeiko* is seen in Southern General Robert E. Lee's letter to his troops concerning the surrender at Appomadox: "After four years of arduous service, marked by unsurpassed courage and fortitude, the Army of Northern Virginia has been compelled to yield to overwhelming numbers and resources." The nuance of *hupeko* is not a structure to which one automatically submits (like submission to civil government). Rather, it is submission after a process, struggle, or even a battle, has occurred. Submission does occur, but the picture is one of serious discussion and dialog prior to one party giving way.

Thus, God's flock is to be open to being persuaded by (*peitho*) its shepherds. In the course of on-going discussion and teaching the flock is to be open to being convinced (*peitho*) by its leaders. Mindless slave-like obedience is not the relationship presented in the New Testament between elders and the church. However, there will be those times when someone, or some few, in the flock can't be persuaded of something and an impasse will arise. When necessary to break the grid-lock, dissenters are to give in to, to yield to (*hupeiko*), the wisdom of the church leaders.

Thus, in the final analysis, churches are to be elder *led* more so than elder *ruled*. Consensus congregational rule is the New Testament pattern. The times when a church might be temporarily elder-ruled is when one or a few within the church become self-willed, unreasonable, obstinate, divisive, enslaved to sin, or deceived into false doctrine (Heb 13:17). Even this submission, however, is to come after dialogue, discussion and reasoning.

CONCLUSION

What we have argued for might be compared to government by a parliamentary monarchy. King Jesus is our Monarch. The church is His consensus-based Parliament. Every church member is a Member of Parliament (in the House of Commons). The elders are also Members of Parliament, but serve as party whips with policing roles. (Remember, of course, that any analogy breaks down if pressed too far!) The general idea is church polity by elder-led congregational consensus.

— Steve Atkerson

NOTES

1 Henry Woolf, ed., *Webster's New Collegiate Dictionary* (Springfield, MA: Merriman, 1973), 200.

2 Joseph Thayer, *Greek-English Lexicon of the New Testament* (Grand Rapids, MI: Baker, 1977), 196.

3 Bauer, Arndt, Gingrich, Danker, *A Greek-English Lexicon of the New Testament and Other Early Christian Literature* (Chicago, IL: University of Chicago Press, 1979), 240.

4 Lothan Coenen, "Church," *The New International Dictionary of New Testament Theology,* Vol. 1, Colin Brown, General Editor (Grand Rapids, MI: Zondervan, 1971), 291.

5 Wayne Gruden & John Piper, *Recovering Biblical Manhood and Womanhood* (Wheaton, IL: Crossway Books, 1991), 150.

6 Bauer, 639.

7 W.E. Vine, *An Expository Dictionary of New Testament Words* (Iowa Falls, IA: Riverside Book and Bible House, 1952), 124.

DISCUSSION QUESTIONS

1. What is the difference between episcopal, presbyterian, and congregational church polity?
2. What did the Greek word *ekklesia* originally refer to?
3. Why do you suppose that Jesus chose such a politically loaded word like *ekklesia* to describe His followers?
4. What are some examples in the New Testament of God's people making decisions as a body?
5. What is the difference between majority rule and congregational consensus?
6. What is the difference between consensus and unanimity?
7. What provisions has God made to help a church achieve consensus?
8. Where and how do elders factor into church government by corporate consensus?
9. According to Jesus, how much authority should church leaders have (Lk 22:24-27)?
10. In Hebrews 13:17, believers are encouraged to "obey" and "submit" to church leaders. How does this square with congregational rule?
11. What types of people and situations do you suppose Hebrews 13:17 is designed for?
12. How should both local congregational consensus and universal church consensus apply to interpreting the Bible?

Note: NTRF also offers a teacher's resource to help lead a discussion of New Testament church life. Request *The Practice of The Early Church: A Theological Workbook (Leader's Guide)* from www.NTRF.org.

PART ONE

That the original church held its meetings primarily in private homes is common knowledge and without dispute (Ac 16:40, 20:20, Ro 16:3-5a, 1Co 16:19, Col 4:15, Phlm 1-2b, Jam 2:3). Less well known is the fact that the early church continued this practice for hundreds of years, long after the New Testament writings were completed. G.F. Snyder observed, "the New Testament Church began as a small group house church (Col. 4:15), and it remained so until the middle or end of the third century. There are no evidences of larger places of meeting before 300."[1] For longer than the United States has existed as a nation, the nearly universal practice of the church was to meet in houses. Again quoting Snyder, "there is no literary evidence nor archaeological indication that any such home was converted into an extant church building. Nor is there any extant church that certainly was built prior to Constantine."[2] Why were house churches the norm for so long?

PERSECUTION?

The most common explanation for the existence of early house churches was the pressure of persecution, similar to the situation that exists today in China. However, could there also have been other, equally compelling, reasons for having living room oriented fellowships? Suppose there had been no first century persecution. Are we to assume that church buildings would automatically have been constructed, and that individual congregations would have swelled to enormous size, limited only by the dimensions of the biggest building locally available?

It is often overlooked that the followers of Jesus sometimes met in homes while simultaneously "enjoying the favor of all the people" (Ac 2:47, NIV). Persecution was not always a factor. Based on 1 Corinthians 14:23 ("if the whole church comes together and . . . some unbelievers come in," NIV), it is possible that unbelievers also attended church meetings, so where they met was not always a secret to outsiders. It is simply not true that early believers were always persecuted everywhere and all the time. Persecution prior to around A.D. 250 was sporadic, localized, and often the result of mob hostility (rather than the empire-wide decree of a Roman ruler). Surprisingly, Roman officials are often presented in a somewhat favorable light by the New Testament writers since they intervened to protect Christians from unlawful local harassment by unbelieving Judaism (Ac 16:35, 17:6-9, 18:12-16, 19:37-38, 23:29, 25:18-20, 25:24-27, 26:31-32). Prior to 250, Christianity was illegal, but generally tolerated. The simple fact is that widespread persecution did not occur until Emperor Decius in A.D. 250, followed by Gallus (251-253), then Valerian (257-259) and finally Diocletian (303-311).[3] Someone, somewhere, could have constructed a special church building in the 200 years prior to Decius, but significantly, *no one ever did*. (Even in China today some believers manage to construct church buildings.) This suggests there might have also been a theological purpose behind home meetings.

When persecution did erupt, meeting in homes did not keep Saul from knowing exactly where to go to arrest Christians (Ac 8:3). The church in Rome later responded to government persecution by meeting underground, in the more protective catacombs. Even the presence of persecution, however, would not necessarily rule out a deeper, purposeful preference for smaller, house-sized congregations. The fact remains that everything in the New Testament was written to a living room sized church, and arguably the New Testament ideal for church life is best realized in a smaller, family like setting.

Poverty?

Could poverty have been a deciding factor in explaining the total absence of church buildings during New Testament times and for centuries afterwards? Many of the earliest converts to Christianity were from Judaism. The construction of synagogues was common throughout the Mediterranean world. Presumably these same people would also have had the means to construct church buildings. The communalism of Acts 4:32-36 reveals that many early converts owned lands and houses. The bulk of converts in later years were of Gentile stock, whose fellow pagans somehow managed to erect huge temples to their gods. Would not Gentile Christians also have been able to afford to construct places for the church to gather?

That some rich were among God's elect is made clear by the advice that Timothy received to "instruct those who are rich in this present world not to be conceited or to fix their hope on the uncertainty of riches, but on God, who richly supplies us with all things to enjoy. Instruct them to do good, to be rich in good works, to be generous and ready to share, storing up for themselves the treasure of a good foundation for the future, so that they may take hold of that which is life indeed" (1 Ti 6:17-18,

NASV). Also, James warned against showing favoritism toward those who came to the church gathering wearing a gold ring and fine clothes (Jam 2:1-4), indicating such persons were indeed involved with the church.

Further evidence of the presence of wealthy believers can be seen in Paul's rebuke to the rich in Corinth for slighting the poor by refusing to eat the Lord's Supper along with them: "Or do you despise the church of God, and shame those who have nothing? What shall I say to you? Shall I praise you? In this I will not praise you" (1Co 11:22, NASV). Poverty alone clearly was not a deciding factor in the lack of church buildings during those early centuries.

PROGRESSION?

Some think that God intended for the practice of meeting in homes to be a legitimate phase of the church's early development, an initial but transitory step toward later maturity. Thus house churches were characteristic of the church in its infancy, but not in its maturity. It was right and natural, they argue, for the church to grow beyond these early practices and develop ways that are far different than, but in the spirit of, the practices of the apostles as recorded in Scripture. Thus the erection of cathedrals, large worship services, the rise of one bishop presiding over a city of churches, the development of the modern hierarchical presbytery system, even the eventual merger of church and state after Constantine, are seen as good and positive developments.

Yet the apostles seem to have intended for churches to adhere to the specific patterns that they originally established. For instance, the Corinthians were praised for holding to the apostles' traditions for church practice (1Co 11:2). Sweeping appeals for holding to various church practices were made based on the universal practices of all the other churches (1Co 11:16, 1Co 14:33b-34). The Thessalonians were directly commanded to hold to the traditions of the apostles (2Th 2:15). The apostles were handpicked and personally trained by our Lord. If anyone ever understood the purpose of the church, it was these men. The practices that they established for the church's corporate activities would certainly be in keeping with their understanding about the purpose of the church. Respect for the Spirit by whom they were led should lead us to prefer their modes of organization to any alternative that our own creative thinking might suggest.

Also telling is the total absence of any instruction in the New Testament regarding the construction of special buildings for worship. This is in contrast to Old Covenant Mosaic legislation, which contained very specific blueprints regarding the tabernacle. When the New Covenant writers did touch upon this subject, they pointed out that believers themselves are the temple of the Holy Spirit, living stones that come together to make up a spiritual house with Jesus Christ as the chief corner stone (1Pe 2:4-5, Ep 2:19-22, 1Co 3:16, 6:19). Thus at the very best, church buildings are a matter of indifference to our Lord. At the worst they can be a carnal throwback to the shadows of Mosaic law. The real issue is not where a church meets, but where and how it can best do what God requires of it. A major reason that church buildings are erected is in order to hold more people than will fit into a typical living room. Yet one must wonder at the wisdom behind constructing a large church edifice, since having too many in attendance can serve to defeat the very purpose for holding a church meeting in the first place! Large crowds are great for worship services, evangelistic meetings or to hear preaching, but church is to be about something completely different than these activities (see below).

A PURPOSEFUL PATTERN?

Might the apostles have laid down a purposeful pattern of home churches? What practical effects would meeting in a home have on one's church life? It is a design axiom that form follows function. The apostles' belief concerning the function of the church was naturally expressed in the form that the church took on in the first century. Some of the distinct practices of the early (house) church are worth considering.

1. The over arching significance of the house church lies in its theology of community. The church was depicted by apostolic writers in terms which describe a family. Believers are children of God (1Jn 3:1) who have been born into his family (Jn 1:12-13). God's people are thus seen as part of God's household (Ep 2:19, Ga 6:10). They are called brothers and sisters (Phm 2, Ro 16:2). Consequently, Christians are to relate to each other as members of a family (1Ti 5:1-2; Ro 16:13). (In fact, in China today, house church is called family church.) Out of this theological point that God's children are family arises many church practice issues. The question becomes, what setting best facilities our functioning as God's family?

2. Many scholars are persuaded that the Lord's Supper was originally celebrated weekly as a full, fellowship meal (the Agape Feast). Each local church is to be like a family (1Ti 5:1-2), and one of the most common things families do is to eat together. Early church meetings, centered around the Lord's Table, were tremendous times of fellowship, community and encouragement (Lk 22:16-19, 29-30, Ac 2:42, 20:7, 1Co 11:17-34). Rather than a funeral-like atmosphere, the Lord's

Supper was in anticipation of the Wedding Banquet of the Lamb (Re 19:6-9). The larger an individual congregation, the less family-like it becomes, and the more impersonal and impractical the Lord's Supper as a true meal can become. Thus in later centuries, as the church abandoned home meetings, the Lord's Supper was eventually stripped of everything save the token ingestion of a small piece of bread and one swallow of wine.

3. Early church meetings were clearly participatory (1Co 14, Heb 10:24-25, Ep 5:19-20, Col 3:16). Any brother could contribute verbally. The prerequisite for anything said was that it be edifying, designed to strengthen the church. Since public speaking is a great fear for many people, participatory meetings are best suited to living room sized gatherings, composed of people who all know each other and are true friends. Participatory meetings are impractical for large numbers. Once the living room setting was replaced by the sanctuary, interactive meetings were replaced by worship services.

4. The Scriptures are full of the "one another" commands. Church is to be about accountability, community, and maintaining church discipline (Mt 18:15-20). These ideals are best accomplished in smaller congregations where people know and love each other. Church is to be about relationships. A large auditorium of people, most of whom are relative strangers to each other, will not easily achieve these goals. Nominal Christianity is harbored as it becomes easy to get lost in the crowd. Churches that meet in homes best foster the simplicity, vitality, intimacy and purity that God desires for his church.

5. The New Testament church had clearly identified leaders (elders, pastors, overseers), yet these leaders led more by example and persuasion than by command. The elder-led consensus of the whole congregation was paramount in decision making (Mt 18:15-20, Lk 22:24-27, Jn 17:11, 20-23, 1Co 1:10, 10:17, Ep 2:19-20, 4:13-17, Phlp 2:1-2, 1Pe 5:1-3). Achieving consensus is possible in a church where everyone knows each other, loves each other, bears with one another, is patient with one another, and is committed to each other. However, the larger the fellowship, the more impossible it becomes to maintain relationships and lines of communication. In a large congregation, the pastor necessarily functions more like the CEO of a corporation.

6. The first century church turned their world upside down (Ac 17:6), and they did so using the New Testament house church. House churches are low cost, generally lay led, can reproduce quickly, and have great potential for growth through evangelism. We need to think small in a really big way! God does not equate bigness with ability.

Paul reminded that "God chose the foolish things of the world to shame the wise; God chose the weak things of the world to shame the strong. He chose the lowly things of this world and the despised things — and the things that are not — to nullify the things that are, so that no one may boast before him" (1Co 1:27-29, NIV).

7. The New Testament urges the generous support of missionaries, evangelists, qualified elders, and the poor (1Co 9, 1 Ti 5:17-18, 3 Jn 5-8). Which group of believers would better be able to fund church planters and assist the poor, a thousand believers organized in a single traditional church that meets in their own church sanctuary, complete with a Sunday school complex and family life center (gym), or a thousand believers networked together in cooperating house churches? Surveys of Protestant congregations in America reveal that on average 80% of church revenues goes toward buildings, staff and internal programs; 20% goes to outreach. In house church networks, those percentages are easily reversed. Being freed from the burden of constructing church buildings and their resulting expenses would also allow greater sums of money to go toward the support of church workers and the needy.

8. Since they met almost exclusively in private homes, the typical congregation of the apostolic era was small. No specific number is ever given in Scripture, but there were generally no more people than will fit comfortably into the average living-room. The pattern is for smaller, rather than larger, churches. Regarding the size of first century homes, Fuller seminary professor Robert Banks, wrote that "the entertaining room in a moderately well-to-do household could hold around 30 people comfortably — perhaps half as many again in an emergency . . . it is unlikely that a meeting of the "whole church" could have exceeded 40 to 45 people, and may well have been smaller . . . In any event we must not think of these as particularly large . . . Even the meetings of the "whole church" were small enough for a relatively intimate relationship to develop between the members."[4]

CONCLUSION

We are not arguing for meeting in houses simply for the sake of meeting in houses. We are suggesting that the apostolic church did not erect church buildings in large part because they simply didn't need them. God intended the typical church to be living room sized. The letters which were written to the various New Testament churches were in fact written to house churches. Because they are written to house churches the instructions contained in them are geared to work in a smaller congregation — they were never meant to work in a large group setting. Consequently, they don't work well in such a setting. To attempt to apply New Testament church practices to a contemporary large church is just as unnatural as pouring new wine into old wineskins (Mt 9:17).

— Steve Atkerson

PART TWO

Why do we keep insisting that churches ought normally to meet in people's houses? Won't anywhere else do? A lot of churches that practice in the way we advocate meet in Christian book shops and coffee shops that have a lounge area just like in someone's private house; what's wrong with that? Well, I suppose that in some parts of the world Eskimos might meet in igloos and Red Indians in teepees; and of course on a nice day (and we even get them occasionally here in England too) what possible objection could there be to meeting in the garden (that's the 'yard' to my American readers) or in a field somewhere? And to the above I have no objections whatsoever, but merely wish to bring us back to the essential point that the format for church gatherings in the New Testament kept each individual church small in numbers, and was therefore simply perfectly suited to everything occurring in people's home. What more, after all, does a biblically based church need for its gatherings than the homes of those who are part of it? And when it comes to biblical churches meeting in lounge areas of book shops and coffee shops – or indeed, in any other public building – there is actually a big problem that will (hopefully) have to eventually be faced, but of which some seem to be completely unaware.

Now it is certainly true that a church could meet in a public building of some kind and still remain small enough in number to function as scripture teaches; and if such a building can be arranged with a nice cozy lounge area and made to feel "like home," then all the better. Indeed, assuming there are kitchen facilities then there isn't even a problem regarding sharing the love-feast together. But there is a problem to be faced, and a big one too, and it is simply this: A first-generation biblical church may well be able to come together and meet in such a way without any problem - but what of the situation once growth occurs and other churches need to come into being from it? (I am assuming that, being biblically based, this imagined church does indeed want to grow numerically, as the Lord enables, and not just remain the same personnel its whole life.) So, do you see the problem? That church can't just keep getting numerically bigger (even though larger numbers can easily be accommodated by virtue of the fact of it meeting in a public building) because it could then no longer function in the way the New Testament teaches that it should, and another church needs to come into existence. And here is the point: Where will that church meet?

Now there may, of course, be an abundant supply of Christian coffee houses and book shops round about with nice lounge and kitchen areas, and so I guess new churches could just go and hire them out; but I still think that an important question remains: Why not just meet in each others houses? I mean, what is the problem with simply doing that? It is, after all, what every church in scripture did. (Every time individual churches are given a location in the New Testament it is always, and without fail, in someone's home.) So why, oh why, would you want to be different? Why be a church that is biblically based in every other respect, having bought into the notion that we should do things just like they did back then, and then break ranks over this?

Could it possibly be (though surely not) that behind this is a feeling that opening our homes to each other is a bit too inconvenient? Too close for comfort, even? The apostles of Jesus taught believers to open their homes to each other and to actually have their church gatherings in each others homes. After all, am I truly known as I should be if my home-life isn't wide open to those with whom I have fellowship? Can people know me properly, truly and deeply, if they don't regularly see my home life and family life and have it shared with them? Are we really to believe that meeting in homes was a purely incidental aspect of the blueprint for church life we find in scripture, or is it as significant and important as the other aspects such as open, participatory gatherings, having the Lord's Supper as a full meal and practicing biblical leadership and consensual church government? I put it to you that the burden of proof very much lies with those who seem to think it unimportant!

However, let me say too that where homes are literally too small to have more than three or four people visiting at any one time (Tokyo, perhaps?), then by all means make other appropriate provision. The irony is that in the very place where this trend is particularly prevalent, America, homes are very definitely on the large size. (At least they are by our standards here in England where, incidentally, at our church we pack each other into our homes, come what may, even though it means that in some of them, mine included, you can't even see the carpet any more.)

So if you are a biblical church meeting in a coffee house some-where then fine; that sure is better than being an unbiblical church meeting in someone's home. However, do take on board the simple fact that, should you grow and become too large numerically to remain one church any longer (and as I have already indicated, you should most certainly desire for such to be the case), then how ridiculous to be trying to find more and more Christian coffee houses and the like to rent rather than just locating each church's gatherings in the homes of those who are part of them. How ridiculous as well to end up with a new church gathering in people's homes, whilst the original one continues to meet in the coffee house, or book shop, or public hall, or whatever.

Which ever way you look at it, it seems quite illogical to not just do things the way the New Testament churches, under the direction of the apostles, did them. A church can indeed meet in a public building and yet remain truly biblical in every other way as far as practice is concerned. Yet the question remains: When it is quite feasible, all things being equal, to meet in each others homes, and given that this was the universal practice of the New Testament churches as taught and directed by the apostles of Jesus, then why on earth would any otherwise biblical church want to decide not to do likewise?

— Beresford Job

PART THREE

How can a church keep from wearing out the host family and their home? New Testament writings indicate that the same couple hosted the church every week. This was probably due to the fact that larger homes, needed to host scores of people, were in short supply. Some people really do have the gift of hospitality and won't mind hosting the church every week, but admittedly this can be quite taxing. This is especially a problem if one spouse is out of tune with the other. Typically, the tuned-out spouse (usually a man) will be clueless to the miseries that the other one (usually the wife) is suffering in hosting the church weekly. Church members could come over to help clean up both before and after the meeting. Another alternative is for the meeting location to be rotated on a weekly basis, with all who have suitable dwellings sharing the load. It is good for others to learn hospitality! Further, each home could have its own house rules, such as: please take off your shoes when entering the house, no children jumping on the furniture, no eating in the living room, etc.

What if the homes are tiny and just too small for a meeting? This can be a real problem. One alternative is to add on to a home to make the meeting room bigger, or knock out a wall, or remove much of the furniture from the church meeting room, or close in a garage. If all else fails, renting an apartment clubhouse or some similar arrangement can work, as long as the objective is not to hold more people than could fit into a moderately well-to-do home. The typical first century house church was composed of scores of people, not hundreds of people.

How can we keep the neighbors from complaining about the cars? Rotate the church meeting from week to week between different homes, park only on one side of the street, be sure to fill up the drive way to get as many cars as possible off the street, park at a nearby school or closed store, etc. Remember too that the idea is to start a new church after the existing church starts to get crowded. There should not be all that many cars pulling up to park.

What type of property damage can hosting the church cause? Spilled drinks, food dropped on upholstery, crayon markings on the floor and table cloth, tracked in mud, etc. During one home church meeting a teenage girl ran through a closed sliding glass door. Be mentally and (medically) prepared for accidents.

How would you handle a situation where visitor's children, or the children of a newly attending couple, are not well behaved? Some couples' standards of acceptable social behavior are vastly different from others' standards. It may shock and amaze you at how indifferent some parents are to the destructive actions of their children. In such cases you must calmly, politely, and directly ask them to control their children. (And, expect them to be offended no matter how tactfully you approach them!). Doubtless, they will not have a good idea on how to control their children, so be prepared to help them with child training. Have a good supply of child training books on hand that you can give out.

Home meetings are not easier, but they are the New Testament way.

— Steve Atkerson

NOTES
[1] Graydon F. Synder, *Church Life Before Constantine* (Macon, GA: Mercer University Press: 1991) 166.
[2] Ibid., 67.
[3] Williston Walker, *A History of The Christian Church* (New York, NY: Charles Scribner's Sons, 1970) 43.
[4] Robert Banks, *Paul's Idea of Community: The Early House Churches in Their Historical Setting* (Grand Rapids, MI: Wm. B. Eerdmans Publishing Co., 1988), 41-42.

Discussion Questions

1. Why were house churches the norm in the New Testament and for so long afterwards?

2. What evidence is there that persecution and poverty were not the only reasons that the early church met in homes?

3. Some argue that house churches were characteristic of the church in its infancy, but not in its maturity. It was right and natural, they argue, for each church to grow beyond the house. How do you feel about this?

4. Why might the apostles have laid down a purposeful pattern of home churches?

5. What practical advantages would meeting in a home have on one's church life?

6. What of a situation where growth occurs and the congregation is getting too big for the home?

7. Are we to believe that meeting in homes was a purely incidental aspect of the blueprint for church life, or is it as purposeful as the other aspects such as participatory gatherings, having the Lord's Supper as a full meal and congregational consensus? Why?

8. How would the number of people impact a church's ability to have a participatory meeting or achieve congregational consensus?

9. What advantages for growth and reproduction would a house church approach have over a church building centered approach?

10. How was each of the early churches able to grow numerically and yet still meet in a private home?

11. What inconveniences will occur if homes are opened up for church meetings?

12. What should be done in a situation where a home is simply too small to host a church meeting?

13. What psychological impact might where we hold church meetings have on the actual meetings and people themselves?

Note: NTRF also offers a teacher's resource to help lead a discussion of New Testament church life. Request *The Practice of The Early Church: A Theological Workbook (Leader's Guide)* from www.NTRF.org.

6

TEN REASONS FOR HOUSE CHURCHES

Anglican evangelist David Watson observed that "For the first two centuries, the church met in small groups in the homes of its members, apart from special gatherings in public lecture halls or market places, where people could come together in much larger numbers. Significantly these two centuries mark the most powerful and vigorous advance of the church, which perhaps has never seen been equaled. The lack of church buildings was no hindrance to the rapid expansion of the church; instead, in comparison to the situation after A.D. 200, it seemed a positive help"[1]

It is obvious from the New Testament that the early churches generally gathered at homes (Ac 2:46, Ro 16:3, 5, 1Co 16:19, Col. 4:15, Phm 2). There was a massive expansion of the universal church when they gathered regularly and locally as small communities. The move of the Holy Spirit was awesome in and through these small communities of the early church. These small communities were like dynamite in their locale. Every member seemed to be active in the body of Christ as they met together in private homes and the Kingdom of God had spread mightily through the whole people of God.

Should *we* gather in houses simply because the early church had gathered so? Is it wrong to gather in a building? Certainly not! The early church didn't have vehicles to travel fast, seminars with PA system, guitars, phones, computers, etc., but does that mean we shouldn't use them? We don't gather in houses, having a narrow focus, just because the early church had so gathered. There are many good reasons to understand why gathering in houses is a good choice, helping us especially to function biblically. The following are the ten reasons why gathering in houses is an effective strategy for a healthy church.

ONE ANOTHER MINISTRY

Sometime back I received an article on church growth entitled, "Turning Visitors into Attenders." I wondered where in the Holy Bible it says about attending the church! According to the Holy Scriptures the church is comprised of functioning believers who actively participate for the edification of the body of Christ. Biblically thinking, there is a great need of messages that would address on, "Turning Attenders into

Participators." Church is not about attending formal services with a passivity; it is not a program but people. It is not going to service but doing service to one another. It is about intimate fellowship with one another. It is about actively encouraging one another. It is about inter-dependently functioning for the edification of all. Regretfully, in the structure and the order of the church today, we are often missing the very purpose of church gathering — the fellowship and encouragement of *one another* (Heb 10:25).

Robert Banks wrote, "The purpose of church is the growth and edification of its members into Christ and into a common life through their God-given ministry to one another (1 Cor. 14:12, 19, 26)."[2] Regretfully in our day, in stark contrast to New Testament church gatherings, the significance of every member functioning in the body of Christ is virtually lost. The theology of the priesthood of all believers appears to exist only in theory. The church has retreated and reverted back to the old Judaic and Roman Catholic makeup, which breeds the prevalent passivity. It is sad that today's church buildings functionally resemble temples, pastors dictate as priests and the New Testament church pattern has been discarded for the Old Testament temple system. David Watson rightly observed, "Ever since the Old Testament symbols were fulfilled in Christ and in His church, the church has faced constant temptations to bring back the institutions that Christ has fulfilled and removed; and she has, to a large extent, fallen to these temptations."[3]

There is a great need for a reformation in our church today that will restore the significance and the priestly functioning of each member in the body of Christ. It is said that the early church was "one another" fellowship, not "one man over others" service. Because of the lack of every member ministry, the church is not only in a passive state but also many leaders are suffering from stress and burnout. The church is supposed to be a team, not an audience, wherein all work together for its growth. The leaders are called not to model "superstar ministry" but to motivate "every member ministry" (Ep 4:11-12). Do we find one man having the dominant function in the early church? Is there a balance between teaching and every member participation in today's typical church gathering?

How are the leaders of the church motivating every member to function actively in the body of Christ and to effectively witness to the world? Is there the privilege and encouragement for every member to participate in the gathering of the church? William Barclay writes about the early church gathering, "The really notable thing about an early Church service must have been that almost everyone came feeling that he had both the privilege and obligation of contributing something to it."[4]   It seems that we have lost the sacred recognition that every member in the body of Christ is a precious, potential and powerful instrument of the Holy Spirit. In the early church the ministry belonged to the whole people of God.

In his challenging book *Rich Christians in an Age of Hunger,* Ronald J. Sider made a good point. He said, "The early church was able to defy the decadent values of Roman civilization precisely because it experienced the reality of Christian fellowship in a mighty way . . . Christian fellowship meant unconditional availability to and unlimited liability for the other sisters and brothers-emotionally, financially and spiritually. When one member suffered, they all suffered. When one rejoiced, they all rejoiced (1 Cor. 12:26). When a person or church experienced economic trouble, the others shared without reservation. And when a brother or sister fell into sin, the others gently restored the straying person (Mt. 18:15-17; 1 Cor. 5; 2 Cor. 2:5-11; Gal. 6:1-3). The sisters and brothers were available to each other, liable for each other and accountable to each other. The early church, of course, did not always fully live out the New Testament vision of the body of Christ. There were tragic lapses. But the network of tiny house churches scattered throughout the Roman Empire did experience their oneness in Christ so vividly that they were able to defy and eventually conquer a powerful, pagan civilization. The overwhelming majority of churches today, however, do not provide the context in which brothers and sisters can encourage, admonish and disciple each other. We desperately need new settings and structures for watching over one another in love."[5]

We need to understand that structure and systems exist for a purpose; they are not end in themselves. There is a great necessity for us to have structures and systems in a way that will benefit the effective functioning of the church. Gathering in houses facilitates much participation, interaction, discussion and one-another ministry. Also, it is in such a setting that teaching can be done more like a dialogue rather than like a monologue; it is more pervasive and most effective.

To function as effectively as the early church functioned, the structure, size and system matter a lot. The structure should be informal, the size of the community ought to be small and the system or order must be flexible. Since every member's participation and ministry was highly valued and encouraged in the early church, a home is a good setting wherein every person can comfortably contribute and function for the edification of the whole body of Christ.

Ten Reasons for House Churches

INTIMACY AND ACCOUNTABILITY

God's Word reveals that a church is a family of God and we are the members of God's household (Ep 2:19, 1Ti 3:15, Ga 6:10). Since the church is a family, everyone has the responsibility toward the welfare of all the members. Paul wrote, "If one part suffers, every part suffers with it; if one part is honored, every part rejoices with it" (1Co 12:26). How do we suppose this could happen in the church if we are not closely knit together as a family? How many believers are starving spiritually due to lack of good fellowship? Though we come together physically, isn't there a sense of lack of intimacy and accountability between one another? Are we really walking in love with intimate relationship? Early believers were so closely knit together as a family that they were falsely accused as being immoral and incestuous (because they called one another brother and sister, had love feasts, and greeted one another with a holy kiss).

There is a necessity to cultivate a family atmosphere in church gathering, rather than a sober and formal environment. The church is not a religious service but a family unit. Do the believers view the church as a family, having a sense that they belong to that family? Is there a familial atmosphere when we come together as a church? Don't we realize the necessity to emphasize relationship and fellowship between and among one another? We only seem to be having good services without genuine fellowship. How can we practically foster such an intimate fellowship when the church comes together? In a chapter entitled Small Is Beautiful, prolific author Robert Banks wrote, "Home churching enables us to come to know, love, and serve a manageable group of people who will come to know, love, and serve us as well. In such a group we can gradually let down the masks we wear in public and begin to share our weaknesses, doubts, and fears as well as our strengths, certainties, and abilities. Thus we start to overcome the ironic situation of being less open and less honest in church than we are elsewhere. In small home-church groups we learn to give and receive, to teach and understand, to carry others' burdens and receive help with our own, to love and be loved. In such a group we can become more like Christ and assist others to become more like Christ too. In doing so we develop a common Christ-like attitude, character, and way of operating. We become integrated into Christ more closely and more firmly."[6]

In a small community, intimacy and accountability become quite feasible and viable. The level of one's spirituality becomes obvious in small communities, thereby lending more room to encourage one another so that no one would be hardened by the deceitfulness of sin (Heb 3:13). We can relate to one another intimately, know one another, share with one another, exhort one another and stimulate one another to love and good deeds (Heb 10:24, 25). Gerald Oliver urged the church, "It is time that all become involved in small groups that are bound together by love which pray, study the Bible, fellowship, and hold each member accountable for the 168 hours of each week."[7] The privilege of stirring up intimacy and staying accountable to one another can be well practiced in this kind of small communities. We believe an informal place like a house is an effective place to practice all the above essentials.

THE LORD'S SUPPER

Michael Green pointed out that "communion (i.e. the Lord's Supper) in those days would be much more of a meal than it is today, and an opportunity for much informal worship and fellowship. The meal time was called an *agape*, a love-feast, and in later times it fell into disuse because it was much abused."[9] However, Paul did not put an end to the meal because of the abuse in the Corinthian church. Instead, he taught them about the right participation in the Lord's Supper.[10] The Lord's Supper is a significant practice for the gathered church for it directs our focus both on the vertical relationship (remembrance of the Lord's death and His coming) and the horizontal relationship (fellowship with the believers as a family).

Earlier in this book, it was pointed out that the early church gathered as a family, celebrating the Lord's Supper in the context of a fellowship and communal meal, remembering the Lord's death, reminding the Lord of His coming and rejoicing for bringing them together as one body and family. Concerning the Lord's Supper, J.I. Packer and Merrill C. Tenney wrote in *Illustrated Manners and Customs of the Bible* that "early Christians ate the symbolic meal of the Lord's Supper to commemorate the Last Supper, in which Jesus and His disciples observed the traditional Jewish Passover feast. The themes of the two events were the same. In the Passover, Jews rejoiced that God had delivered them from their enemies and they looked expectantly to their future as God's children. In the Lord's Supper, Christians celebrated how Jesus had delivered them from sin and they expressed their hope for the day when Christ would return (1 Cor. 11:26). At first, the Lord's Supper was an entire meal that Christians shared in their homes. Each guest brought a dish of food to the common table. The meal began with common prayer and the eating of small pieces from a single loaf of bread that represented Christ's broken body. The meal closed with another prayer and the sharing of a cup of wine, which represented Christ's shed blood."[11] It is difficult to have the Lord's Supper as a family meal in a large, impersonal gathering and formal structure. A home is the ideal location to celebrate the Lord's Supper in a meaningful way.

SIMPLE CHURCH

To gather as a church in a house is about as simple as it gets. Not much money is required to do this kind of church planting work. Like the early church, a simple house is enough for the fellowship of the church. Money has become a primary factor in many a ministry today. It has become a major concern, topic of conversation and source of conflict. Without a lot of money, it seemly has become almost impossible to do the Lord's work. However, when we examine the early church, money was not a primary issue at all. The early disciples planted churches in homes, had simple gatherings in homes and multiplied into other houses as the fellowship grew.

In nations like India (where I live), buying a piece of land and constructing a building is not an easy thing. Most of church buildings here are constructed with the help of foreign funds. An accusation Christian workers often face from unbelievers is that Christian ministry and conversion is done by and for the money that comes in from abroad. Those ministries are really at risk that rely on foreign funds. The early churches were generally indigenous fellowships, yet when there was a need they stood with one another and helped each other. Blessed is the nation wherein most of its churches and ministries have grown on the concept of self-support, self-propagation and self-governing.

In doing a church-planting ministry, if we follow the current expensive model, wherein we require a lot of money for building (which we use once in a while), its maintenance and salaries, it is highly difficult to plant numerous churches. Many suppose there is no church without a sacred building. It is regretful to see how the New Testament view of the church and the temple is distorted by idolizing a building as a sacred place of God and stitching up the curtain of the Old Testament temple that was torn by the finished work of Christ on the cross (Mt 27:51). Arthur Wallis said, "In the Old Testament, God had a sanctuary for His people; in the New, God has His people as a sanctuary."[12] Through Christ Jesus, we *ourselves* are God's temple and God's church (1Co 3:16, Ac 20:28). Let us give heed to the penetrating words of John Havlik: "The church is never a place, but always a people; never a fold but always a flock; never a sacred building but always a believing assembly. The church is you who pray, not where you pray. A structure of brick or marble can no more be the church than your clothes of serge or satin can be you. There is in this world nothing sacred but man, no sanctuary of man but the soul."[13]

Therefore, although there is nothing wrong to have a special building, it is not a requirement for the gathering of the church since we can gather simply at homes like the early church. I have seen how Christian workers run here and there to beg money for the construction of church building. Some even ask unbelievers for such a task. Much disgrace has been brought to the name of the Lord because of the preachers' emphasis on money to give to their ministry. In this way, we are not going to accomplish much for the Lord.

Donald McGavran, who is considered to be an expert on church growth, remarkably stated, "Obtaining a place to assemble should not lay a financial burden on the little congregation. The house church meets all these requirements effectively. House churches should always be considered, both for initial planting and for later extension."[14] To do saturation church planting, by which the cities and villages will be filled with churches, we need a simple strategy. Gathering as a church in houses is a simple and effective method.

BI-VOCATIONAL LEADERS

We learn from the early church pattern that the shepherds or overseers of the church arose from the church's own community (Ac 14:23, 2Ti 2:2, Titus 1:5). They were homegrown, having and operated under a plurality of leadership in each church.[15] The leadership of the early church was of two kinds — local and itinerant.[16] These days, ministry is confined to full-time work without a secular job. However, when we explore the New Testament church, the local leaders were generally bi-vocational workers and the itinerant leaders were financially supported.

Being local leaders, the pastors were generally bi-vocational workers. Paul, though an itinerant worker, set himself as an example to others by working with his own hands (Ac 20:17, 33-35; 1Th 4:11-12, 2Th 3:6-12). Of course, there are exceptions where some are worthy to receive hospitality and voluntary offerings because of their labor in preaching and teaching (1Ti 5:17). Addressing today's situation, Is giving sermons for an hour (or more) once a week on Sunday and on other special occasions what we call laboring in preaching and teaching? Robert Baker, in *A Summary of Christian History*, noted, "These leaders usually worked to earn a living and were not supported by the church. No artificial distinction was made between clergy and laity."[17] The *International Standard Bible Encyclopedia* states that "The ministry of the early church received no stipends. The ministry were office-bearers, to whom ecclesiastical obedience was due in virtue of their call and election and their being set apart by prayer, and perhaps by laying on of hands, for sacred office; but they were at the same time merchants, artisans, or engaged in other secular callings, and supported themselves . . . If office-bearers received a share, it was only on account of their poverty and because they were on the roll of widows, orphans and helpless poor. The introduction of ministerial stipends and the implication that a paid ministry was expected to give its whole time to the service of the church made the distinction between clergy and laity more emphatic. When we investigate the matter, it is evident that the fact that the clergy are paid complicates the question; for the earliest lists are evidently those who are entitled to share in the funds of the church, and widows and orphans figure as members of the ordo or clerus."[18]

Hence, it is not a requirement that local elders resign their secular jobs and give themselves exclusively to the affairs of the church. However, they are free to devote themselves exclusively for the ministry of the church if they have a genuine personal guidance from God for extensive ministry beyond the local church. It is sorrowful to witness many Christian workers unnecessarily suffering financially due to unbiblical perspective about the church ministry. A "call to ministry" is by default automatically understood as abstinence from secular work.   Do we have any biblical basis for this ingrained belief?   Alex Rattray Hay observed that Paul "definitely counseled the Ephesian elders to support themselves (Ac 20:32-35), and that, eventually, was the general practice."[19] Certainly some elders will be fully supported by the church, but these are the exception, not the rule.

Moreover, church planting and church multiplication becomes difficult if all local pastors expect to completely rely on the church for their survival. Rather, they are generally to work in the secular field and lead the small community of believers. Finance is not a major problem in a simple, small community in a house, since pastors can easily support themselves and simultaneously lead the church. It would be a wonderful opportunity for both the pastors and believers to support itinerant missionaries and evangelists on the field, including the poor and needy. Therefore, we believe house church is a wise approach wherein pastors can be bi-vocational workers, leading small communities in an effective way.

EASE OF ACCESS FOR UNBELIEVERS

I was once asked, "People see the mosque as a holy place for Muslims and the temple as a sacred place for Hindus. Don't you think it is important to have a special building for Christians which is considered to be sacred?" Christianity is unique because the church itself, the whole people of Christ, is God's temple and every member a priest of God (1Co 3:16, 1Pe 2:5, 9). In our attempt to identify ourselves with other pagan religions we must be careful not to lose our uniqueness. In contextualizing the message we should not compromise with unbiblical perspectives. Frank Senn pointed out well that "Christians of the first several centuries lacked the publicity of the pagan cults. They had no shrines, temples, statues, or sacrifices. They staged no public festivals, dances, musical performances, or pilgrimage . . . Indeed, Christians of the first three centuries usually met in private residences that had been converted into suitable gathering spaces for the Christian community . . . This indicates that the ritual bareness of early Christian worship should not be taken as a sign of primitiveness, but rather as a way of emphasizing the spiritual character of Christian worship."[20]

Every religious structure is seen as a sacred place of a respective religious group and the unbelievers who belong to a different religious group feel very much uncomfortable in such a place. A pastor friend of mine once shared, "I've made friendship with lot of unbelievers and they feel quite comfortable to come to my house. But if I tell them to come to a special building, which people suppose it to be a sanctuary, they find it extremely uncomfortable to come. The house is a good place for them to be invited to come and join in a fellowship." A house is such an informal place that even unbelievers feel comfortable to come, witnessing how we live as a community and love one another. Is it not this love that identifies Christ's disciples to the world, even giving us an opportunity to witness unto them (Jn 13:35)?

Donald McGavran once said, "The congregation should meet in the most natural surroundings, to which non-Christians can come with the greatest ease and where the converts themselves carry on the services."[21] We cannot expect unbelievers to come to a religious building, though at times they may come occasionally. The early church gathered at homes and there were occasions wherein unbelievers used to attend (1Co 14:23-24). The houses were used for hospitality and also for church gathering. Michael Green has mentioned, "One of the most important methods of spreading the gospel . . . was by use of homes."[22] House church provides an informal and friendly atmosphere for the unbelievers to stay at ease in the gathering of the church and experience the love and fellowship of Christ Jesus through His children.

Ten Reasons for House Churches

PERSECUTION

One day I read in the newspaper that a church had been burned down. I was not shaken because the church, the people of God, was not harmed. It is the building wherein the church usually gathered, that was burned. Many Christians and unbelievers alike think that a building is the church while actually it is the Christ's redeemed people that are the church and the sanctuary of God. During times of persecution, church buildings, which are regarded as a religious place for Christians, often become primary targets for assault. It is not safe for the people of God to gather in such a place when situations are hostile.

The church gathering in a house is much better in times of persecution. This doesn't guarantee that persecution will not come at all. The early church faced persecution despite gathering in houses, yet gathering in houses is much safer during times of persecution than gathering in a supposedly religious building. In many parts of the world, especially in the third-world countries, believers gather for fellowship in a network of underground house churches — small communities that secretly gather in the living rooms of believers.[23]

Furthermore, it is interesting to notice that during persecution, both in the early church and in the modern-day, the house churches spread rapidly. God often uses persecution to bend our knees and to make our feet active. The church often becomes active, both in prayer and network, at difficult times. House churches usually play a vital role in hostile conditions. The churches in China, as well as in some parts of India, are growing vastly through the network of house churches. One reporter wrote about the house church movement in China that "It is difficult to estimate exactly how many Christians worship and serve in these house churches. In 2000, an unconfirmed report stated that there are approximately 80 million believers in the house-church movement. Clearly the house-church movement has been the mainstream of Protestant Christianity in China.[24]

It seems persecution is rapidly spreading in many countries. The opponents are seeking to stop the Christian work wherever it is actively functioning. There is a great need to do the Lord's work wisely in such situations. Much prayer, much encouragement and much diligence are required. The fellowship of the church is very much necessary to encourage one another to stay strong in the Lord. Therefore, we believe, gathering as a church in houses is an effective model even during times of persecution.

NOURISHMENT AND MULTIPLICATION OF CHURCHES

I was talking with a man who is a member of an old church that gathered in that place for more than hundred years. I asked him courteously, "How many churches have you people planted?" He said, I think, about two. This is because of a greater financial budget required to plant and build churches. This is not how God's Kingdom can spread rapidly. The church ought to penetrate into the society. The church should be "Go-centered", not "Come-centered." For the church to spread into every part of the world, careful nurturing and multiplication is essential.

As it was said to the first man and woman, "Be fruitful and multiply" (Ge 1:28), likewise it is commanded to the church to multiply by going and making disciples of all nations (Mt 28:19-20). Which is the better and efficient way that has a greater scope for the multiplication of the church? How many church members are living unfruitful life due to improper nourishment and motivation? Gathering in houses has a great potential for spiritual nourishment and multiplication. As the fellowship grows strongly more than the required size in a house, the church will inevitably multiply and spread to different places. In this way, churches can easily and rapidly multiply throughout the city or village.

Howard A. Synder observed the effectiveness of multiplying churches and described, "Not mere numerical growth but the multiplication of local churches is the test of a healthy, growing church. The biblical ideal is neither to produce a host of new Christians who live unattached, separated lives, nor to expand existing local churches until their membership bulges into the thousands. The biblical pattern is to form new converts into local congregations and to multiply the number of congregations as new converts are added. The ministry of Paul and other New Testament evangelists was a church-multiplying ministry. Converts in many cities quickly ran into the thousands; yet for nearly two hundred years no church buildings were erected. Such growth under such conditions can be explained only as the multiplication of small congregations."[25]

Saturation church planting can be done in an effective way in a model like this, if we work with diligence and with the wisdom and power of the Holy Spirit. The church that grows only in one place may be good for boasting about the numbers but it usually lacks qualitative fellowship, spiritual nourishment and the motivation to spread. I know many members who belong to a large "number gathering" church but do not have any motivating relationship with the overseers and with one another.

Ten Reasons for House Churches

Does attending Sunday service for two hours make someone a part of the body of Christ? Are we the members of the church only in name? Is this the kind of church Jesus died for? What does it mean to be a part of the body of Christ? Are we passionate to spread God's Kingdom or see His Kingdom grow in one place?

The churches that are well nourished and scatter are the ones that easily prosper, both numerically and spiritually. One of the major reasons the early church greatly prospered is because of the spiritually nourished scattered believers (Ac 8:1, 4, 11:19ff). Church multiplication is more effective than church planting. There is a great need to emphasize more on church multiplication than church planting. Church multiplication is contagious. It is like a fire in the forest. But how can this all happen? Wolfgang Simpson wisely wrote, "In house churches, the people are the resources, Jesus is the program, fellowship is the reason, multiplication is the outcome, and discipling the neighborhood the goal."[26] He wrote elsewhere that "The church is changing back from being a Come-structure to being again a Go-structure. As one result, the Church needs to stop trying to bring people 'into the church,' and start bringing the Church to the people. The mission of the Church will never be accomplished just by adding to the existing structure; it will take nothing less than a mushrooming of the church through spontaneous multiplication of itself into areas of the population of the world, where Christ is not yet known."[27] Therefore, we believe, gathering in a house as a small community creates much room for the church to have quality spiritual nourishment and compels the church to multiply.

DISCIPLESHIP AND MULTIPLICATION OF LEADERS

There is a great need for the multiplication of biblical leaders in the churches today. Multiplication of leaders leads to an explosive growth of the Kingdom of God through the church. This happens when the church is properly discipled. Jesus did not say, "Go and have good services and meetings." He said, "Go and make disciples" (Mt 28:19-20). Discipleship is an intimate kind of equipping. The gathering of the church is an opportunity for discipleship. One of the effective ways to witness the multiplication of leaders is in making disciples.

The growth of the believers and the multiplication of leaders, through the process of discipleship, are the healthy signs of a biblical church. As the leaders disciple the church, the church will disciple one another and penetrates the world with a vision for discipleship. Sadly, in our modern-day system, discipleship is not a significant and a necessary task of the church. It is supposed to be the work of the discipleship training centers or bible colleges. Dietrich Bonhoeffer aptly stated, "Christianity without discipleship is always Christianity without Christ."[28]

When there is no discipleship, the potentiality of the church is buried and the prospective leaders are unidentified, unmotivated and thus ignored. Will it not be shocking news if a survey is taken about how the churches are discipled, and the way churches are raising and sending leaders in a year or in at least in five years? Did not our Lord Jesus tell us, "The harvest is plentiful but the workers are few. Ask the Lord of the harvest, therefore, to send out workers into his harvest field" (Mt 9:37-38)? Are we praying, equipping, mobilizing and sending the leaders into the harvest field? How are the churches setting goals and strategies for leadership multiplication?

The growth of the small communities through discipleship often results in the growth of more leaders. Leaders are born and developed, not often out of public preaching but out of personal discipleship. Quality mentoring and overseeing is manifested more in such small gatherings, thereby identifying and motivating more potential leaders. Grace Wiebe rightly pointed out, "House churches can be a vital part of raising up, training and multiplying many servant leaders (resulting in much less burnout of leaders)."[29] In this kind of informal setting, there is a great possibility for the multiplication of disciples, consequently leading to the multiplication of leaders and churches. Therefore, we believe, gathering in house is an effective way for the church to get discipled and to raise, equip and send many leaders.

THE POOR, THE NEEDY AND MISSIONS

A careful reading of the Holy Scriptures reveals that money in the early church was used in large part to assist the poor and needy.[30] Each church was autonomous and an independent social organization. Even during the middle part of the second century, the collection was primarily taken to help the poor and needy people. According to the information found in *First Apology* by Justin Martyr and in the *Didache*, church historian Earle E. Cairns mentions that at the end of the fellowship of the church, "they finally took up a collection for aid to widows and orphans, the sick, the prisoners, and strangers. The meeting was then dismissed, and all the people made their way to their homes."[31]

The early church also gave towards missions. However, many of the exhortations given to the churches about giving are toward helping the needy people. This is almost neglected these days. Why there is a great emphasis on helping the poor and needy as well as missions? Let us think - What is it worth to preach the gospel to the people while neglecting to share the love and compassion of Christ in deed? John wrote, "If anyone has material possessions and sees his brother in need but has no pity on him, how can the love of God be in him? Dear children, let us not love with words or tongue but with actions and in truth" (1Jn 3:17-18).

Mahatma Gandhi once said, "There are people in the world so hungry that God cannot appear to them except in the form of bread."[32] The gospel of Christ meets both the spiritual and physical needs. In His parable on "The Good Samaritan," Jesus taught that 'loving our neighbor' means 'helping the needy' (Lk 10:25-37). Even the pastors were exhorted by Paul to help the needy people. It is actually to them that Paul said, "In everything I did, I showed you that by this kind of hard work we must help the weak, remembering the words the Lord Jesus himself said: 'It is more blessed to give than to receive" (Ac 20:17, 28, 34-35).

When the believers brought the money from the sales of the property and put it at the apostles' feet, they distributed it to needy people (Ac 4:32-35). It is interesting to notice that the early church even sold their properties to help those who were in dire need. The famous words, "God loves a cheerful giver" are written to the church of Corinth in the context of helping the needy saints of the church (2Co 9:1, 7).

John MacArthur pointed out well, "The primary purpose of giving, as taught in the New Testament, is for the support of the saints, the church. A Christian's first obligation is to support fellow believers, individually and collectively. The church's first financial responsibility is to invest in its own life and its own people (cf. 2 Cor. 8:1-5; 9:12-15; Phil. 4:14-16). Obviously that is not the only economic obligation we have. The parable of the Good Samaritan makes it clear that we should minister personally and financially to anyone in need, regardless of religion, culture, or circumstances (Luke 10:25-37). Paul also teaches that we should 'do good to all men' (Gal. 6:10). But in the same verse he goes on to say, 'And especially to those who are of the household of faith' (cf. 1 John 3:17). In 2 Corinthians 9:13 the apostles calls for a generous distribution 'to all.' Support of the poor and needy in the world in the name of the Lord is a high-priority Christian activity by Scriptural standards."[33] What percentage of the money raised from the church is actually going to the poor and needy people? Even in the Old Testament, a special tithe was raised once in three years to assist the orphans, widows and other poor people (De 14:28-29). How are the tithes of the churches used today?

It is said that most of the money today is generally going toward maintenance and administration, with less money going toward missions. In many churches, there is no special consideration to help the poor and needy. Are both the poor and missions a priority in the financial budget of traditional churches? What percentage of the money, collected from a traditional church is going to help the needy and missions? The authors of the *Life Application Bible Commentary* on the Gospel of Mark, warned, "If our churches spend large amounts on their physical buildings and ignore missions, evangelism, and care for the poor, they will likewise come under God's judgment."[34] Since gathering in a house is a simple model (i.e. money is not required for building and its maintenance), money can be used to help the poor and needy, including support to missions.

Final Words

To justify their practices, many ignorantly and unreasonably oppose this teaching (as I once did) without a careful study and examination about how the early church functioned. There is so much good to speak about the modern day church. Yet a reformation is needed to help God's people function more effectively and biblically. Gathering in houses is not a perfect solution wherein we don't have any problems at all. It is only a better and more effective approach. In saying this, I mean it has more advantages and less disadvantages. Of course the problems that occur, based on different situations, places and culture, must be dealt prayerfully and wisely according to the wisdom of the Holy Spirit and with the counsel of experienced godly people.

Also, let the reader not mistake that the church is confined to gather in a house. It can gather in an office, hall, class room, hut, tent, etc. as long as the size of the community is small wherein every-member participation is possible and mobilized. The structure is not as important as is the functioning of the church. This chapter could actually be titled, "Ten Reasons For Small Communities." Since the house is an informal place wherein people can generally gather as small communities, I have used it often in this chapter. Christ's people are free to gather wherever they feel convenient and yet still function according to the New Testament church pattern.

Finally, may we never forget that any church paradigm is weak and lacks life without the empowerment of the Holy Spirit. The Spirit of God is the life of the church; without Him any church is dead. Let us seek to be clothed with the power from on high as we constantly seek to establish His Kingdom on earth. May the Lord abundantly pour out His Spirit upon His body, the church!

Ten Reasons for House Churches

I close this chapter with a comment worth contemplating by an Anglican commentator David Prior. He wrote, "It is better to be bothered about quality rather than quantity: a tiny diamond is far more valuable than a lorryload of stones. It is for that reason that we are going to work with groups and small communities rather than with large crowds . . . we are only concerned with small communities made up of people who know they are the Church. It is with these that we are going to set about the work of spreading the Gospel, of proclaiming in word and deed that Christ came to free us from wretchedness and oppression, whether that be spiritual or material. Work in small groups is far more worthwhile. A spoonful of sugar dissolved in a small cup sweetens the coffee, and that is the way with the Gospel in a small community. But put the same spoonful of sugar into a huge pot of coffee and its taste simple gets lost."[35]

— Stephen David

NOTES

[1] David Watson, *I Believe in the Church* (Great Britain: Hodder & Stoughton, 1978), 121.

[2] Robert Banks, *Paul's Idea of Community* (Massachusetts: Hendrickson Publishers), 90.

[3] Watson, 117.

[4] William Barclay, *The Letters to the Corinthians*, Revised Edition (Westminster Press, 1977), 135.

[5] Ronald Sider, *Rich Christians in an Age of Hunger* (Illinois: InterVarsity Press, 1977), 190-191.

[6] Robert & Julia Banks, *The Church Comes Home* (Massachusetts: Hendrickson Publishers, Inc., 1998), 84.

[7] Taken from an unpublished article, "Services Versus Service."

[8] *Dictionary of Biblical Imagery* (India: OM-Authentic Books), 828.

[9] Michael Green, *Evangelism Now & Then* (Illinois: InterVarsity Press, 1979), 103-104.

[10] Paul mentions the problem in 1Co 11:20-21 and finally gives the solution in verse 33-34.

[11] J. I. Packer and Merrill C. Tenney, *Illustrated Manners and Customs of the Bible* (Nashville: Thomas Nelson Publishers, 1980), 540-541.

[12] Frank Viola, *Pagan Christianity* (Present Testimony Ministry, 2002), 99.

[13] John Havlik, *People Centered Evangelism* (Nashville: Broadman Press, 1971), 47.

[14] Robert Fitts, *The Church in the House* (Salem, OR: Preparing the Way Publishers, 2001), 18.

[15] Ac 11:30; 15:2, 4, 6, 22, 23; 14:23; 20:17-28; Php 1:1; 1Th 5:12-13; 1Ti 4:14; 1Ti 5:17; Tit 1:5; Jam 5:14; 1Pe 5:1-3; Heb 13:7, 17, 24.

[16] Gordon Fee, *Gospel and Spirit* (Massachusetts: Hendrickson Publishers, Inc., 1991), 139.

[17] Robert Baker, *A Summary of Christian History* (Nashville, Tennessee: Broadman & Holman Publishers, 1994), 11.

[18] *Power Bible CD* [CD-Rom] V4.5. Bronson: Online Publishing, 1999-2005.

[19] Alex Rattray Hay, *The New Testament Order for Church and Missionary* (1947), 299.

[20] *Christian Liturgy*, 53.

[21] Fitts, 18.

[22] Michael Green, *Evangelism in the Early Church* (1970), 207.

[23] www.bibleleague.org/church/planting/china.php

[24] Eternal Perspective Ministries, www.epm.org/articles/Chinesetorture.htm.

[25] Howard Synder, *The Community of the King* (Illinois: Inter-Varsity Press, 1978), 122.

[26] Wolfgang Simpson, *Houses that Change the World* (Chennai, India: Mission Educational Books, 1998), 142.

[27] Ibid, 21-22.

[28] www.choosethelife.com/041100_article.html

[29] The Network for Strategic Missions, www.strategicnetwork.org/index.php?loc=kb&view=v&id=8614&fto=1269&

[30] Ac 2:45; 4:32-37; 6:1-4; 9:36; 20:34-35; Ro 12:13; 1Co 16:1-3, 15; 2Co 8:1-5; 9:1-2, 7; Ga 2:6-10; 6:9-10; Phm 7; Tit 3:8; Heb 6:10-11; Heb 13:2-3, 15-16; Jam 1:27; 2:15-17; 1Pe 4:9; 1Jn 3:16-18.

[31] Earle E. Cairns, *Christianity Through The Centuries* (Grand Rapids: Zondervan Publishing House, 1996), 84.

[32] Wheel Words, www.texaschapbookpress.com/wheelwords.htm.

[33] John MacArthur, *The MacArthur New Testament Commentary 1 Corinthians* (Printed in India: 1984 by The Moody Bible Institute of Chicago), 451.

[34] Bruce B. Baton, et al., *Life Application Bible Commentary on Mark* (Illinois: Tyndale House Publishers, Inc., 1994), 319.

[35] David Prior, *The Church in the Home* (Great Britain: Marshall Morgan and Scott Marshall Pickering, 1983), 163-164.

Ten Reasons for House Churches

1. What evidence is there that the lack of church buildings is not a hindrance to the rapid expansion of the church?
2. How does the structure, size and system of a church impact the one another aspect of ministry?
3. How does the size of a congregation influence whether its members see the church as a corporation or as a family? How would this effect intimacy and accountability?
4. What was the primary purpose of the early church gathering? And how is it different from the way we are gathering today?
5. What does it mean to be a part of the body of Christ? What is your function in your church?
6. Why is it difficult to have the Lord's Supper as a family meal in a large, impersonal gathering and formal structure?
7. In what context did the early church have the Lord's Supper and for what purpose? What difference will it make if we practice alike in our day?
8. How does the church gathering in houses make the church planting simple?
9. What are the advantages of house churches having bi-vocational pastors?
10. Why do you think the local leaders were generally bi-vocational whereas the itinerant leaders were generally supported by the church?
11. What are the advantages of house church having some full time elders?
12. In what way does the church put unbelievers at ease by gathering in houses?
13. List five points on the advantages of house churches during times of persecution.
14. How is the nourishment and multiplication of the church more likely to occur in a smaller community rather than a larger one?
15. Do you believe discipleship should be the core responsibility of the church? If so, in what kind of setting and in what ways discipleship can be done effectively?
16. Why are micro churches the best environment for the multiplication and training of new leaders?

17. Contrast New Testament giving objectives with modern church spending? What changes do you suppose we need to bring in order to use our finance biblically?
18. Why is it better to be bothered about quality rather than quantity?

Note: NTRF also offers a teacher's resource to help lead a discussion of New Testament church life. Request *The Practice of The Early Church: A Theological Workbook (Leader's Guide)* from www.NTRF.org.

7

CHILDREN IN CHURCH

At a Virginia house church conference, before a panel discussion was about to begin, I whispered to a friend that I bet the first question was going to be: "How do we handle the children?" Sure enough, it was. This, in my opinion, is the number one question asked by those contemplating the house church. It is a tremendous stumbling block, but it shouldn't be. This chapter will examine three things: first, the differing philosophies or mind sets that the institutional and house church have toward children and the church; second, practical issues that arise; and third, the advantage to children of the church in the home.

In an article I once wrote, I asked the question: "What do you do *for* the children?" I am ashamed to say that the first draft of that article read: "What do you do *with* the children?" I had subconsciously succumbed to the philosophy or mind set of much of the institutional church: children are a problem, they interfere with the almighty "service," where important, paid professionals in robes or coats and ties give important speeches, and where serious, quiet, and holy listeners sit deathly still in pews. So, the question becomes, what do we do with the children while we are doing the important things in the "service"?

Neither Jesus, nor the apostles, ever worried about what to do with the children. Jesus never, ever said: "Suffer the little children to be packed away in the nursery." Can you imagine the children being led to Children's Church during the Sermon on the Mount?

The Scripture doesn't say much on handling children when believers gather. But I can't imagine that the believers back then didn't have children. I imagine not much was ever said, because the early Christians didn't make such a big deal about the issue. The churches were in the home; families lived in homes; children met with the church in the home.

Although the Scriptures don't say anything directly concerning the children and the gatherings of believers, there are glimpses. For example, children are explicitly stated to have been present at the feeding of the five thousand, and the feeding of the four thousand (Mt 14:21, 14:38.). On a missionary journey, "all the disciples and their wives and *children"* accompanied the apostles, as they left, to pray on the beach (Ac 21:5b). Finally, when Paul's letter was read to the Ephesians, it addresses the children directly: "children, obey your parents in the Lord"

Children In Church

(Ep 6:1-2). How could the children hear that exhortation read in church, unless the children were in the church meeting?

And despite the relative Scriptural silence on kids and church, I can guarantee one thing: there weren't any Sunday Schools and Children's Churches. If Sunday Schools are essential adjuncts to church life, why is the Bible silent on this subject? His building plan, the Bible, is complete in every detail. Where is the Christian who would deny that the Bible is a perfect blueprint? Interestingly, there is not even a hint of Sunday Schools in God's blueprint.

Sunday Schools were not even originated to teach Bible stories or Christian morality, but were started in nineteenth century England to give poor children of mill and mine laborers a chance to read and write. Who had primary responsibility for training children before the appearance of Sunday Schools? The family. I think it is the contention of most house churches that the family still has the primary responsibility for the instruction and nurturing of Christian children. That may be the reason most home churches (just like the biblical New Testament church) don't have Sunday Schools. And this really is a barrier to Christians who contemplate leaving the institutional church for the home church. It is amazing how many Christians worry about the spiritual welfare of their kids to the point that the parents will poison themselves to death on the corrupt religiosity of some institutional churches, just so long as there's a good youth program. I am convinced that many institutional churches realize this, and capitalize on it by providing jam-up "youth ministries," in order to keep their "tithing units" from leaving. (Of course, I realize that often there are other, sincere motives involved, too).

Although it is the family's primary duty to raise children up in the Lord, it does not follow that the home church should be uninterested in their welfare. Quite the contrary. If kids see their parents' church as a drag, they'll tend to think Jesus is a drag, too. Thus we must discuss practical ways for the home church to make children know that the church belongs to them as well as to their parents.

In discussing practical ways to integrate children into the life of the home church, we must understand at the onset that if parents bring the traditional mind set of the institutional church into the house church, nothing will work for the kids. The institutional church has the mentality of juvenile segregation: push them out into the Sunday School wing, so everything can be Holy and Quiet. This, of course, is unbiblical. How quiet do you think the kids were during the Sermon on the Mount? The institutional church is liturgically rigid in its "order of service," and kids, being as unprogrammed and unpredictable as they are, can never fit within that rigidity. So the first practical thing to do in the church in the home is to relax – there's going to be more noise and interruption in the house church. People with children need to quit feeling guilty about it, and people without children need to exercise more tolerance than they would in the institutional church.

The second practical thing to do is to develop close relationships between each adult, and between all adults and all children. This development is possible in the home church, in a way that it is not possible in the organized church. With close relationships, when little Johnny is about to flush the cherry bomb down the toilet, an adult who is not Johnny's parent can firmly request that the little hellion extinguish the wick, without fear of alienating little Johnny or little Johnny's mom. Close relationships are extremely important.

The third practical thing that should be done is to find creative, workable ways to involve the kids in the meeting with the adults. Where did the idea come from that the meeting (or the church) belongs exclusively to the adults? I know of one house church in which the children are generally musically gifted. The young folks play guitars, violins, and flutes, and feel free to lead out in song or music. Other home churches encourage kids to share testimonies, or to recite memorized Scripture, or to ask for prayer requests. During a meeting in my home church, someone conducted a "Sunday School lesson" for the young children with the adults present. The adults were forced to adapt to a young child's viewpoint (something that all adults should do periodically), and the kids were able to have fun with their parents as they learned the spiritual lesson being taught.

The fourth practical thing I would suggest is not to be hidebound by "house church theology." Sure, we don't believe in Sunday Schools, but the world's not going to end if someone has something special for the kids, or if he takes them aside in another room once in a while. And we don't believe in pacifying the kids with entertainment to keep them out of our hair, but there's nothing wrong with showing them a video once in a while (even, heaven forbid, if the video is a Bugs Bunny cartoon, and not spiritual).

A fifth practical suggestion that one house churcher has suggested is for each meeting home to have announced house rules, so that children and parents might not inadvertently harm anything (for instance, "no eating in the living room.").

A sixth practical suggestion is to tolerate fussing infants as much as you can, but if they get too loud, make sure the parents understand that the baby should be taken out of the meeting until he cools off. If a parent doesn't do this, the parent should be communicated with. Remember, relationships are important. We need to constantly put ourselves in the shoes of our brothers and sisters – and our kids are, in the body of Christ, our brothers and sisters. Let's prefer them in love.

My seventh, and last, practical suggestion, is never to let the meeting become boring – neither for the children, nor for the adults. If the meeting is dead or too long for the adults, imagine what its like for the kids! Their attention span is probably about half of ours. We need to constantly put ourselves in the shoes of our brothers and sisters – and our kids are, in the body of Christ, our brothers and sisters. Let's prefer them in love.

We finish these thoughts on children and the house church by presenting the manifest advantages of the home church for young folks. We should not look upon children as an obstacle to getting folks into the house church. We should look at the advantages of the house church for kids, and point out these advantages to potential house church converts.

One big advantage of the home church for young people is that the youth get to see their parents in loving, supportive relationships with one another. They get to see their parents open their hearts to God in a real, personal, nonreligious, un-phony fashion.

Another tremendous advantage is that the kids are not given second-class status in the church: they are not segregated, put out of sight, out of mind in nurseries, Sunday Schools, and youth ministries.

One of the biggest advantages, in my view, is the close relationships that develop between adults and children of other adults. In my home church, I constantly pray for the children involved. There are only six couples in the church, and only fourteen children. It's very easy to find out what's going on in the kid's lives, and easy to pray for them daily, individually, by name. I submit to you that this doesn't happen very often in the mega-church.

CONCLUSION

I close with a brilliant spoof by Doug Phillips of Vision Forum on his church's "Youth Program." Although not describing a living-room sized church, his points are still quite relevant:

"I have the privilege of worshiping in a small, family-integrated church. When asked about our various church programs, I explain that we are blessed with more than thirty different organizations to which our members belong - they are called families. I further explain that we have more than sixty youth directors - they are called parents. In fact, we have such a full schedule of events that there is a mandatory activity every day of the week - it is called family worship . . .

With so much responsibility on their hands, our youth directors have to really get their collective acts together . . . They have to study God's Word more than they have ever studied before so they can wisely lead their organization. They have to be creative so they can solve the diverse problems of their special interest groups. They have to learn to be patient. They have to learn to love. They even have to reprioritize their lives.

This last part is crucial. Only by reprioritizing life, and structuring their organizations properly, will our youth directors be successful. They know that. They also know there is a price to pay. But most of them are willing to pay the price, because they have decided that the greatest activity they can do in this life is to be a youth pastor and to run a special interest organization called the Christian family.

Here is what we are discovering: The more we commit to faithfully shepherding our mini-congregations, the more blessing we experience. Moreover, the more we study what God's Word says about these little congregations, the more we see the wonder and the brilliance of God's plan of equipping the Church and transforming the entire culture through these often forgotten, twisted and even maligned organizations called Christian households."[1]

— Dan Walker

NOTES

[1] Douglas W. Phillips, "Our Church Youth Group" (San Antonio, TX: Vision Forum Ministries, 2002) www.visionforumministries.org/ issues/uniting_church_and_family/our_church_youth_group.aspx.

Children In Church

1. Why is it unfathomable to envision the children being led to a first-century equivalent of "children's church" during the Sermon on the Mount?
2. What scriptural examples exist of children being present in religious gatherings?
3. What was the origin of the Sunday School?
4. Who had primary responsibility for training children before the appearance of Sunday Schools?
5. Who is responsible for a child's religious training, the church or his parents? Explain.
6. Who are the proper youth directors within any church?
7. Why do many parents not want their children with them in church or Bible study?
8. Why do many parents insist their children stay with them in church or Bible study, rather than Sunday School or youth groups?
9. What role can children/teenagers play in a 1 Corinthians 14 participatory church meeting?
10. Infant mortality rates in the ancient world were dismal. Some argue that today's larger families justify obtaining a facility that will hold more people than a private home (due to the larger number of children). Do you agree? Why?

Note: NTRF also offers a teacher's resource to help lead a discussion of New Testament church life. Request *The Practice of The Early Church: A Theological Workbook (Leader's Guide)* from www.NTRF.org.

8
Thoroughly Biblical Church

What are the irreducible requirements for a church to be biblical? It was argued earlier in this book that the practices passed on by the apostles have the force of biblical command. From the New Testament as a whole we can piece together a clear picture of just what this apostolically commanded church practice actually was:

•*Believers met as churches on the first day of the week. (It is instructive to note at this point that this is the only apostolic practice that the early church fathers didn't mess around with and change. The reason for this is that it doesn't in any way touch on the actual nature of what a church is, and therefore didn't affect the wrong teachings and changes to church practice they introduced one way or the other. They therefore left this one thing unchanged and it remained as the apostles had originally established.)*

•*When churches came together they met in houses.*

•*When they came together in their houses their corporate worship and sharing together was completely open and spontaneous (1 Corinthians 14:26 describes the proceedings as, "each one has"), with no one leading from the front. The early believers didn't have anything that even approximated a church service.*

•*As part of these proceedings they ate the Lord's Supper as a full meal, indeed as their main meal of the day, commonly referring to it as the love-feast.*

•*They understood each church to be an extended family unit (the idea of churches being institutions or organizations would have been totally alien to them), and practiced non-hierarchical plural male leadership that had arisen from within the church they would subsequently lead. This indigenous eldership (elder, pastor/shepherd, bishop/overseer being synonymous terms in the New Testament) sought to lead consensually wherever possible, and was understood to be purely functional and not in any way positional.*

The Bible clearly reveals how the apostles, who were the recipients of Jesus' full revelation and teachings, established churches to operate and function. The question before us is this: How much of their blueprint can be changed yet still leave a church fundamentally biblical in its nature and functioning? (I use this phrase because nature and functioning are interrelated, being actually different sides of the same coin. As in the rest of life, form follows function and is just the way things unalterably are! Parents and children, for instance, function together differently than colleagues at the work place, and it's the difference in nature that makes the difference in function so important. A family where parents and children relate together more like work mates than blood relatives would be an example not of a normal family, but a dysfunctional one. So likewise, churches that function as institutions or organizations, rather than extended families of the Lord's people, are examples of dysfunctional churches and not, biblically speaking, normal ones.) So let us proceed in earnest to the answering of the question we posed, and see what parts of the apostolic blueprint, if any, are nonessential in maintaining both the nature and functioning of a biblical church. We'll start with the issue of which day churches ought to meet.

Now as far as nature and function are concerned this is indeed entirely neutral, and as I pointed out formerly, the early church fathers realized this and so saw no need to make changes. They knew that you could alter the functioning and nature of churches without reference to the day on which they met, and so in that regard left things as apostolic *status quo*. Conversely, a biblical church could change the day on which it met yet remain everything it already was, and continue to practice and function in the same manner in every other respect. I would be the first to say that being (nature) and doing (function) church biblically is more important than the day on which you meet in order to so be and do, and would rather be part of a church that was biblical in practice and function but which met midweek, than one that met on Sundays but which wasn't biblical according to our earlier definition. But here is my question: When even the early church fathers themselves chose not to change the day of the gathering of believers, on what basis, and for what possible reason, ought we? I repeat though that I do accept without reservation that a church meeting on a different day of the week to Sunday can be otherwise fully biblical. Further, if it ever became illegal to meet on Sundays, but not Thursday, then I would probably, under such circumstances, be quite happy to make the necessary changes. But outside of such extenuating circumstances, why change the day on which the early church, under the guidance and care of the apostles, met?

At this point let me just answer the legitimate point that in the world of the New Testament the Jews started a new day in the evening, which means that the first day of the week for them started on our Saturday evening. Therefore, if any church met on Saturday evenings specifically for that reason, then I would accept it as a biblical thing to do.

However, it must still be said that this would seem to be illogical in countries where each day is reckoned to commence in the morning. For most of us the first day of the week is the time period from when we get up on Sunday morning until we go to bed again, so I would still maintain that meeting as churches on Sundays remains the biblical norm as far as we are concerned. Further, the verse in Acts 20 which gives us the information about the churches meeting on the first day of the week is written by a Gentile (Luke) concerning a Gentile situation (Troas), and it is unlikely that he would therefore be thinking in terms of the Jewish way of reckoning a day. But let's move on now to the question of meeting in houses.

That the early church did meet in houses no one with an ounce of Bible knowledge is going to deny. The nature and functioning of the meetings they had when believers came together as a church simply meant that there was never any need for them to do otherwise. Numbers in each church were, by definition, supposed to be small; and their interactive gatherings, with no one leading from the front (the New Testament church didn't have anything even vaguely resembling a church service), and with a meal thrown in for good measure, were just perfect for a house setting. After all, what better place could there possibly be? And so once again we see form following function, as it always does in the New Testament. The eventual move from houses into specially sanctified religious buildings was, as with all the other changes we are considering, made by the early church fathers. It is interesting to note as well that this was the final change they made to the apostolic blueprint, and that meeting in houses was actually the original apostolic practice that survived their reinvention of the Christian church the longest.

But let us now consider the plight of twenty Eskimos in a village some where near the North Pole who have just become Christians, and who therefore want to become a church, but whose largest igloo can only fit eight people in it. Now if they therefore decided to hire a slightly larger igloo with the express purpose of using it for their gatherings as a church, then assuming they still meet as the Bible describes, and don't therefore change the nature of what their gathering together ought to be, then I would see no problem. Indeed, I would rather be part of a biblical church that met outside of homes for their main gathering — assuming though that the other biblical practices were in place — than part of a church that met in homes but which was unbiblical in every other respect. You can, if you really have to, maintain the nature and functioning of a church whilst meeting somewhere other than in a home. Indeed, the church of which I am a part used to sometimes utilize a rented hall for the bit of our gathering together that included the singing, this being out of love for neighbors when we heard of their complaints about the noise. But we sat in a circle, just as if in a home, and what we did in that hall was completely open with everyone free to spontaneously take part, and without anyone leading from the front. And when we were done we returned to one of our houses for the love-feast. But let me underline that we must make sure that we don't let deviations from the biblical norm, permissible only because of extenuating circumstances, actually become the norm. Let me illustrate what I mean by this from what the Bible teaches about baptism.

Biblical baptism, like the apostolic tradition concerning the way a church functions, is a command from the Lord. And although its actual mode isn't anywhere commanded in the pages of Scripture, we know from the way the early church did it (apostolic tradition again) that it was to be done upon conversion, with no time lapse, and in water. (And of course the immersion bit we get from the simple fact that the actual word baptism in English is simply a transliteration of the Greek word *baptizo* which literally means to dip, dunk or immerse.) And many of us would be greatly concerned at any idea that we are free to make changes to this, whether regarding who is to be baptized, the mode of their baptism or it's timing; and remain painfully aware of how the church at large has massacred baptism in each of these ways for far too long. So our position would be that, in order to comply with the teaching of the Word of God, a person should be baptized upon profession of faith in Jesus, as soon as possible, and by full immersion in water.

Let us now address an instance of someone coming to the Lord who is bedridden because of disability. Baptism, as biblically commanded and exampled in the New Testament, is clearly out of the question as far as he is concerned, so would not coming up with some other more appropriate mode (sprinkling?) therefore be incumbent upon us? And of course we would respond to this in the affirmative! In such a circumstance one would technically be out of step with the teaching of Scripture as to the mode of baptism, yet still be in complete harmony with its intent and spirit. But here is the vital point: Nothing of what I have just said could possibly apply to the conversion of an able bodied person, and the normal mode would need to be employed in order for things to be as the Lord wants. And neither could anyone argue for baptism for someone who hadn't responded to Jesus by faith, because that would attack the very nature of baptism, even though its external mode might still be in accordance with the Scripture.

This is what I mean when I say we must not make biblically permitted deviations, necessitated because of extenuating circumstances,
become the norm. If the church of which I am a part had access to the
size of houses that similar churches have, for instance, in America, then
we would never even have thought of using a hall for part of our gathering together. (The neighbors obviously wouldn't hear the singing from
a detached house separated from next door by a large piece of land and
so the need to appease them would never have arisen.) And if we return
for one moment to our postulated brothers and sisters at the North Pole,
should it turn out that they do have igloos big enough to fit a good
number of people in after all, then what possible need would they have
of hiring a large public building-type igloo for their church gatherings?

Of course the truth of the matter is that any process of negotiating
away any of these factors, which together make a church biblical, is
usually a lead up to attempts at smuggling in alternatives to the other
three things I listed:

•*Open worship and sharing with no one leading from the front*
•*The Lord's Supper as a full meal*
•*Non-hierarchical plural male indigenous leadership*

Let me make it quite clear that with what we have said about meeting in houses, plus the above three things, we are indeed now looking at
the non-negotiable and irreducible bare minimum requirements for a
church to be said to be biblical. But let me make it clear as well that I do
not by this mean that everything has to be in place from the word go.
There is often, and frequently, the need for instruction, development
and spiritual growth first. Yet it still remains the case that these things
must be at least where a church is heading for, it's destination so to
speak, even if it has not arrived there. Of course the Lord's Supper as a
full meal ought to be in place from the very start as there is just no
possible reason for such not to be the case, but eldership, for example,
would normatively arise much later. And it is often the case as well that
someone might take an initial lead in the corporate weekly gatherings
until the others learn how to begin playing their part. But the thing to
grasp is that it should nevertheless be quite clear where the church was
heading in regards to how it functions and goes about things.

The issue here is ultimately that anything that touches on these
things does indeed impact on the very nature of what a church is. Change
things here and you cause a church to begin functioning in a way that is
not only different from what the New Testament reveals, but completely
alien to it. Indeed, virtually it's opposite! To return to our example of
baptism, we might say that here we have an equivalent to baptizing an

unbeliever. The very nature of the thing is changed and the Lord's intention for it made void and cancelled out. Indeed, it is virtually done away with! It boils down to this: Why would anyone who understands these last three parts of the blueprint want to play around with the first two (meeting on Sundays in houses) in any case, unless there were the most pressing of extenuating circumstances forcing them into it? I have yet to hear it put better than by my good friend Steve Atkerson, "The question is not so much why we should do things the same way the apostles did; but rather, why would we want to do anything differently?"

I rather think that says it all!

— Beresford Job

Discussion Questions

1. In your opinion, what are the irreducible requirements for a church to be biblical?
2. How much of the apostolic blueprint can be changed yet still leave a church fundamentally biblical in its nature and functioning?
3. Why is what a church does more important than where or when it does it?
4. What are some extenuating circumstances that justify a deviation from the biblical pattern?
5. Why did the author cite the example of the Eskimos and the quadriplegic?
6. Just because a church happens to meet in a home does not make it biblical. What did the author mean by biblical church?

Note: NTRF also offers a teacher's resource to help lead a discussion of New Testament church life. Request *The Practice of The Early Church: A Theological Workbook (Leader's Guide)* from www.NTRF.org.

Part II
CHURCH MINISTRIES

9

PREACHING & TEACHING MINISTRIES

What role did preaching and teaching play in the early church? God's people need in-depth teaching from God's Word. Acts 2:42 reveals that the early Christians devoted themselves to the apostle's teachings. Teaching is listed as one of the gifts of the Spirit in 1 Corinthians 12. Paul urged that if any man has the gift of teaching, "let him teach" (Ro 12:7). Those elders who work hard at teaching and preaching are to be supported financially by the church (1Ti 5:17).

1 Corinthians 14 contains a detailed prescription for the typical church meeting. One of the lessons to be learned from 1 Corinthians 14 is that church meetings are not to be dominated by any one person, no matter what his spiritual gift. Each one of the brothers is to have the opportunity to contribute to the meeting. Teaching was clearly included in the list of activities that can occur, but it was tossed into the mix in an amazingly cavalier way (14:26). Clearly, early church home meetings were not focused primarily on Bible study. In this context, if a gifted teacher exercised his gift weekly in a in-depth manner, it would necessarily squelch the expressions of the other gifts. Equal weight is to be given to a variety of input: singing, testimonies, prayer, prophecy, tongues, teachings, etc. Thus any teachings would need to be shorter, rather than longer, to allow for all the gifts to be freely exercised. If the 1 Corinthians 14 meeting is not the time for supernaturally gifted teachers to present comprehensive teachings, then when is that time?

The answer is simple. Intense, long teachings are to be done at special ministry meetings, not the regular Lord's Day church meeting. Weekly gatherings of a local church are to be focused on the Lord's Supper, followed by an participatory time of orderly, verbal one anothering (1Co 11:17-22. 14:23). The goal for all that is done is edification (1Co 14:26). Such church meetings are to be smaller (scores of people) rather than larger (hundreds or thousands of people), and not dominated by any one person.

In contrast to church meetings, ministry meetings generally are focused on one (or a few) individual's gifts, and can be as large a gathering as accommodations will allow. If 5,000 believers want to assemble to hear someone expositor the Scriptures, great! However, it is important to make sure that everyone involved realizes that such a gathering is not church. It is merely a ministry meeting.

For instance, for two years Paul held daily discussions in the lecture hall of Tyrannus with the result that all who lived in the province of Asia heard the word of the Lord (Ac 19:9-10). When in Rome, Paul rented his own house and from it boldly and without hindrance preached the kingdom of God and taught about the Lord Jesus Christ (Ac 28:30-31). These ministry meetings did not replace the regular meeting of the local church, but were in addition to them. Another example of larger ministry meetings is the public healing ministry that the apostles carried on in Solomon's Colonnade (Ac 5:12-16, 42). Large crowds gathered to hear the Gospel and bring their sick for healing. Yet these large daily preaching and healing services did not supplant the smaller, regular, house church meetings (Ac 2:46, 8:3).

There are many modern examples of ministry meetings. Bill Gothard traveled and presented his Institute in Basic Youth Conflicts in major cities all over America. Literally thousands would go hear him, often filling the local civic center to capacity. Present in the audience were Christians from every denomination in the area. Yet it was not a church; it was a teaching time designed to equip the church at large. Another example is when Billy Graham would come to a city, rent the stadium, and hold an evangelistic crusade. Believers from many different churches would participate in His crusade. Yet the crusade was not a church meeting; it was evangelism. Those who came to Christ through the crusade were channeled into local churches. A third example is the music ministry of Bill and Gloria Gather. God's people flock to their concerts and worship the Lord with great enthusiasm. God's people then return to their local churches uplifted and full of praise. Images of the worship described in Revelation 19:1-10 come to mind. It is good to be blessed by such gatherings.

All ministry meetings should be designed to strengthen the local church, not supplant it. True churches have the right to exercise church discipline, have their own elders, and celebrate the Lord's Supper. None of this is true of properly functioning ministry meetings. One of the great errors of modern Christendom is confusing large ministry meetings with true church meetings. Indeed, that which is truly church has been replaced entirely by ministry meetings. After visiting the Western church, Chinese Christian Watchman Nee observed that most Western Christians had never actually been to a church meeting — that all they had experienced was ministry meetings!

The Western way of conducting a church service is very much like a New Testament ministry meeting. It is dominated by one gifted person, with large numbers of people in attendance to benefit from his gift. These ministry meetings might revolve around bible teaching, evangelism, praise, healing, encouragement, etc. Such meetings are very helpful and have a rightful place. Yet such meetings are ultimately secondary and optional. Primary and indispensable are the meetings of the local church. Local church meetings are to be smaller, participatory, not focused on any one person's gift, and centered around the Lord's Supper.

— Steve Atkerson

PART TWO

In the New Testament we find churches meeting on Sundays, in people's houses, with a twofold purpose. First, they had completely open, participatory and spontaneous sharing together and worship which wasn't led from the front in any way. Second, they ate the Lord's Supper together as their main meal of the day. Given such a set up, and it is indeed how the apostles universally set churches up, then certain other things would subsequently find no place.

For instance, in such a set up there is not the slightest need for sacred buildings. Hence it will come as no surprise that we find the churches in the New Testament meeting exclusively in people's homes. Something else you won't find in the New Testament is a Sunday service, led from the front, with those attending sitting audience style in rows and participating only in singing and, maybe, a bit of open prayer. Neither will you find in the New Testament anything that even faintly resembles a sermon. Such a practice would go completely against what the very essence of a church gathering on Sundays was originally seen to be. The apostles set churches up in such a way that when they came together on the Lord's Day the rule was strictly, "each one has . . . for you may all prophesy one by one" (1Co 14:26, 31). They set churches up in such a way that would positively encourage all those gathered to participate, and therefore brought about a situation where the Lord would be free to move by His Spirit through each part of His body. Any idea of the Lord's Day gathering of the church revolving around the ministry of any one individual flies completely in the face of Scripture and contradicts it outright.

This is not to say, however, that there isn't a place for the type of teaching amongst God's people whereby one person predominates in giving it. The Lord does indeed provide people in churches who are gifted in this very thing, and the New Testament makes it clear that teaching is a calling and gift of the Holy Spirit. Indeed, in the church of which I am a part we meet for Bible Study on Tuesday evenings, and we work very hard at furthering our understanding of God's Word. But in the New Testament the coming together of a church on Sundays was not the time when such gifts were exercised in that particular way, and the push was always for mutual participation; for lots of people to share something, including a short teaching, rather than for one person to predominate or lead in any way.

And this helps us to at last take the emphasis away from leadership, and from our inclination to just revolve around those who are gifted in teaching and public speaking ability and to consequently make *big men* of them. It helps to keep us safe from the evil of the whole *clergy/laity* divide thing, and from the completely unbiblical two-tier system of *leaders* and *led* which creates hierarchy. Hierarchy is something no church should ever have. The only hierarchy found in the pages of the New Testament, pertaining to church life, is simply Jesus and everyone else. Even elders — for that is what a biblically based church will either have or be moving towards, a plurality of co-equal, male elders who have been raised up from among those they serve — are strictly in the *everyone else* category.

Moreover, this biblical way of doing things creates a set up in which people feel free to question whatever is being taught in order to test and understand it more fully. It also makes those who teach realize that the onus is on them to do so in such a way as to persuade people that what they are saying is actually biblical. It helps minimise the danger of those who are taught being expected to just passively accept things because it's what the leaders teach. It brings about a situation wherein people are much more likely to actively and questioningly understand rather than merely passively accept things as being the case and just agree. It creates, in short, what many leaders in many churches fear most, *people with open Bibles and free-thinking minds who don't accept things merely on the authority of a leader's say-so, but who question and challenge until they are persuaded that something is or isn't biblical.* It further releases the corporate insight and wisdom of all in the church, and engenders an atmosphere of humility and the willingness for everyone to learn from anyone. It recognises the vitally important fact that the Lord is in *all* His people, and can therefore speak through any of those in the church and not just some *chosen and verbally gifted elite.*

But I must deal now with what might, in some people's minds, be perceived as biblically-based objection: Paul's preaching. Take a look at a particular Sunday that Paul the Apostle spent with the church in

Troas: "On the first day of the week we came together to break bread. Paul spoke to the people and, because he intended to leave the next day, kept on talking until midnight" (Ac 20:7).

Here we have the believers in Troas coming together for their main weekly gathering, and we can note certain things. (By the way, no Bible scholar would disagree with any of the following observations I am going to make. They are a simple matter of textual fact.).

•*The church is gathering on the first day of the week, on Sunday.*
•*They were gathering together in someone's house.*
•*The Greek text here conveys that the main purpose given for their coming together was for the breaking of bread.*
•*The phrase breaking of bread refers to eating a full meal, here the Lord's Supper.*

The thing I want to focus on here is that Paul spoke to the people and kept on talking until midnight. That certainly makes it sound as if Paul is doing the talking and that everyone else is just listening. So if that is the case then there isn't much open, un-led participatory stuff going on here as we might expect to see, assuming of course that what I've written so far isn't complete nonsense. But there's worse to come, because in some translations of the Bible this verse actually reads, "Paul preached unto them . . . and continued his speech until midnight."

That doesn't just sound like a Sunday sermon, that sounds like the very mother and father of all Sunday sermons either before or since! Paul, if this verse is to be believed, not only preached to the church, but continued to do so until midnight. What on earth can I say to that in the light of the burden of this article? Well, it's actually very simple. The original Greek doesn't say here quite what the English translation conveys. Luke doesn't use any of the various Greek words for *preach* at all. He rather describes what Paul was doing here until midnight with the word *dialogemai*. And *dialogemai*, as any Greek scholar will tell you, means *to converse, to discuss, to reason* or *dispute with*. It denotes a two-way verbal trafficking between different parties and is actually the Greek word from which we get the English word *dialogue*.

Preaching is a monologue, and in certain settings of church life that may well be fine. Midweek Bible studies, for example, may very well be conducted at times by one person doing a monologue followed by questions. But in the New Testament, when the Lord's people come together on Sundays as a church, it's strictly *dialogue* that goes on, and this is precisely what Paul is doing here. He is most certainly teaching the church, and it goes on most of the night because they wanted to learn all they could from him, but it was a discussion-type format and not a

monologue of some kind. It was participatory and interactive, and therefore completely in keeping with the way the apostles set up Sunday
gatherings of churches to be like. In short, Paul was simply conversing
with them. It was a dialogue, and he and the assembled church were
reasoning together. It was two-way mutual communication. It was question and answer, point and counterpoint, objection and explanation! Paul
isn't here standing on some raised platform with everyone sitting silently
just listening to him speaking *to* them. No, he is rather sitting on the sofa
in the lounge talking *with* them.

There is of course a time, as I have already said, for something of a
more formal lecture type format, but even then let it be clear that whoever is teaching must be completely and fully open to questions concerning their subject matter. I don't by that necessarily mean in the middle of
the teaching, but when the speaker has finished then let the questions
and comeback flow. Let it be clear as well that whoever does do teaching, and the more brothers amongst whom this task is shared out the
better, is just one of the brothers, and is not *special* or *spiritually el-
evated* just because that person is gifted in a particular way. (At our
Tuesday night Bible Studies at the church of which I am a part we also
do lots of discussion and interactive type teaching sessions as well, and
use the lecture type format as just one of various approaches.)

Let me end by making clear that I am not in the slightest down
playing Bible teaching in the life of Christian churches. Far from it!
Indeed, none of us would be going on about any of these things in the
first place were it not for the fact we are into good solid Bible teaching
ourselves, and keen to both receive it and pass it on to others. No, we
are simply saying that we have got to start doing things biblically. We
must in this, as with everything else, get back in line with what the Word
of God teaches rather than just sticking with age-old, yet completely
unbiblical, traditions.

Churches need ongoing teaching, of that there can be no doubt.
But they need other things too! To do some biblical things at the expense
of other equally biblical things is, believe me, a big mistake. The apostles
expected that, when believers met in their respective churches on the
Lord's Day, it would be a case of, "When you come together each one
has" (1Co 14:26). That, then, is the way it should be! Nothing more and
nothing less!

Got it? Good! It's pretty simple really, isn't it? After all, whose
ideas and way of doing things have got to be the best? Jesus and His
apostles? Or someone else's?

— Beresford Job

PART THREE

Amid all of our emphasis on home-sized fellowships, it is important to emphasize that the Scriptures also describe a much bigger attitude and congregation: membership in the church universal. It is unhealthy for believers to exist exclusively in one isolated house church. Each house church, properly speaking, is a part of the much bigger city church in whatever town it is located. Though they may never all meet together in one place, and though there is to be no outward ecclesiological authority controlling them, all the congregations in a given area constitute the one body of Christ. We are to cultivate an attitude of oneness, acceptance, love, concern, and cooperation with all the other believers in our city.

What has all this "big church" talk got to do with preaching and teaching? Simply this: in Bible teaching and interpretation we must not ignore the rest of the church as a whole. The Bible is our final authority, but it is not our *only* authority. The Holy Spirit has actively guided and worked in God's people for the past 2,000 years. When the church of history has studied a matter and reached consensus on it, that becomes authoritative for us as well. Do we really have the right to dispute the theology of the church of the ages? As one church historian put it, "It is said that the Acts of the Apostles are more correctly described as the 'Acts of the Holy Spirit'. But it is all church history which should be written under that title and be appreciated as such. Any Christian movement which neglects this story loses the dimension of the solidarity with Christ's church in all ages. The slogan 'Back to the New Testament!' represents only part of the truth. 'Onwards with the Spirit!' is the other half of this truth; together they make up the authority of the Reformers — which was always that of 'Word and Spirit'. It is the same Spirit who inspired the Bible who is alive in the church, creating the tradition and bringing afresh to every age the authority of the once-given Word."[1]

Who has the authority to decide upon the correct interpretation of the Bible, a single church (i.e. Rome), the individual believer, or the universal church as a whole? At one extreme, Roman Catholics will declare that as an individual you are not supposed to interpret your Bible, but rather that you should accept what Rome declares it to mean. At the opposite extreme, though, many Evangelicals have replaced Rome with a new Pope in the form of each individual believer. "Just me and my Bible." Is this much different?

The authors of this book advocate historic Christian orthodoxy poured into the wineskin of New Testament patterns for church life. We believe that the original teachings of the apostles are preserved in the essential doctrines of the historic Christian faith. Jesus said that it was actually to our advantage that He went away, for in His place He sent the Holy Spirit to live in and guide us. Confidence in the Spirit's ability to teach and direct God's people makes us conclude that in the essentials of theology, the church of history has been taught of the Spirit When certain basic doctrines are agreed upon today by Christians from every conceivable background, and also by virtually all those who went before us in the faith, that should get our attention. That is authoritative. Some of these basics include a belief that the sixty-six books of the Bible do finally and completely comprise God's written revelation to us, the doctrine of the Trinity, the deity of Christ, the propitiatory nature of Jesus' work on the cross, justification by grace through faith unto good works, the future bodily return of Jesus, the future tomb-emptying resurrection of the dead, and the future judgment.

The original Protestant doctrine of *sola scriptura* included the belief that whereas the Bible is our final authority, it is not our only authority. The church as a whole is also an authority (albeit a secondary one). As Paul wrote to Timothy, the church is "the pillar and foundation of the truth" (1Ti 3:15). When the entire church arrives at the same conclusions regarding theology, that is authoritative. Teachings contrary to doctrine universally agreed upon by the church at large are not to be entertained.

The church of history has passed on to us various creeds and confessions. The word "creed" is from a Latin root that simply means, "I believe." Did you know that there is even a post-New Testament, church-made creed printed in your Bible? It is called the "Table of Contents." The books of the Bible were not finally compiled and settled upon until quite some time after the apostolic era. How can we trust the church of history to give us the right collection of books that are supposed to be in our Bibles and yet not also trust her to give us right theology about what that same Bible teaches? The main people who resist an acceptance of the basic creeds of the church are those who hold to aberrant theology, denying one or more of the essentials listed above.

Since they are not inspired, it should be acknowledged that the creeds and confessions of various churches are liable to error. That this is so is obvious from the fact that they differ from one another in places. However, what should get our attention all the more is when the creeds and confessions *do line up* in uncoerced agreement at various points. It is somewhat naive, arrogant even, to think that a new truth has been discovered that 99% of all others who have ever studied the Bible failed to see. We must cultivate an historical humility, a spirit of mutual submission with the church at large and with the church of ages past. Pastors, teachers, laymen, historians, catechists, and theologians all coming to the same conclusion regarding a basic theology is significant. Although church practice is beyond the scope of the creeds, it is important to consider that scholars from every denomination are in general agreement regarding such practices of the early church as house churches, participatory meetings, Lord's Supper fellowship meals, non-hierarchical church leadership, and the support of qualified elders, itinerant evangelists and church planters.

Throw out the interpretations of the church as a whole, and you are left with individual subjectivism. Keith Mathison, throughout *The Shape of Sola Scriptura*, has aptly pointed out that modern American Evangelicalism has redefined *sola scriptura* in terms of secular Enlightenment rationalism and rugged democratic individualism. This modern reinterpretation grants autonomy to each individual believer's reason and judgment. The result is the relativism, subjectivism, and theological chaos that we see in modern Evangelicalism today. Mathison points out that each of us comes to the Scripture with different presuppositions, blind spots, ignorance of important facts, and, most importantly, sinfulness. Since we are far from neutral, each of us reads things into Scripture that are really *not* there and also misses things that *are* there. Reason and conscience become the final interpreter. The universal and objective truth of Scripture is made virtually of no effect, because instead of the Church proclaiming with one voice what the Bible teaches, every individual interprets Scripture as seems right in his own eyes. The unbelieving world is left hearing a cacophony of conflicting voices rather than the Word of the living God. In the final analysis, each individual is responsible for establishing *his own creed.*[2]

Faddish theological ideas will continue to sprout like weeds in a garden. Devilish doctrinal winds will always blow and toss the ungrounded to and fro. These challenges must be put into perspective. Which would you rather throw out the window, a recent novel theological position of very few people or the theological convictions of the universal Christian church of all ages? The choice is between the tried and proven faith of the collective body of God's people and the private judgment of a few individual objectors. False teaching could be broadly defined as anything which falls outside of the historic orthodox faith as upheld by the general consensus of the Christian Church for the last two millennia.

The church as a whole has clearly spoken concerning the correct interpretation of the foundational doctrines of the Christian faith. To deny these is to deny the teachings of the Bible. Those who do not hold to sound orthodoxy are not to be allowed to teach their false doctrine (1 Ti 1:3), and are not to be recognized as apostles, elders, teachers, or deacons (1 Ti 3:9, Titus 1:9). Individual churches are not like little row boats out on Lake Placid. Instead, we will go through storms on the high seas. Challenges will come. Aberrant teaching will wash up on deck. It is not a matter of if, but when. In opposing heretical theology, elders and teachers must declare, like captains of war ships, "Repel all boarders!" We are to gently instruct those who oppose, "in the hope that God will grant them repentance leading them to a knowledge of the truth, and that they will come to their senses and escape from the trap of the devil, who had taken them captive to do his will" (2 Ti 2:25-26).

— Steve Atkerson

NOTES

[1] Tom Dowley, ed. *Eerdman's Handbook to the History of The Christianity* (Grand Rapids, MI: Wm. B. Eerdman's Publishing Co., 1977), 16.

[2] Keith Mathison, *The Shape of Sola Scriptura* (Moscow, ID: Canon Press, 2001).

DISCUSSION QUESTIONS

1. What role did preaching and teaching, respectively, each play in the early church?

2. If the 1 Corinthians 14 meeting is not the time for supernaturally gifted teachers to present comprehensive teachings, then when is that time? Explain.

3. What is the difference between a church meeting and a ministry meeting?

4. Why is it important to be able to question something that is being taught? When is it not appropriate to question a teaching?

5. Biblically, what is the difference between preaching and teaching?

6. What role should consensus play in the correct interpretation of the Bible?

7. One historian wrote that 'Back to the New Testament!' represents only part of the truth. 'Onward with the Spirit!' is the other half of this truth. What did he mean by this?

8. Who has the authority to decide upon the correct interpretation of the Bible, a single church (i.e. Rome), the individual believer (whether you or the Pope), or the universal church as a whole? Explain.

9. What role should the early creeds play in our belief system?

10. Which would you rather throw out the window, a recent novel theological position of very few people or the theological convictions of the universal Christian church of all ages? Why?

11. What can we do to be sure our church remains in alignment with historic Christian orthodox?

12. If you find yourself in a house church that has no gifted teachers, what can you do to expose your family to solid teaching?

Note: NTRF also offers a teacher's resource to help lead a discussion of New Testament church life. Request *The Practice of The Early Church: A Theological Workbook (Leader's Guide)* from www.NTRF.org.

THE NICENE CREED

This authoritative statement of Christian orthodoxy was the consensus of church councils that met in Nicea (A.D. 325) and Constantinople (A.D. 381). The wording of the Nicene Creed comes largely from the New Testament. It is the most widely accepted and used brief statement of the Christian Faith.

We believe in one God, the Father, the Almighty, maker of heaven and earth, of all that is, seen and unseen.

We believe in one Lord, Jesus Christ, the only Son of God, eternally begotten of the Father, God from God, Light from Light, true God from true God, begotten, not made, of one Being with the Father. Through him all things were made. For us and for our salvation he came down from heaven: by the power of the Holy Spirit he became incarnate from the Virgin Mary, and was made man. For our sake he was crucified under Pontius Pilate; he suffered death and was buried. On the third day he rose again in accordance with the Scriptures; he ascended into heaven and is seated at the right hand of the Father. He will come again in glory to judge the living and the dead, and his kingdom will have no end.

We believe in the Holy Spirit, the Lord, the giver of life, who proceeds from the Father and the Son. With the Father and the Son he is worshiped and glorified. He has spoken through the Prophets.

We believe in one holy catholic* and apostolic Church.

We acknowledge one baptism** for the forgiveness of sins. We look for the resurrection of the dead, and the life of the world to come. Amen.

* In this context, "catholic" means "universal."

** "For" here means "because of" as in "She cried for joy." Just as circumcision was the outward seal of the righteousness that Abraham had already received by faith (Ro 4), so too water baptism is the outward sign of the salvation every believer already has because of his faith in the risen Lord Jesus and the work that He did for His people on the cross.

It was argued earlier in this book that the ideal is government by the consensus of the whole congregation, and that churches should be elder-led more so than elder-ruled. If this really is the case, are elders really even needed in a church? What function do they serve?

ADVANTAGES OF HAVING ELDERS

It would be a serious blunder to conclude that elders are unimportant to the life of a church. Paul warned that "fierce wolves will come in among you, not sparing the flock." (ESV, Ac 20:29). Some wolves are schismatic, others promote false doctrine, and still others practice immorality. Too often, house churches without qualified elders fall in a type of spiritual malaise. No one takes leadership responsibility. There is no 'point man" to offer direction. Things just coast along. Discipleship is minimal. In many cases, it becomes a case of the blind the blind. Pooled ignorance in "teaching" becomes the norm. Evident sins are overlooked. Social problems are not dealt with. The church can become vulnerable to wolves in sheep's' clothing.

During the World War Two battle of Midway, a lone American air torpedo squadron (VT-8), from the aircraft carrier *Hornet,* attacked the Japanese invasion fleet. Tragically, the squadron was ordered to attack without fighter escort. Like the charge of the Light Brigade, it proved suicidal. Only one airman survived. Elders are to the church what the American fighter planes would have been to the bombers: protection. One important ministry that elders offer is defense against savage wolves. For instance, elders are men who can "refute" those who oppose sound doctrine (Tit 1:9).

The reality of the situation is that house churches are not yet mainstream in Western Christianity. As such, a house church is likely to attract every unattached heretic, rebel and social misfit in the county. Without elders willing to stand at the gate to intercept and deal with such persons, a house church is particularly vulnerable to abuse, strife, frustration, and even disbanding.

Besides fending off wolves, elders serve the body in many other ways. In many respects, a church without an elder is much like a family without a father. Qualified elders provide direction, teach, disciple, help the church achieve consensus, promote the saints' growth into maturity, train future leaders, lead by example and guard the truth (Ac 20:25-31, Ep 4:11-13, 1Ti 1:3, 3:4-5, 5:17, 6:20, 2Ti 1:13-14, 2:2, 15, 3:16-17, 4:2-4, Ti 1:9, 13, 2:15 and Heb 13:17). Church leaders are men of mature character who oversee, shepherd, teach, equip and coach. Every now and then they will need to call on the obstinate to submit to their leadership (Heb 13:17).

ELDER-LED CONGREGATIONAL CONSENSUS

One very important ministry elders provide is leadership. All are agreed that the Lord Jesus is the head of the church (Col 1:15-20). Thus, the church ultimately is a dictatorship (or theocracy) ruled by Christ through His written Word and the influence of the Holy Spirit (Jn 14:25-27; 16:12-15; Ac 2:42; Ep 2:19-22; 1Ti 3:14-15). Once we follow the organizational flow chart down from the head, where does the line of authority go?

In speaking to the elders of the Ephesian church, Paul said, "Keep watch over yourselves and all the flock of which the Holy Spirit has made you overseers. Be shepherds of the church of God which He bought with His own blood" (20:17, 28). The use of the terms overseers and shepherds certainly suggests a supervisory position for elders. When writing to Timothy about the qualifications for an elder, Paul asked, "If anyone does not know how to manage his own family, how can he take care of God's church?" (1Ti 3:5). This again implies a management role for elders. Peter asked the elders to "be shepherds of God's flock that is under your care, serving as overseers" (1Pe 5:2). Once more elders are painted in a leadership mode.

1 Timothy 5:17 refers to elders who direct the affairs of the church well. 1 Thessalonians 5:12 asks the brothers to respect those "who are over you in the Lord and who admonish you." Hebrews 13:7 commands, "Remember your leaders." Following that, Hebrews 13:17 adds, "Obey your leaders and submit to their authority. They keep watch over you as men who must give an account." All of this indicates that there are to be human leaders in the church. These leaders are most often referred to as elders or overseers.

As to the difference between an elder, overseer ("bishop" in the KJV), and pastor (shepherd), an examination of Acts 20:17, 28-30, Titus 1:5-7, and 1 Peter 5:1-3 will show the synonymous usage of these words. All three refer to the same person or ministry. Any modern distinction between them is purely artificial and without scriptural warrant.

The biblical references to "rule" by overseers could, if taken in isolation, easily lead to a wrong view of how elder rule should operate.

There is more to the equation than at first meets the eye. Consider the steps of church discipline in Matthew 18:15-17 as it relates to a church's decision making process (see also 1 Corinthians 5:1-5; Galatians 6:1). Notice that the whole congregation is to be involved in the decision to exercise discipline. Notice also that the leaders are not especially singled out to screen the cases before they reach the open meeting nor to carry out the discipline themselves. It is a congregational decision.

This corporate process is also glimpsed in Acts 1:15-26. The apostle Peter placed the burden for finding a replacement for Judas upon the church as a whole. In Acts 6:1-6, the apostles turned to "all the disciples" (6:2) and asked them to choose administrators for the church's welfare system. Both these examples point to congregational involvement.

Paul wrote to "all" (1:7) the saints in Rome, and made no special mention of the elders. The letters to the Corinthians were addressed to the entire "church" (1Co 1:2, 2Co 1:1). Again there was no emphasis on the overseers. This is all the more remarkable when one considers that Corinthians deals with church discipline, marriage, the Lord's Supper, and interactive meetings. The greeting in Galatians 1:2 focuses on the "churches" in Galatia. The message was not first filtered through the leaders. The "Saints in Ephesus" (1:1) were the recipients of that letter (Ep 1:1). In Philippians 1:1 the saints were given equal billing with the overseers and deacons, who are finally mentioned in a salutation.. In Colossians 1:2, the salutation went to "the holy and faithful brothers in Christ." All of this implies that the elders were themselves also sheep. The elders were a subset of the church as a whole. There was no clergy/laity distinction.

This lack of emphasis on the leadership is also seen in 1 Thessalonians 1:1; 2 Thessalonians 1:1; James 1:1; 1 Peter 1:1; 2 Peter 1:1; 1 John 2:1, 7, and Jude 1:1. In fact, the book of Hebrews was written to a group of believers and it was not until the very last chapter that the author asked them to "greet all your leaders" (13:24). He did not even greet the leaders directly!

Much may be gleaned from the way that New Testament writers made appeals directly to entire churches. They went to great lengths to influence ordinary rank and file believers. The apostles did not simply bark orders and issue injunctions (as a military commander might do). Instead, they treated other believers as equals and appealed directly to them as such. No doubt local church leaders were led in much the same way. Their primary authority lay in their ability to influence with the truth. The respect they were given was honestly earned. It was the opposite of military authority wherein soldiers respect the rank but not necessarily the man.

Hebrews 13:7 reflects the fact that the leadership style employed by church leaders is primarily one of direction by example: "Remember your leaders . . . Consider the outcome of their way of life and imitate their faith." Along this same line, 1 Thessalonians 5:12-13 reveals that leaders are to be respected, not because of automatically inferred authority of rank, but because of the value of their service — "Hold them in highest regard in love because of their work." Jesus said, "You know that the rulers of the Gentiles lord it over them, and their high officials exercise authority over them. Not so with you. Instead, whoever wants to become great among you must be your servant, and whoever wants to be first must be your slave" (Mt 20:25-28).

The word church in the New Testament is used a few times to refer to the universal church. Most occurrences, however, refer to organized local churches. No organized church should be any bigger than a single congregation, and no church has official jurisdiction or authority over any other church (though there naturally will be interchurch cooperation and assistance). Each house church is ideally to be guided by its own elder(s). Each elder is equal in authority to any other elder. There is to be no senior pastor nor presiding bishop over a city. A leader's primary authority is based on his ability to persuade with the truth. He is to lead by example, not lording it over the church (1Pe 5:3). Church polity is thus a dynamic process of interaction, persuasion, and right timing between the shepherds and the sheep.

Jesus' comments on leadership truly must be the starting point and final reference in our understanding of an elder's authority (Lk 22:24-27). Dr. Hal Miller has insightfully observed, "Jesus' disturbing teaching about authority among his followers contrasts their experience of it with every other society. The kings of the Gentiles, he said, lord it over their subjects and make that appear good by calling themselves "benefactors." They exercise their power and try (more or less successfully) to make people think that it is for their own good. But it should never be so in the church. There, on the contrary, the one who leads is as a slave and the one who rules is as the youngest (Lk 22:24-27). Lest this lose its impact, you should stop to reflect that the youngest and the slaves are precisely those without authority in our normal sense of the word. Yet this is what leadership among Jesus' people is like."[1]

Though they were technically apostolic workers, Timothy and Titus clearly functioned as substitute elders until permanent local men were appointed. The elders that were later appointed could be expected to do the same types of things that these temporary apostolic workers had done on the local level (1Ti 1:3, 4:11, 5:17, 6:17, Tit 1:12-13, 2:15, 3:10). From this it is clear that it is proper an for elder, in exercising servant leadership, to authoritatively reprove, speak, teach, and guide. An elder is to "rule well" and "oversee" the church, taking the initiative in prompting and guarding. As a mature believer, his understanding of what constitutes right or wrong behavior and doctrine will most probably be correct. An elder naturally will often be among the first to detect and deal with problems. He is to be proactive, not merely reactive. However, if those he confronts refuse to listen, the elder's final recourse is to then present the matter to the whole church in accordance with the Matthew 18 process. Though a elder is critical to the consensus process, authority, ultimately, still rests with the church corporately (congregational consensus).

There is a delicate balance to be reached between the leadership role of elders and the decision making responsibilities of the congregation. Too far one way and you have a pope. Too far the other and you have a ship with no rudder. In essence, both the arguments for the leadership of the elders and for the corporate responsibility of the entire church are valid. On one hand, you have elders leading by example, guiding with teaching and by moderating the give-and-take discussion of the assembly. On the other hand, you have the flock. The church corporately makes the final decision, yet they are exhorted to follow their elders and to allow themselves to be persuaded by their leaders' arguments (Heb 13:17). Elders' words have weight only to the extent that the people give it to them. Elders deserve honor due to the position in which God has placed them (1Ti 5:17).

THE APPOINTMENT OF ELDERS

How should elders be appointed? All potential overseers must meet a lengthy list of qualifications (1Ti 3:1-7; Tit 1:5-9). That a man is both willing and able to be an elder is obviously the work of the Holy Spirit (Ac 20:28). Once these prerequisites are met, the would-be elder is then appointed. In Ac 14:23 Paul and Barnabas apparently did the appointing, and Titus was left in Crete by Paul to appoint elders (Tit 1:5). As Nee observed, "they merely established as elders those whom the Holy Spirit had already made overseers in the church."[2]

After the apostles (missionaries/church planters) appointed elders and moved on, there is virtual silence as to how subsequent elders were, or ought to be, chosen. Operating from the principle of Acts 1:15-26 & 6:1-6, one could conclude that the succeeding elders were chosen by the whole congregation (following the requirements laid out in 1 Timothy 3:1-7), under the leadership of the existing elders, and under the advisement of any itinerant ministers that have earned the right to be heard by that local congregation.

THE PRESBYTERY

The New Testament pattern is for each house church to be led by a body of equal brothers (some of whom are elders), depending upon one another, accountable to one another, submitting to one another, and living out a mutual ministry. Is there supposed to be one elder per church, several elders per church, or several churches per elder? According to Acts 14:23, Paul and Barnabas "appointed elders in each church." The biblical evidence seems to support a plurality of elders in every church.

However, a bit of confusion arises because the New Testament sometimes speaks of only one church in certain cities. For instance, Acts 8:1 mentions "the church at Jerusalem." Paul wrote to "the church of God in Corinth" (1Co 1:2) and to "the church of the Thessalonians" (1Th 1:1). Jesus told John to write to "the" church in Smyrna, "the" church in Pergamum, etc. (Re 2:1, 8, 12, 18; 3:1, 7, 14). It is possible that these examples reflect the doctrine of something called the city church. As there is biblically only one church universal, so too some argue that there is philosophically only one church per city. Yet just as the universal church is an abstract reality with no outward organization, so too the city church concept would be an abstract reality, without earthly organization. An examination of the New Testament will reveal that, though all churches were united under Christ as head, there was no outward ecclesiastical organization uniting them. Though cooperating voluntarily together, each church was autonomous. Theirs was a strong inward bond, a spiritual oneness of life in the Lord. Though independent of outward government, they were interdependent in responsibility to one another (see 2Co 8-9). Thus, philosophically, there would be only one church in Atlanta, one in London, one in Moscow, etc. Each abstract city church would be made up of many local, organized, autonomous house churches. If this approach is accurate, the plurality of elders referred to in the Scriptures could flag a plurality per city, but not necessarily in every house church.

Did the plurality of elders serve the city-wide church as a whole, or only individual house churches? That elders worked together is clear from Philippians 1:1, 1 Timothy 4:14 and Titus 1:5. Yet it would be a mistake to conclude that they collectively were over multiple churches as some sort of ruling presbytery. Since any elder's authority lies primarily in his ability to persuade with the truth, and since any respect due him is earned via personal interaction, there is no way a presbytery of elders could rule over a group of churches anyhow. Ideally, each house church should have its own elder(s). In those transitional situations where a house church has no one qualified to be an elder, temporary leadership could be sought from a respected church planter, a missionary, an elder in a nearby church, or an itinerant pastor-teacher (Ep 4:11).

CONCLUSION

Harvey Bluedorn offers this excellent biblical summary of the ministry and authority of elders:

1. **The New Testament Standard** — As the pattern of things shown to Moses established the standards for the tabernacle (Ex 25:9,40; 26:30; 39:42,43; Ac 7:44; Heb 8:5), and as the pattern of things shown to David established the standards for the temple (1Ch 28:11-13,19), so the pattern of things shown in the New Testament establishes the standards for the assembly, the temple of God (1Co 3:9,16,17; 6:19,20; 2Co 6:16; Ep 2:21,22; 4:13-16; 1Ti 3:15; 1Pe 2:5,9; Re 1:6; 3:12; 5:10; 20:6).

2. **Servant Leaders** — Leaders are a functional necessity for the assembly. The Lord Jesus raises up men from among the members of the body, and equips them to meet stated qualifications. They will inevitably emerge from among the membership and become apparent to the assembly, and the assembly must formally recognize the Lord's calling in those whom the Lord has truly gifted and qualified to serve as guides, teachers, and examples to the whole body. Such servants are called elders and overseers, or shepherds and teachers (Tit 1:5, Ep 4:11).

3. **Multiple Elders** — A plural number of elders will ordinarily emerge from the membership of an assembly (Ac 14:23), although in a newly formed assembly it may require some time to pass before the Lord fully equips and qualifies elders (Lk 12:42; 1Co 4:2; 1Ti 3:6,10; 5:22; Tit 1:5; Heb 5:12,13). Among the pastor-elders there are some who especially toil in discourse and teaching (Ep 4:11; 1Th 5:12,13; 1Ti 5:17).

4. **Decisions by Full Agreement** — Decisions are made by the full agreement of the assembly, as represented in the men of the assembly, under the advice and counsel of their servants, the elders. Presumably, the men may, by full agreement, delegate certain on-the-spot-type decisions to someone, including to elders, but they must always reserve the right to make the decision themselves, or to deter-

mine the policy for such decisions, and they must require of those to whom they delegate decisions a full report and accountability to the assembly.

5. **Elders are Servants, Not Lords** — The Word of Christ rules by His Spirit in the midst of His people, through the regenerate hearts and renewed minds of the members of the assembly as He brings them to complete mutual agreement, unanimous accord, or consensus. Elders lead by the moral authority of a servant who provides word and example, and who commands respect for what he gives, not for what he requires. Elders do not rule as independent authorities. Their role is advisory and supervisory, not the lordly authority of command and conform. Elders are instrumental, through their leadership, teaching, and example, in bringing about consensus in the assembly, but all authority rests in Christ alone. All members — including elders — submit to the Lord, then to one another in the Lord — including elder members, who submit to other members, including to other elder members. In other words, there is no chain of command — God, then Christ, then elders, then members — but only a network of submission, and elders have the greatest burden of submission and accountability because they are servants to the whole assembly. Only those who humble themselves to the level of servants before the Lord and His assembly may be raised to this level of accountability. By the nature of the case, those who would exalt themselves to a position of authority over all, have necessarily disqualified themselves from a position of service.

6. **The Saints are Kings and Priests** — It is a severe violation of the adult conscience to treat the saints as children under the over-lordship of elders. The ultimate effect of treating the saints as children is that they will either remain children in their understanding as they submit to bondage, or they will rebel. Elders exercise appropriate authority as fathers within their own households, but their role in the assembly is not as fathers and lords over children and servants, but as elder brothers in the faith and humble servants to the whole.

7. **A Deliberative Assembly** — The gathered assembly is a deliberative body. The men in the assembly are encouraged to interact in an orderly manner with the reading, exhortation, and teaching in the assembly, regardless of what form that interaction assumes - informative lecture, thoughtful consideration and discussion of propositions of Scripture, logical debate of different sides of a question, or consultation on practical issues. This is not a Quaker-like meeting of "whenever-the-spirit-leads," nor is it a family-friendly-style meeting of token

affirmations by heads of household, nor is it a worship-centered meeting of lively entertainment, but it is a genuine discipleship learning process which edifies and brings the whole assembly to maturity in Christ through the interaction of the men of the assembly.

8. Independent Congregational Accountability — Each congregation constitutes its own communion and is independently accountable to the Lord, but all true congregations exist within the same spiritual kingdom. They depend upon the same Lord, and they cooperate as much as circumstances require and allow, both on the level of individual persons and on a congregational level. There should be no ungodly jealousy between brother believers, nor between sister assemblies.

— Steve Atkerson

NOTES

[1] Hal Miller, "As Children and Slaves: Authority in the New Testament," *Voices*, (Salem, MA: March/April 1987), 6-7, 20-21.

[2] Watchman Nee, *The Normal Christian Church Life* (Colorado Springs, CO: International Students Press, 1969) 41.

The Ministry of Elders

1. Why are elders needed in a church? What function do they serve?

2. Following the church organizational flow chart down from Christ the head, where does the line of authority go?

3. What is the difference between an elder, and overseer (bishop) and a pastor?

4. Why were church leaders not mentioned in the greetings of the epistles, and often not even mentioned or written to in entire letters?

5. What examples did Jesus give, in Luke 22:24-27, of the authority that church leaders have over the church?

6. Why were elders not mentioned in the church discipline process of Matthew 18?

7. How should elders be appointed?

8. Did the plurality of elders serve the city-wide church as a whole, or only individual house churches?

9. Is a church without an elder really a church?

10. Which point from Harvey Bluedorn's summary of the ministry of elders did you find the most interesting?

11. In general, what type of man should a church look for to be an elder, based on 1 Timothy 3 and Titus 1?

12. Are the qualifications for elders primarily those of character or ability (1 Ti 3, Titus 1)? Explain.

13. Why is it important that a man meet the qualifications of 1 Timothy 3 and Titus 1 in order to serve as a elder?

11
FULL TIME MINISTERS

Famous are the words of Jesus, "It is more blessed to give than to receive." Not so familiar is the context in which this truth was recorded. Jesus' words are not found in any of the four Gospels. These words of Jesus were quoted by the apostle Paul while speaking at a pastor's conference (Ac 20:32-35). Amazingly, Paul was instructing those pastors to be in the position of *giving* silver, gold and clothing to the church, rather than receiving such from it!

ACTS 20

In light of what Jesus said, should pastors earn their living from the church? In Acts 20, Paul gave the Ephesian elders specific instructions on their duties as elders. Concerning finances, Paul stated that he had coveted no one's silver or gold and that he had, in fact, paid his own way by working hard with his hands (20:34-25; compare 18:1ff). Following Paul's example, the elders were also to earn their living from secular jobs so as to be able to help the weak and live out the words of the Lord Jesus that it is more blessed to give than to receive. Thus, from Acts 20:32-35, it is clear that elders are generally to be in the financial position of giving to the church, not receiving from it. However, Acts 20 is not the only passage that deals with this subject.

1 CORINTHIANS 9

What of 1 Corinthians 9:14, where it is stated that those who proclaim the gospel should receive their living from the gospel? We can observe from 1 Corinthians 9 that at least three groups made their livings from their ministries during New Testament times: apostles (9:1-6), the Lord's brothers (9:5) and evangelists (9:14). According to Paul, various factors combined to justify this truth:
•*A human point of view (soldier, vineyard keeper, shepherd), 9:8*
•*The Law of Moses (oxen, temple priests), 9:9-10, 13*
•*Spiritual principle/logic (spiritual seed/material harvest), 9:11*
•*The words of Jesus, 9:14*

From a merely "human point of view" (9:8) Paul asked: "Who serves as a soldier at his own expense? Who plants a vineyard and does not eat of its grapes? Who tends a flock and does not drink of the milk?"

(9:7). The answer is obvious. All make their livings from their work, and so should apostles/church planters/missionaries/evangelists.

Then, from the Law of Moses (9:8-9), Paul quoted: "Do not muzzle an ox while it is treading out the grain." Applied to apostles, Paul asked "Is it about oxen that God is concerned? Surely he says this for us, doesn't he?" (9:9-10). If oxen can eat from what they do, so can apostles. In 9:13, Paul brought in the example of Old Testament priests, asking, "Don't you know that those who work in the temple get their food from the temple, and those who serve at the altar share in what is offered on the altar?" (9:13).

Paul also high lighted an important spiritual principle of reaping and sowing: "If we have sown spiritual seed among you, is it too much if we reap a material harvest from you?" (9:11). Paul concluded that this is a "right" and should be his "all the more" (9:12).

Paul's final argument was found in the words of our Lord who "commanded that those who preach the gospel should receive their living from the gospel" (9:14). If it is true for evangelists, it is true of apostles, too.

1 Corinthians 9 specifically concerns the rights of an apostle, someone commissioned by either Jesus or the church to travel around evangelizing and establishing churches (the word missionary is never used in Scripture; such people were called apostles and evangelists). As is clear from the text, all such people have the "right" (9:12) to financial support.

Unexpectedly, after writing convincingly of an apostle's rights in 1 Corinthians 9, Paul then added, "But I have not used any of these rights. And I am not writing this in the hope that you will do such things for me." (1Co 9:15). If Paul did not write this with the hope that the Corinthians would give him support (1Co 9:15), then why did he write it? In essence, 1 Corinthians 9 is a parenthetical remark. Paul's main topic began in 1 Corinthians 8 and concerned not being a stumbling block to others (food sacrificed to idols, 8:9). Paul's waver of his right to full-time support (1Co 9) illustrated just how far Paul was willing to go to so as to "not hinder the gospel" (9:12b, 15). Then, in 1 Corinthians 10, Paul continued on with his main topic, concluding with "Do not cause anyone to stumble, whether Jews, Greeks or the church of God" (1Co 10:31-32). Thus, Paul's objective in writing 1 Corinthians 9 was neither to limit nor extend the categories of those who had the right to support from the church. It was merely an illustration. As such, it reveals that Paul had a very liberal approach to supporting church workers: "Is it about oxen that God is concerned?" and "If we have sown spiritual seed among you, is it too much if we reap a material harvest from you?"

Individual believers have the privilege and responsibility of giving generously toward the support of missionaries and evangelists. In so doing, the giver is co-laboring along with the Christian worker. Without such full time workers, the advance of God's kingdom could be hampered. Pray for such ministers. Find creative ways to encourage them in their labor of love. Purpose to give sacrificially and consistently toward their support.

Is it wrong to apply this passage to elders? Since Paul waived his apostolic "right" to get his "living" from the gospel (9:15, 18), the example he showed the Ephesian elders in Acts 20 seems all the more compelling (see also 1Th 2:9; 2Th 3:7-9).

1 Corinthians 9 deals specifically with the rights of an apostle, not an elder. However, based on the principles expressed in 1 Corinthians 9, would it be committing the unpardonable sin for an elder to make his living from the church? Of course not! Based solely on Acts 20, it would seem that pastors (elders) will generally not receive full time financial support for their ministries. However, since Acts 20 is not the only passage dealing with this subject, 1 Corinthians 9 (above) must be factored in, as must 1 Timothy 5 (below).

1 Timothy 5

Temporarily stationed in Ephesus was Timothy, Paul's traveling companion and fellow apostle (1Th 1:1; 2:6), whom Paul left there to squelch strange doctrines (1Ti 1:3). Concerning the same Ephesian elders as in Acts 20, Paul wrote that elders who did a good job directing the affairs of the church and who worked hard at preaching and teaching were worthy of something called "double honor" (1Ti 5:17). Then, using almost the exact same reasoning as in 1 Corinthians 9:9, 1 Timothy 5:18 states, "For the Scripture says, 'Do not muzzle the ox while it is treading out the grain,' and 'The worker deserves his wages.'" This parallel should not be minimized. The implications are clear.

Does honor mean pay? No. From the Greek word *time*, it primarily means "respect." There is a specific Greek word for pay (*misthos*) and, significantly, it is used in 1 Timothy 5:18 (about employees), but not in 1 Timothy 5:17 (about elders). *Time* can in certain contexts mean price, but since a price is the quantity of one thing that is demanded in sale for another, it hardly makes sense in this passage (are elders for sale?). This same word (*time*) is also used immediately following in 1 Timothy 6:1, "All who are under the yoke of slavery should consider their masters worthy of full respect (*time*)." Are slaves to pay their masters? One practical application of this honor is that an accusation brought against an elder is not to be received unless it is substantiated by more than one witness (1Ti 5:19). 1 Timothy 5:19 logically follows 5:17-18 if honor refers to respect (an accusation involves dishonor), but follows awkwardly if honor refers to pay. A good parallel verse is 1 Thessalonians 5:12-13, wherein the church in Thessalonica was asked to "respect those who work hard among you, who are over you in the Lord and who admonish you. Hold them in the highest regard in love because of their work."

However, *time* is also used immediately prior to this passage about elders. According to 1 Timothy 5:3, honor is to be given to widows who are really in need (the NIV renders it as "proper recognition"). This occurrence of *time* obviously means granting the widow more than respect. Giving the widow food, helping her with her house and yard work, visiting her, offering her living quarters if needed, and of course even monetary assistance, is the idea. Honor was also clearly understood by Jesus to refer to material support in Mark 7:10. The Law of Moses required, "Honor your father and your mother." Unhappy with the religious leaders of Judaism, Jesus said, "But you say that if a man says to his father or mother: 'Whatever help you might otherwise have received by me is Corban' (that is, a gift devoted to God), then you no longer let him do anything for his father or mother. Thus you nullify the word of God by your tradition that you have handed down" (Mk 7:11-13). Thus, it is clearly within the realm of possibility that honor to an elder might include giving him a love offering, an honorarium.

So why did Paul use *time* (honor) instead of *misthos* (wages) in 1 Timothy 5:17? Perhaps because the elder's relationship to the church is not to be as a hireling. Nor is he to charge a fee for his services. Jonathan Campbell wisely stated, "There is a difference between being paid to do a job and being released to do a work."

Concerning voluntary giving (an honorarium) versus a salaried position, Dan Walker warned, "The widows of 1 Timothy 5:3-16 weren't earning a salary, they were receiving charity. And 'the laborer is worthy of his hire' quote in Luke 10 referred obviously not to disciples receiving a salary or wages, but hospitality (eat and drink what's set before you, etc.). The word wages in the Old Testament quotation (1Ti 5:18) is obviously metaphorical (just like the unmuzzled ox eating straw is metaphorical). If you push that metaphor too far, we'll have Christian workers eating straw! In another example of the metaphorical use of wages, Paul wrote to the Corinthians that he had robbed other churches so as not to accept wages from Corinthians. Vines states that the word wages in 2 Corinthians 11:8 is clearly metaphorical, which, of course, it is. I don't think it's anybody's business if a Christian worker (whether apostle,

154

prophet, elder, teacher, or whatever) receives voluntary offerings from anybody for whatever reason. But the minute a salary or wages is paid, the principle of voluntary giving of service to the body is violated, the principle of clergy-less Christianity is violated, the priesthood of all believers is violated, etc. I'm not getting on that train, because it's heading over the cliff. The number one stench in the institutional church is money, plain and simple. It is an abomination, a disgrace not only to God, but to the human race. And once we open the door with a hireling clergy, we are finished. In conclusion, if Paul had meant double wages in I Timothy 5:17, why didn't he say double *misthos*, or double *opsonion*, two perfectly clear words which mean wages and would have conveyed what he meant? And if he meant wages, why didn't the early church follow his example?"

London elder Beresford Job comments, "I think it unlikely that there would be much need for anyone to be a full time elder unless he also had a ministry wider than just to the house church of which he is a part. It is significant that when Paul addresses this issue, he assumes that any elders who might need some kind of support were precisely those engaged in preaching and teaching (1Ti 5:17ff). This leads me to believe that he is referring to people who were among the evangelists and pastor-teachers listed in the fourfold trans-local ministries of Ephesians 4:11. I therefore conclude that there are men who are called to share themselves out amongst more than one church who won't necessarily have time to do a secular job as well. Assuming they aren't millionaires, or have a business that supports them and which functions pretty much without needing their attention, they are going to have to be funded from elsewhere.

However, the apparent contradiction we seem to have in Scripture is that although the laborer is indeed worthy of his hire (such men have bills to pay and families to support too), ministry is nevertheless free of charge and we see nothing whatsoever in the New Testament of salaried positions. Indeed, the idea of churches employing someone is perfectly at odds with the teaching of the New Testament as a whole. If someone feels called to a ministry which prohibits him the time to earn money from other employment, then he can well trust the Lord to provide his needs. It will, of course, be through the freewill offerings of the Lord's people, but nothing must be done by the one called into full time service to ever procure money because that would transgress scriptural teaching that all ministry is free of charge.

I have been in full-time ministry for twenty-five years and don't charge money, don't take collections, have never requested that collections be taken on my behalf, have never mentioned expenses incurred, never sent out a prayer letter or made needs known to others in any way. I finance everything I do myself and simply respond to whatever I believe the Lord would have me do, whether it's driving locally to teach or buying plane tickets for my family and I to come over to the States to minister. I do knowing that if I work free of charge then the Lord will provide for my family and I in answer to prayer. I call it 'living by faith properly' as opposed to 'living by faith - and hints and prayer letters and collections.' "

It is clear from Scripture that individual believers in local churches owe honor (esteem) to all elders, and double honor (as in a regular hono-rarium) to those elders who are particularly gifted in oversight and teaching. Initiative should be taken by those who are blessed from the spiritual ministry of an elder to reciprocate that blessing materially.

Among American Christians, there are many questions about a house church incorporating with the government, or having its own bank account. We would caution against this. First, U.S. churches are already tax exempt, according to the Constitution. Further, having a church budget and bank account is just something else for the carnal coral to quibble over. If anything, it is the qualified elders who should incorporate as a 501c3 ministry. That way, tax exempt status can be gained, and free-will gifts to the elder would qualify as tax deductions, and the elder would not be on a salaried position from the church. The pastor-teacher would, in essence, be like any other self employed brother in the assembly. As has been pointed out above, he probably would have to have a ministry wider than one house church.

1 PETER 5

What did Peter mean in 1 Peter 5:2 when he exhorted the elders to shepherd God's flock voluntarily and not for sordid gain? "Sordid gain" is from a single Greek word, *aischrokerdos*. *Aischros* means shame or disgrace and *kerdos* means gain, profit, or advantages. A related term, *aischrokerdes*, is used in Titus 1:7 where elders are required not to be fond of sordid gain. 1 Timothy 3:3 parallels this with a requirement that elders be free from the love of money. Thus, *aischrokerdes* is a virtual synonym for being greedy for money. Peter's warning suggests that money *did* occasionally go along with the ministry of elder, and being in it for the money was not a good reason to be an elder!

R.C.H. Lenski pointed out that since elders were usually bi-vocational, Peter's warning was that elders not use their position to seek the trade of the church in business matters.1 (How many businessmen have joined First Church primarily to climb the social and economic ladder?).

Another way to look at Peter's words is to see them as a caution for the elder who is already successful in his secular career and at the height of his earning potential. Such an elder is to be willing to forgo potentially lucrative time spent at work and instead give his time and energy to serving as an overseer.

SYNTHESIS

Jesus commanded that those who preach the gospel (evangelists) should make their living from the gospel. Paul, in an illustration, applied this same principle to apostles (1Co 9). Finally, using the same arguments found in 1 Corinthians 9, it was applied to qualified elders (1Ti 5).

Acts 20 is addressed to elders in general. In general, elders are normally going to be bi-vocational and will thus be in a position of giving monetarily to the church, rather than receiving from it. The exception to this generalization is 1 Timothy 5, written with reference to those elders who not only "direct the affairs of the church well" (5:17) but who also "labor in the word and doctrine" (NKJV). Though all elders are worthy of honor (1Th 5:12-13), some elders are worthy of double honor. This double honor most likely is a reference to financial support from the church. Blending Acts 20 with 1 Timothy 5 would also suggest that even those elders worthy of double honor (financial support) be willing and trained to work some secular vocation if local conditions require it (i.e., in times or areas of economic depression, in very small churches, because of persecution, etc.).

CAUTIONS

1. Suggesting that individual believers are obligated to support those elders deemed worthy of double honor (pastor-teachers) does not mean that the full time elders are somehow higher in rank than the other elders. One elder may be more gifted than another, or more influential, but there is no such thing in the New Testament as an official senior elder, nor of a hierarchy of elders, nor of a presiding bishop over the other elders. The pastor-teacher mentioned in Ephesians 4 is not in any way to be over all the churches of a city. Instead, he is the servant to all the churches of the city.

2. To be avoided are elders (especially those worthy of double honor) who dominate the 1 Corinthians 14 meeting. If an elder receives financial support that enables him to study the Word, it's possible that he will have so much more to teach, and be expected to do so,

that the other brothers won't feel as free to teach. That would squelch the priesthood of believers and violate the spirit of 1 Corinthians 14:26. Such meetings are not to be pastor-centered. Instead, a gifted elder's in-depth teaching ministry should occur during a midweek Bible study or other special ministry meeting.

3. Even though qualified elders may make their livings from their ministries, there is to be no clergy-laity distinction. Authority generally resides in the church as a whole, not usually with its leaders. The leaders are to be humble servants, not lords. Rusty Entrekin warns: "Although we know that pastor-teachers are supposed to be servants and not in a special clergy class, those who are not pastor-teachers will still have a tendency to regard them that way, especially because of our modern institutional church mind-set regarding professional pastors. Even if the pastor-teacher doesn't think that way about himself initially, if he doesn't watch himself, he could very easily begin to gradually, perhaps imperceptibly, adopt that mind-set. Since the godly, sincere, and vibrant believers of the late first century and early second century church fell victim to this mind-set, just think of how easily we could today with the peer pressure of conventional wisdom, centuries of traditions, and lukewarm spirituality encouraging us to do so! We need to be very careful not only to guard against the priesthood being robbed of their God-given rights, but also to exhort them not to give their rights away."

CONCLUSION

What can be concluded about the idea of full-time church workers?

1. There is no historical pattern in the New Testament either for or against full-time elders. It is silent with regard to example. There are, however, direct teachings on the subject.

2. There is a general command in Acts 20 for elders to follow Paul's example of supplying their own needs so as to be in a position of giving silver and gold and clothing to the church, rather than receiving from it.

3. All elders are worthy of honor (esteem), 1 Thessalonians 5.

4. Qualified elders, those who rule and teach well, are worthy of double honor (voluntary financial support, 1Ti 5).

5. Elders are not to be motivated by the desire for "sordid gain" from their ministry (i.e., not just in it for the money, nor using the office to gain sales or business clients), 1 Peter 5.

6. Each church member needs to financially support those who are evangelists, apostles, and pastor-teachers, per 1 Corinthians 9 and 1 Timothy 5. It is the New Testament pattern to give to support such people.

— Steve Atkerson

NOTES

1 R.C.H. Lenski, *The Interpretation of the Epistles of St. Peter* (Minneapolis, MN: Augsburg Publishing, 1966) 219.

DISCUSSION QUESTIONS

1. Why did Paul remind the Ephesian elders that it is more blessed to give than to receive (Ac 20)?

2. Based on 1 Corinthians 9:1-14, what right does every apostle (missionary) have?

3. What examples were given in 1 Corinthians 9 of those who made their living from the church?

4. Why did Paul ask, "If we have sown spiritual seed among you, is it too much if we reap a material harvest from you?" (1Co 9:11).

5. How have you personally obeyed the Lord's command of 1 Corinthians 9:14?

6. According to Romans 15:26-27, what do you owe to those who have brought you a spiritual blessing?

7. Explain how you personally have obeyed Galatians 6:6?

8. What in the following texts suggest that Paul did not always support himself by tent making (Ro 15:24, 1Co 16:5-6, 2Co 1:15-16, 11:7-9, Php 4:10-19, Phlm 22)?

9. Which elders are worthy of double honor (1Ti 5:17)?

10. What similarities are there between 1 Timothy 5:18 and 1 Corinthians 9:9-10? See De 25:4, Lk 10:7.

11. What does it mean to show double honor to some elders (1Ti 5:17ff)?

12. There is a specific Greek word for "wages" (*misthos*; used in 1 Ti 5:18). Why do you suppose Paul used *time* ("honor") instead of *misthos* in 1 Timothy 5:17?

13. What cautions do 2 Corinthians 2:17 and 1 Timothy 6:3-5 hold for ministers?

14. What did Peter mean when he exhorted the elders to shepherd God's flock voluntarily and not for sordid gain (1Pe 5:2)?

15. Does 1 Peter 5:1-4 imply that receiving money did, in some circumstances, go along with the ministry of elder? Explain.

16. The typical New Testament congregation was no bigger than would fit into someone's living room (a house church). How could a qualified elder make his living from such a small church?

17. What principle did John establish in 3 John 5-8?

18. What can be concluded about the idea of ministers who are fully supported by the church?

Note: NTRF also offers a teacher's resource to help lead a discussion of New Testament church life. Request *The Practice of The Early Church: A Theological Workbook (Leader's Guide)* from www.NTRF.org.

JESUS SHALL REIGN

Jesus shall reign where'er the sun Does his successive journeys run;
His kingdom stretch from shore to shore, Till moons shall wax and wane no
more.

Behold the islands with their kings, And Europe her best tribute brings;
From north to south the princes meet, To pay their homage at His feet.

There Persia, glorious to behold, There India shines in eastern gold;
And barb'rous nations at His word Submit, and bow, and own their Lord.

To Him shall endless prayer be made, And praises throng to crown His head;
His Name like sweet perfume shall rise With every morning sacrifice.

People and realms of every tongue Dwell on His love with sweetest song;
And infant voices shall proclaim Their early blessings on His Name.

Blessings abound wherever He reigns; The prisoner leaps to lose his chains;
The weary find eternal rest, And all the sons of want are blessed.

Where He displays His healing power, Death and the curse are known no
more:
In Him the tribes of Adam boast More blessings than their father lost.

Let every creature rise and bring Peculiar honors to our King;
Angels descend with songs again, And earth repeat the loud amen!

Great God, whose universal sway The known and unknown worlds obey,
Now give the kingdom to Thy Son, Extend His power, exalt His throne.

The scepter well becomes His hands; All Heav'n submits to His commands;
His justice shall avenge the poor, And pride and rage prevail no more.

With power He vindicates the just, And treads th'oppressor in the dust:
His worship and His fear shall last Till hours, and years, and time be past.

As rain on meadows newly mown, So shall He send his influence down:
His grace on fainting souls distills, Like heav'nly dew on thirsty hills.

The heathen lands, that lie beneath The shades of overspreading death,
Revive at His first dawning light; And deserts blossom at the sight.

The saints shall flourish in His days, Dressed in the robes of joy and praise;
Peace, like a river, from His throne Shall flow to nations yet unknown.

— Isaac Watts, 1719

12
THE MINISTRY OF EVANGELISM

We consider the last words of an individual to be of utmost importance. Family members will crowd around a dying man's bed to catch his last words and then recall them again and again for years to come. Similarly, the last words of Jesus Christ before He ascended to heaven were of utmost importance. He gives them to us in all four gospel accounts and in the book of Acts.

Matthew 28:18-20 "All authority has been given to Me in heaven and on earth. Go therefore and make disciples of all the nations, baptizing them in the name of the Father and the Son and the Holy Spirit, teaching them to observe all that I commanded you; and lo, I am with you always, even to the end of the age."

Mark 16:15-16 "Go into all the world and preach the gospel to all creation. He who has believed and has been baptized shall be saved; but he who has disbelieved shall be condemned."

Luke 24:46-49 "Thus it is written, that the Christ should suffer and rise again from the dead the third day; and that repentance for forgiveness of sins should be proclaimed in His name to all the nations, beginning from Jerusalem. You are witness of these things. And behold I am sending forth the promise of My Father upon you; but you are to stay in the city until you are clothed with power from on high."

John 20:21 "Peace be with you; as the Father has sent Me, I also send you."

Acts 1:8 "But you shall receive power when the Holy Spirit has come upon you; and you shall be My witnesses both in Jerusalem, and in all Judea and Samaria, and even to the remotest part of the earth."

Notice that in every case Jesus emphasizes the responsibility of the apostles to extend His kingdom. They are to make disciples of all the nations, preach the gospel to all creation, proclaim repentance for forgiveness of sins to all the nations, be sent by Jesus Christ just as He was sent by His Father, and be witnesses to the remotest part of the earth. Jesus gives the same basic message in five different ways in order that the apostles would have no doubt as to what their job was after He left. He left these words ringing in their ears. He had one thing He wanted to impress indelibly on their minds. It was as if He was saying, "If you forget everything else I've taught you, you must never forget this!" These texts form the marching orders for the Church until Christ returns.

Those of us who meet in home churches must deal responsibly with these final words of Jesus Christ. Theoretically, we should have an advantage over those who meet in more traditional settings. Since we do not typically use our money to hire a pastor or pay for a mortgage on a building, we should have all the finances necessary to do the work of evangelism in our city. Additionally, the house church model is much easier to reproduce than the traditional church. In order to plant another house church we don't need to hire a seminary trained individual, and build a special religious edifice complete with cross, stained glass windows, pulpit, pews and organ. All we really need to plant a house church is a handful of people who love Jesus Christ and want to follow Him together. On the other hand, the whole dynamic of a house church can work against the command of Christ to reach out with His gospel. Often, when someone comes into a house church they enjoy the rich and intimate fellowship with other believers so much, that they tend to focus on that to the neglect of equally important matters, like evangelism, discipleship and church planting. However, we must not let that happen to us. Our churches must not only have an inward nurturing thrust. They must also have an outward missionary thrust.

Too often the church has a fortress mentality. We see the power of Satan and his demons, and wanting to protect ourselves from the power and pollution of sin, we retreat and cloister in fear. However, instead of finding ourselves on the defensive, we ought to be on the offensive! Jesus said that the gates of Hades would not overpower His church (Mt 16:18). In this passage the church is on the offensive, and hell is on the defensive! I understand Jesus to mean that as the church boldly, and aggressively invades Satan's kingdom with the gospel of Jesus Christ, the devil will not be able to successfully oppose our onslaught. We will prevail. We have the power and authority to invade the kingdom of darkness with the truth of the gospel, and hell can't stop us. Let this truth from the lips of Christ encourage and embolden you to new evangelistic exploits!

If all this is true, how should our house churches engage in the task of reaching the lost and planting new churches? Let's take a look at where and how the early church evangelized to get some direction for our own churches.

WHERE DID THE EARLY CHURCH EVANGELIZE?

Often churches today seek to evangelize by inviting non-Christians to one of their meetings. A popular approach is to gear the Sunday church service towards non-Christians by having professional music, drama, and practical messages directed towards the nonbeliever in areas such as finances, stress, work, and family. They hope that unbelievers will be attracted to Christ through such means. After they have been converted, they are encouraged to attend a Bible study during the week where they can grow in their faith. However, the New Testament approach is almost completely opposite. Instead of inviting the lost to church meetings, most New Testament evangelism took place during the week as believers came into contact with unbelievers, or as apostolic workers proclaimed Christ in public places. Church meetings were designed for the edification of believers, not the conversion of unbelievers (1Co 14:3, 5, 12, 17, 26). Of course, on occasion unbelievers did attend church meetings (1Co 14:24-25). Nevertheless, the meetings were not designed for them but rather for the strengthening of the church. It seems that the Biblical model is to proclaim Christ to others as the Lord provides opportunity for our witness, and when someone comes to faith in Christ, to then invite him to begin meeting with other believers in our corporate gatherings.

HOW DID THE EARLY CHURCH EVANGELIZE?

The early church took Jesus' words at face value and sought to obey them. They did so in two different ways. Speaking in broad, general categories, apostles (church planters) and evangelists sought to reach those they did not know through public proclamation, while the other members of the church sought to reach the lost through daily interaction with people they did know. Apostolic workers proclaimed Christ in synagogues, market places, and riversides (Ac 13:5, 14; 17:17; 16:13). The rest of the church on the other hand, witnessed primarily through their daily, regular contact with unbelievers. That's why Paul wrote to them and said, "Conduct yourselves with wisdom toward outsiders, making the most of the opportunity. Let your speech always be with grace, seasoned as it were, with salt, so that you may know how you should respond to each person" (Col 4:5-6). Peter exhorts likewise, "...but sanctify Christ as Lord in your hearts, always being ready to make a defense to everyone who asks you to give an account for the hope that is in you, yet with gentleness and reverence" (1Pe 3:15). Early church members were to *respond* to outsiders, and be always ready to make a defense to everyone *who asks*. These passages seem to indicate that the early Christians usually witnessed to the life transforming power of the gospel to those they already knew (life-style evangelism), whereas the apostles (church planters) took a more aggressive approach in proclaiming Christ to those they did not know.

What implications does this have for how our house churches should reach out to the lost? It means that those in our churches whom God has gifted and called to work in evangelism (evangelists and church planters) will look for venues to present the gospel of Christ to those they don't know. Perhaps they will engage in open air preaching, street evangelism, door to door witnessing, and tract distribution. Perhaps they will be given opportunities to speak at various events and functions. Because I am a bluegrass banjo player I have been given several opportunities to preach the gospel to largely secular audiences at concerts and festivals.

On the other hand, other members of the congregation should be praying and looking for opportunities to speak a word for Christ to those they interact with, like classmates, neighbors, work mates, relatives, customers or other acquaintances. Additionally we need to regularly seek to put ourselves in places where we can interact with non-Christians. We can join a neighborhood watch program, civic group, or square dancing group to meet people. We can open our homes during the holidays and invite our neighbors in. We can invite unbelievers into our homes for dinner. We can start an investigative Bible study for any of our unsaved friends who are open to learning what the Bible has to say. We can ask our unbelieving friends what we can be praying for in their lives. I have been surprised to find out how many of our neighbors were actually lonely people and welcomed a loving friendship. When God gives an opportunity for us to befriend an unbeliever, we need to just be ourselves, and let our light shine. The opportunities abound to love people and thus make an eternal difference in their lives.

In addition, our churches should pray for and give generously to those God has gifted and called to evangelize and plant churches. The apostle Paul often urged local congregations to pray for him in his evangelistic and church planting labors (Ep 6:19-20; Col 4:3-4). In the texts just cited, Paul is urging believers to pray for him that God would give him boldness to proclaim the mystery of the gospel, and that God would open to him a door for the word that he could speak forth the mystery of Christ. Furthermore, Paul consistently commended those churches who generously gave of their finances to support his evangelistic work (Php 4:14-19; 2Co 8:1-5). Let's pray for and give to those whom God has raised up as evangelists and church planters today.

Out of all the people the church witnesses to, there will be some whom God has prepared to receive Christ and be saved. What then? Well, the person who led the individual to Christ, if possible, should begin to disciple him by spending time with him, encouraging him, answering questions he has about how to live for God, and providing an example for him in serving Christ. As God saves new believers we can either add them to the existing church, or begin a new church plant. Since house churches have a built in size limitation (as many as can fit in a house), you will probably start to experience difficulties meeting together when the numbers approach 35 or 40 people. At that point plan to plant a new church! You can plant the new church either by splitting the previous church in two, or hiving off a few people and starting a new church plant, while leaving the previous church pretty much intact. I personally prefer the latter method. When people begin to form strong friendships in a church, it can be traumatic to tear them apart. It may be much less stressful to take a few new believers and a brother gifted in church planting and have them begin meeting in a new location. The church planter can begin to teach these new believers how to function as a church, and how to reach their social circle with the gospel of Christ. Hopefully, over time, God will raise up from these new converts mature brothers who can serve as elders to shepherd the flock. The church planter is now free to devote himself to planting a new church, and so the process begins all over again.

Oh, may God stir those of us involved in house churches to labor to fulfill the Great Commission that Jesus might receive glory and His kingdom extend around the world!

— Brian Anderson

Some believers are supernaturally gifted in evangelism and or church planting. Their existence and ministry is a New Testament pattern, especially in pioneer areas. However, it does not follow that every new church must be started by a bona fide church planter, else it is not a true New Testament church. While their ministry is a great help in the plant of a new church, it is not absolutely essential, particularly in areas where the gospel has already been preached and the church firmly established. — Editor

The Ministry of Evangelism

1. Why would Jesus say that His people are the salt of the earth (Mt 5:13)?

2. Based on Matthew 5:17- 7:29, how can we let our light shine before men in such a way that they praise our Father in heaven (Mt 5:13-16)?

3. What did Jesus predict about the gospel in Matthew 24:14? Compare Mk 13:10, Lk 24:46-47.

4. Based on what Jesus said in Mark 4:1-20, what evangelistic results might we anticipate?

5. In John 4:34-38, what can we learn about the *process* that is involved in bringing someone to faith in Christ? Compare 1Co 3:5-9, Ga 6:9-10.

6. What final mission did Jesus give the apostles before He ascended into heaven (Mt 28:18-20, Mk 16:15-16, Lk 24:46-49, Ac 1:8)?

7. How can those of us who meet in home churches deal responsibly with the final words of Jesus Christ?

8. What should we ask God to do whenever we pray for evangelists and missionaries, based on Matthew 9:35-38, Ephesians 6:19-20 and Colossians 4:3-4?

9. Why did Paul commend the churches in Philippi and Macedonia (Php 4:14-19; 2Co 8:1-5)?

10. What should a house church do when more people come than the home can accommodate?

11. According to Acts 11:19-21, 13:48, & 16:14, why was their evangelism so effective?

12. Should you see yourself as an ambassador for Christ (2Co 5:11-21)? How might envisioning this change your life-style?

13. What evangelistic advice did Paul offer in Colossians 4:5-6?

14. Based on the context of 1 Peter 3:8-22, why would someone ask to hear a reason for the hope that we have (1Pe 3:15)?

15. Why does the whole dynamic of a house church tend to work against the command of Christ to reach out with His gospel?

16. How are local church members, as opposed to the apostles and evangelists, supposed to evangelize?

13

MINISTRY HOUSEHOLDS — KEY TO HEALTHY CHURCHES

In modern culture we have increasingly come to evaluate virtually everything from an individualistic perspective. We find our identity in ourselves individually, by our individual accomplishments, position, possessions, etc. We increasingly have difficulty relating to the notion that we are part of something bigger than ourselves.

Yet the Bible portrays a very different paradigm. People are to find their identity in being part of a corporate whole: a lineage, a family or, most importantly, the body of Christ. But many of us struggle to apprehend this corporateness. For example, most Westerners have no more than a theoretical understanding of Jesus' claim (Mt 19:6; Mk 10:8) that a husband and wife "are no longer two but one flesh" or Paul's contention (Ro 12:5) that "we, being many, are one body in Christ, and individually members of one another."

I have always embraced these truths academically. But experientially I couldn't grasp how my wife and I were one in more than the most rudimentary sense of physical intimacy. Similarly, most of my church experience has reflected the assumption that the church is a conglomeration of individuals attending the same function.

As the Lord is leading many to see the New Testament apostolic pattern of gathering in private homes, I suspect that like me, most bring with them the baggage of their past experience and understanding. But the Lord is apparently restoring the understanding and experience of the corporateness of the body of Christ among many house churches today. He is moving us past a solely theological assent to the truth of unity, to the reality of being experientially knit together into a whole that is bigger than its parts.

One way He is doing this is by restoring the foundation of household unity and identity. I theorize that one of the reasons for the homeschool movement (an apparently separate work of God, but one I suspect is linked in God's coordinated purpose) is to prepare households to function unitedly in the church. Historically, as individualism gradually shaped self-perceptions in Western society, the church incrementally lost its awareness of "The Spiritual Power of Ministry Households" (the title of a spoken message from which this chapter springs).

As God deposited in the nineteenth century church the vision for foreign missions, an insidiously destructive seed began to sprout and flourish. Missionary families were concerned about the education of their children. As institutional education became the assumed norm, this created a perceived conflict for many missionaries and the agencies that sent them. Gradually, an educational infrastructure of missionary boarding schools was developed to meet the seeming need. By the twentieth century, it was typical for missionary parents to be separated from their children for extended periods, often beginning at very early ages. As special boarding schools for missionaries' kids (MKs) became more common, a tragic phenomenon became increasingly accepted. The children of missionaries were raised as virtual orphans by loving care-givers who did their best. But many of the sons and daughters of foreign missionaries became bitter about the sacrifices their parents made. Sadly, today there are numerous accounts of MKs who want nothing to do with the Lord, and blame the church for separating them from their parents during a time when, by God's design, they were supposed to be their parents' *primary* ministry (though not their *only* ministry).

To this day there are missions agencies that require missionary candidates to commit to enrolling their children in boarding schools. This is not only rationalized as being for the children's good, but also is overtly intended to free up the *individual* parents to minister on the field with less distraction. Missionary couples are thus seen as partners in ministry, more than as a household unit. The sending agency expects to reap the benefit of utilizing two *individual* workers rather than seeing the couple as a single unit.

This not only has a devastating effect on the children, but on the very notion of the household. In fact, it hastens the spread of individualistic presuppositions, undermining what are ironically sometimes more Biblical cultural family mores in the groups being evangelized. The grievous result is that the new churches being planted are presented an unhealthy and unnatural model of family life. They never get to see an example of whole, healthy households in the lives of those who are discipling them. (During my ministry in Asia, I'm afraid I have frequently observed the prevalent fruit of ignoring, excusing, or even praising unfaithfulness in family life among modern Indian and Chinese churches.)

This sad state of affairs isn't unique to foreign missions, however. During the last few generations the church in the West has increasingly seen Christian workers who have so exclusively focused on their ministry that they have neglected their families. While this phenomenon isn't new, it is becoming pervasive in institutional Christianity. The destructive consequences include the poor reputation of preacher's kids and the undermining of examples of godly family life among God's people.

Before proceeding, let me qualify my exhortation with an acknowledgment that the opposite error is also a trap. Just as it is possible for a man to fall into the idolatry of his own ministry, it is also possible to idolize one's family, or the idea of family. We must always love Jesus Himself above anything, whether our ministry for Him or the family He has entrusted to us. Jesus issued warnings against putting our families above Him (Mt 10:34-37; 12:47-50; 19:29; Mk 10:29-30; Lk 9:59-62; 14:20-26). Yet these scriptures are increasingly used to rationalize an unbiblical neglect of family responsibility. Without neglecting the cautions against inappropriately idolizing family, let's consider what else God's word says about the priority of family ministry, and how it impacts other ministry.

GOD LOVES THE FAMILY

God created families and He expresses His emotions regarding them. In an exceedingly clear expression of his heart, God expresses his passionate feelings about family in Malachi 2:16. "For the LORD God of Israel says That He hates divorce!" I believe God loves the principle of family. He chose family relationships as the dominant metaphor for New Testament Christians' relationship with Him and with one another. Christians become God's children (Jn 1:12; Ro 8:16; 1Jn 3:2) — part of His household (Ep 2:19). Jesus came to, among other things, reveal God as Father (Lk 11:2; Jn 1:18, 16:25). The Holy Spirit was given to, among other things, reveal God as our Abba (Daddy — intimate reference for Father; Ro 8:14; Ga 4:6). One of the most frequently-used identifiers for Christians in the New Testament is the word brothers (Mt 23:8; Ac 6:3; 1Pe 1:22; 1Jn 3:14, 16). One of the most beautiful pictures of the relationship between Christ and the church is the relationship of a Bridegroom and his bride (Mt 9:15; Jn 3:29; 2Co 11:2; Re 19:7-9; 21:2, 9; 22:17). While these metaphors are not completely lacking in the Old Testament, they are all vastly expanded in the New Testament. The Lord intends our healthy family relationships to provide these physical pictures for His use in revealing spiritual realities. If the picture is neglected, we lose part of God's intention for this revelation.

In fact, Paul said every family is designed to be a reflection of the Heavenly Father's patriarchy. In Ephesians 3:14-15 He wrote, "For this reason I bow my knees to the Father [Greek: *pater*] of our Lord Jesus Christ, from whom the whole family [Greek: *patria*] in heaven and earth is named." By His design, families are to be led by fathers and apparently defined by the patriarchal jurisdiction of fatherhood.

Ministry Households — Key To Healthy Churches

Far from abolishing or even minimizing family, the New Testament reinforces and expands what was introduced regarding family in the Old Testament. One of the Old Testament commands quoted most frequently in the New Testament is the command to "Honor your father and your mother" (Ex. 20:12; Le 19:3; De 5:16; Mt 15:3-9; 19:16-19; Mk 7:6-13; 10:17-19; Lk 18:18-20; Ep 6:2). In their letters, the apostles spent a fair amount of time teaching about family practices (1Co 7; Ep 5:22-6:4; Col 3:18-21; 1Ti 3:2, 4-5, 11-12; 5:4, 8-10, 14, 16; Tit 1:6; 2:3-5; 1Pe 3:1-7; Heb 12:5-11).

FAMILY HOSPITALITY

One of the key practices encouraged in the New Testament is hospitality (Ro 12:13; 1Ti 3:2; Tit 1:8; 1Pe 4:9). It should arouse our suspicion of an underlying problem since this is one of the most blatantly disregarded mandates in the modern church. Hospitality is practiced in a family setting. But if our families are being atomized into fragmented individuals, each with his own independent life to pursue, there is very little potential context for being hospitable.

It is instructive that one of the observable qualifications God instituted for evaluating the qualifications of potential leaders in the church is that they be hospitable (1Ti 3:2; Tit 1:8). When I was a young man, I served as a youth pastor and associate pastor in two different institutional churches (each for over a year) in which I never once stepped inside the home of the acknowledged senior pastor. In one case, I never even learned where the pastor lived.

I am not completely faulting these sincere men of God who were supposed to be "examples to the flock" (1Pe 5:3) for this shocking disregard of Scripture. I was nearly as bad. I figured that the neutral territory of the church building was the most appropriate place for fellowship, and that while hospitality was nice, it wasn't essential. Thus there were saints I ministered to who could easily charge me with the same failure. We simply didn't get it!

AN ELDER'S FAMILY

The explicit minimum qualifications for leadership in the body of Christ include other family matters. An elder or bishop (demonstrably the same thing as the pastor in the New Testament church — see *poimaino, presbuteros,* and *episkopos* in Ac 2:17, 28; Tit 1:5, 7; 1Pe 5:1-2) was to be "the husband of one wife" (1Ti 3:2; Tit 1:6). There is some controversy, today, over the application of this. Some simply apply this to polygamy, others suspect it precludes divorced and remarried

172

men from being publicly recognized as exemplary, and still others take it to mean that an elder must be a "one woman type of man."

I suspect the requirement of being "the husband of one wife" not only means a man with *more* than one wife is disqualified, but that a man with *less* than one wife also is not qualified to be recognized as a model for the church. While single men certainly have the benefit of fewer distractions and responsibilities, and thus more freedom, this very lack of responsibility is also a handicap when it comes to leading in the church. It is more likely for a single man to be (or at least be perceived as) a novice, but Paul told Timothy (1Ti 3:6) to choose as elders those who were "not a novice." He further made it clear that the reputation, as well as the reality, of a man's maturity, was important (1Ti 3:7; "he must have a good testimony among those who are outside").

Some time after I married my wife, Connie, I began realizing how unprepared for marriage I had been. I was simply not mature enough for marriage. Yet as I pondered the matter, I concluded that I likely would never have been mature enough for marriage, while I was single. But it seems to me that within months of getting married, I had been stretched in wonderful ways that forced me to mature. I doubt I would ever have grown in those areas as a single man. Marriage made me something I could not have become otherwise. Truly in all but a few cases, "It is not good that man should be alone" (Ge 2:18). There are probably exceptions, but a man who has never been married is not as likely to be a thorough and balanced role model for the body of Christ.

In fact, I suspect that a man who has not experienced fatherhood will be similarly handicapped. Paul told Titus (1:6) to only recognize as elders those men who are "the husband of one wife, *having* faithful *children*." Just as I was not ready for marriage until after I married, I was not ready for fatherhood until after Connie and I were blessed with our first child. Being a father pressed me in certain ways that I would likely never have matured in without having children. As the Lord continued blessing us with more children, and as each of them was trained through different stages of childhood and youth, I was being further prepared for eldership.

The other home schooling fathers and I, in our local congregation, have theorized that God's reason for leading us to disciple our own children at home rather than sending them to school is not exclusively (perhaps even primarily) for *their* benefit. God has called us to teach our own children at least partly because of the maturity this brings to us as fathers. Any teacher will acknowledge that the teachers learn as much or more than the students, in the process of teaching. In fact, I suspect one of God's primary reasons for raising up the homeschool movement in this generation is to prepare truly qualified elders who have learned how to disciple others as a result of discipling their own sons and daughters.

Sadly, as noted earlier, the children of those who are devoted to ministry in the contemporary church often have the worst reputation. I'm blessed to be a PK myself (not Promise Keeper, but Preacher's Kid). But as a child I learned that the acronym PK is often a derogatory term in the contemporary church. While this is not always deserved (many love to find fault in leaders to excuse their own failures), it is too often true that the children of those in public ministry are not examples to the rest of the body of Christ.

I imagine we have all seen men who seem to have a true call of God on their life for public ministry, yet who are so focused on that ministry that they neglect their own family. Paul included, as a qualification for local church leadership, that an elder's children must be well trained. He defines "one who rules his own house well" (1Ti 3:4) as "having his children in submission with all reverence." Then he reasons (1Ti 3:5), "for if a man does not know how to rule his own house, how will he take care of the church of God?"

In his instructions to Titus (1:6) he is more explicit in specifying the expectations of the fruit of an elder's fatherhood. He must have "faithful children not accused of dissipation or insubordination." The children of elders must not only be in submission, but their faithfulness must be so evident that they are not even accused of excesses or disobedience.

Obviously elders' children are going to be selfish and inclined to sin, just as all humanity is. Yet only those men who have proven their capacity to "train up a child in the way he should go" (Pr 22:6) should be publicly recognized as models for the church. The word translated faithful in regard to his children (Greek *pistos*) is elsewhere translated believing. (For example, Jesus used this word as a contrast to Thomas' doubting in John 20:27. See also Ac 10:45; 16:1; 2Co 6:15; 1Ti 4:3, 10, 12; 5:16; 6:2.). It is certainly not a stretch to contend that only men who have trained believing children should be considered for eldership.

Some might point to the examples of Jesus and Paul as unmarried, fatherless men. Such exceptions should certainly motivate us to be cautious in applying the scriptural norm too rigidly. Yet we should also avoid using exceptions to invalidate norms clearly taught in Scripture. Although there are good reasons to conclude Paul was single, some scholars believe he had been married. Even if he was a eunuch, His own Spirit-inspired writing specifies that local church elders (not necessarily itinerant apostles) be "the husband of one wife, having faithful children."

Some might persist by pointing to the other apostles who apparently left their families to follow Jesus. But I suspect we view these accounts through a distorted, modern filter that skews our perception to our own individualistic paradigm. Even the one explicit account (Mk 1:20) of how James and John "left their father Zebedee in the boat with the hired servants," was not likely a dishonoring of their father, in light of Jesus' later extended rebuke (Mk 7:1-13) of the adult Pharisees of "making the word of God of no effect through your tradition" when they rationalized failure to honor their father and mother. Although arguments from silence are suspect, it is not unlikely that James and John had Zebedee's blessing. This is particularly likely given the fact that their mother also seems to have been one of the women who traveled with Jesus (Mt 20:20; 27:56).

But who were these "many women who followed Jesus from Galilee" (Mt 27:55-56; Mk 15:40-41; Lk 8:1-3; 23:49, 55; 24:10)? Some of them are named ("Mary Magdalene, Mary the mother of James and Joses, and the mother of Zebedee's sons."), but apparently there were many others. It's rather surprising that there is no hint of the pharisees accusing Jesus and the apostles of impropriety, given the many women who accompanied them. One possible explanation is that these many women may have included the apostles' wives.

Again, some will protest that this is an argument from silence. Yet the contention that the apostles left their wives and children to follow Jesus is only based on inference, as well. Some are arguing that when Jesus commended those who "left house or brothers or sisters or father or mother or wife or children or lands" for His sake and the gospel's (Mk 10:29), He was making this normative. Yet if this were so, it would be in conflict with the rest of His and the apostles' teaching. Clearly, wife and children are among those we are commanded to hate (Lk 14:26) in comparison to our devotion to Jesus. Yet husbands are elsewhere commanded to love their wives (Ep 5:25; Col 3:19).

WERE THE APOSTLES MARRIED?

We know Peter was married, because each of the synoptic gospels reports that Jesus healed "his wife's mother" (Mt 8:14; Mk 1:30; Lk 4:38). Isn't it amazing that other than this single instance, Peter's wife is nowhere mentioned in the Gospels? But the Gospels' silence about this woman can't be taken to imply some lack of activity or devotion on her part. We know that Peter's wife later traveled with him in ministry (1Co 9:5).

In fact, we find that the other apostles and the brothers of the Lord also traveled with their wives. How many of the other apostles had wives? Paul may be using hyperbole here, but it sounds like he is implying that he, and possibly Barnabas (1Co 9:6) were the only apostles who didn't follow this practice.

We don't know when these other apostles married. It is certainly possible it was subsequent to their three and a half years with Jesus, but it isn't necessarily so, just because their wives are not mentioned in the account. We would only conclude this when reading the account filtered through modern paradigms. Today it would seem highly inappropriate to neglect mentioning the apostles' wives. But if it weren't for the single parenthetical comment by Paul, we would have no direct mention of the apostles' wives at all. If it weren't for that statement, many would assume from the Scripture's silence that they weren't married. Yet this appears to be a relatively recent paradigm.

What about children? It is likely that the apostles' marriages were blessed with the fruit of the womb. Although their children are not mentioned, any more than their wives are, it is only through contemporary frames of reference that we would use this silence to conclude that such children didn't exist, or travel with their parents. In the Hebrew culture, men were assumed to have a wife and children, with few exceptions.

Evidence of another apostle's wife and children comes from a surprising source. Prior to betraying Jesus, Judas was "numbered among the twelve" apostles (Lk 6:13-16; 22:3). And he was married & had children. After his death Peter told the other disciples (Ac 1:16) there was a "Scripture . . . which the Holy Spirit spoke before by the mouth of David concerning Judas." He then went on to quote part of Psalm 109:8, which says, "Let his days be few, And let another take his office." Notice that this Psalm continues speaking of the same person (Ps 109:9-10): "Let his children be fatherless, And his wife a widow. Let his children continually be vagabonds, and beg; Let them seek their bread also from their desolate places." The passage continues talking about his fatherless children and posterity. And Peter claimed this passage was a scriptural prophecy regarding Judas. Thus, arguably, Judas had a wife and children.

While such indications are not some major theme, I am proposing that we moderns have assumed, from the scriptures' silence regarding the apostles' families, that they only followed Jesus individually. It would be more historically valid, given the cultural context, to assume men were married and had children. I am thus persuaded we should use the relative silence regarding the apostles' families as evidence of their existence and that their whole households were following Jesus.

NEW TESTAMENT MINISTRY HOUSEHOLDS

Not only did most of the apostles have families, but the New Testament alludes, more specifically, to several ministry households. Aquila and Priscilla were a couple devoted to the work of the Lord. The Scripture's silence regarding whether or not they also had children as part of their ministry household should not be taken as evidence against the likelihood that they did. Historically it would have been unusual for a couple not to have children, and it would not have been unusual for them to remain unnamed and unmentioned.

The reference (Ac 18:2) to Paul having found Aquila in Corinth, may indicate that he was already acquainted with this family, and was looking for him. At any rate, they welcomed him into their household, even apparently allowing him to be part of their household's tent making business (Ac 18:3). Paul stayed in Corinth a year and a half. When he left for Ephesus, Priscilla and Aquila accompanied him. If they had children, as I suspect is likely, their children would have undoubtedly been part of the household that relocated. Paul only stayed in Ephesus a brief time, intending to return later. But Aquila's household remained in Ephesus (Ac 18:18-19), possibly as a preparation for Paul's anticipated return to that city (verse 21).

During Paul's absence, a man named Apollos began to preach the gospel in the Ephesian synagogue, but his understanding was lacking. So Aquila and Priscilla "took him aside" (Ac 18:26; likely to their own home) "and explained to him the way of God more accurately." Paul later stated (1Ti 2:12) that he did "not permit a woman to teach or to have authority over a man, but to be in silence." How can this be reconciled with the account that Priscilla, as well as Aquila, "explained to [Apollos] the way of God more accurately?"

One solution to this seeming contradiction might be found in the distinction between "explaining" and "teaching." Another might be that Paul's admonition to the silence of women in the church gatherings (1Co 14:34-35) seems to be limited to when "the whole church comes together in one place" (14:23). It is quite likely (or at least possible) that Paul's admonition against women teaching men is in the same context. Thus it would be quite acceptable for women to exercise spiritual gifts in more private settings, or any setting other than the actual gathering of the whole church gathered corporately. So as a significant (prominently mentioned) part of Aquila's ministry household, Priscilla would find appropriate expression of her teaching gift in private conversation, even in helping to meekly correct Apollos' insufficient understanding of the gospel.

We find that when Apollos later left for Corinth there was a body of brethren in Ephesus (Ac 18:27) who corporately "wrote, exhorting the disciples [in Corinth] to receive him." It would appear that Aquila's household ministry was bearing fruit. We definitely know that by the time Paul wrote the epistle of 1 Corinthians (presumably from Ephesus) he sent greetings from Aquila and Priscilla (1Co 16:19), "with the church that is in their house." Their household ministry was obviously bearing increasing fruit.

We can only conjecture how things progressed for the ministry household of Aquila as the years went by, but some time later, when Paul wrote his epistle to the saints in Rome, he specifically said, "Greet Priscilla and Aquila, my fellow workers in Christ Jesus" (16:3). Apparently this household was now in Rome, and it seems the Lord was using their ministry there as well. After further commending them, Paul says, "Likewise greet the church that is in their house" (16:5). As in Corinth and Ephesus, Aquila and Priscilla and their household were clearly ministering together effectively in Rome, for the kingdom of God.

Another interesting ministry household in Scripture is that of Philip the evangelist. He was one of the "seven men of good reputation, full of the Holy Spirit and wisdom" (Ac 6:3) whom the apostles chose to supervise the distribution of food to the widows in Jerusalem. He was later used mightily in bringing the gospel to Samaria, and then led the Ethiopian eunuch to the Lord. The silence of Scripture regarding Philip having a wife is clearly not to be taken as implication he was single. It was not unusual for a man's wife to be in the background. In this case, we conclude Philip had a wife, because his "four virgin daughters who prophesied" are mentioned (Ac 21:9).

This ministry household provided hospitality to Paul and his companions (including Luke). Some assume that because Philip's daughters prophesied, their use of their gifts are arguments against Paul's repeated direction (1Co 14:34-35; he specifically claimed this among "the commandments of the Lord," verse 37) that the sisters "keep silent in the churches." However, there is nothing in the text causing us to think these young ladies prophesied in the church gatherings. Similarly, when another prophet, Agabus, showed up and prophesied that Paul would be bound in Jerusalem (Ac 21:11), there is no reason to understand that this prophecy was given in a church meeting, but rather in the hospitality context of Philip's family entertaining guests. Philip's was a ministry household where prayer, exhortation, and even prophecies were likely common, everyday occurrences by both men and women.

Yet another ministry household mentioned in the New Testament is that of Onesiphorus. Paul wrote (2Ti 1:16-17), "The Lord grant mercy to the household of Onesiphorus, for he often refreshed me, and was not ashamed of my chain; but when he arrived in Rome, he sought me out very zealously and found me." This brother, and perhaps his household, traveled to Rome at least partly for the purpose of finding Paul and ministering to his needs. Whether Onesiphorus' household was with him or not, Paul blessed the whole household. Why?

Paul continued (2Ti 1:18), "you know very well how many ways he ministered to me at Ephesus." Here was a brother who, whether traveling or at home, had a reputation for serving the needs of the saints. Given the reference to his household, it's not hard to imagine that they ministered together with the head of the house in very practical ways. This was another ministry household God was using corporately. Before closing this letter to Timothy he mentions the household of Onesiphorus one more time. He writes (2Ti 4:19) "Greet Prisca and Aquila, and the household of Onesiphorus." Clearly this whole household had a special place in Paul's heart.

A final ministry household I would like to consider is that of Stephanas. Paul baptized this household in Corinth (1Co 1:16). They were Paul's first converts (first fruits) in the Roman province of Achaia, and he commended them (1Co 16:15) as a household that "devoted themselves to the ministry of the saints." He went on to command something I haven't found anywhere else in the New Testament. He directed (1Co 16:16) the Corinthian saints to submit to such. He tells the church there to submit to the whole household of Stephanas. And contrary to some other instances where English translators have used the word submit, in the context of church relationships, this instance uses the Greek word *hupotasso*, a military term referring to subordination and obedience.

APPLICATION

It is clearly more effective to show someone something, than to simply talk about it. The biblical model is for leaders in the body of Christ to be examples to the flock rather than being lords over them (1Pe 5:3). One of the primary areas in which elders are to be examples is in the way they manage their families. To be such an example, those being ministered to must be able to see the household of the leader in operation.

Ministry Households — Key To Healthy Churches

I challenge the body of Christ to seek the Lord for revelation regarding God's heart for families, and to identify the bondage our cultural individualism imposes on us. I urge Christian workers to make their families their first ministry — their own children their primary disciples. Then when we minister to others, we do well to do so, as much as possible, in the presence of our family.

For many years the Lord has led me to avoid traveling alone. Occasionally another brother will travel and minister with me. But usually I bring my wife or one of my children. When a ministry opportunity is close enough to drive, I often take my whole family with me. (As I write this, my whole family — wife and six children — are together on a three-month ministry tour in India.). I have seen the subtle, but definite, impact of having at least part of my family with me in ministry situations. It gives my words much more credibility, when folks see the fruit of my life-style, modeled before them.

My longing is that my family would be, like that of Stephanas, a pleasure to the Lord Jesus as an exemplary, powerful ministry household.

— Jonathan Lindvall

Discussion Questions

1. How has individualism impacted our families and churches?
2. Many Christian workers have so exclusively focused on their ministries that they have neglected their families. What effect would this have on the churches in which these workers minister?
3. What do the scriptures indicate concerning God's attitude toward the family?
4. Give some examples of how God chose family relationships as the dominant metaphor for the New Testament Christians' relationship with Him and with one another.
5. Why is the command for hospitality one of the most blatantly disregarded mandates in the modern church?
6. Why might marriage be an essential prerequisite for being an elder?
7. Why might having well trained children be a prerequisite for being an elder?
8. What does the Bible indicate about the apostles having families and traveling with their wives?
9. What examples of whole households that ministered are there in the New Testament?

Note: NTRF also offers a teacher's resource to help lead a discussion of New Testament church life. Request *The Practice of The Early Church: A Theological Workbook (Leader's Guide)* from www.NTRF.org.

14

THE MINISTRY OF GIVING

Which group of believers is better able to fund church planters and assist the poor, a thousand believers organized in a single traditional church that meets in their own church sanctuary, complete with a Sunday School complex and family life center (containing a bowling alley, racket ball courts, and gymnasium), or a thousand believers divided up to 50 house churches with mostly bi-vocational leaders? A survey of U.S. Protestant congregations revealed that 82% of church revenues goes toward buildings, staff and internal programs; only 18% goes to outreach.[1] In the biblical house church, those percentages can easily be more than reversed!

Since there is no building complex to support, no budget to meet, and no offering plate passed each week, one of the most frequently asked questions from folks new to the biblical house church is, "What do we do with our tithes and offerings?" The answer to this is both fun and liberating. First, God loves a cheerful giver (2Co 9:6-7), and giving the New Testament way can be great fun! Second, it is liberating in the sense that your giving resources are freed up to be given where need most: supporting full time church workers and assisting the needy.

The house church in which I participate rarely takes up a collection. Each family is encouraged to set aside a percentage of every paycheck into their own special giving fund. Week after week each family's funds can accrue there, stored up until a need in the congregation arises. Giving in our church is usually directly from giver to getter, with no middleman involved (though collections are occasionally taken). In this way we give to missionaries, foreign orphanages, the persecuted church, local elders, and the needy. In our case, we have no church bank account nor church property.

COLLECTIONS

Few causes in the New Testament warranted an actual collection from the church corporately. One was to help other believers in need (Ac 11:27-30; 24:17; Ro 15:25-28; 1Co 16:1-4; 2Co 8:1-15; 9:12). Another was to support apostles (church planters) in their work (Ac 15:3; Ro 15:23-24; 1Co 9:1-14; 16:5-6, 10-11; 2Co 1:16; Php 4:14-18; Tit 3:13-14; 3Jn 5-8).

The Ministry of Giving

Whenever believers in other places were undergoing hardship (due to famine, persecution or whatever), the other churches were called upon to supply financial aid. Evidently such collections were not ongoing — they ceased after the need was met (Ac 11:27-30; 12:25; 1Co 16:1-4). To this end we in the Western church would do well to support our brothers in the Chinese church. Local giving to the poor was done in secret and directly (Mt 6:1-4, 19-21; Ep 4:28). Also, a list of local widows who qualified for assistance was kept by a church (1Ti 5:3, 9, 16).

The church was also obligated to support (send out) apostles (church planters). The Greek word for send (*propempo*) is, in the New Testament, associated with helping someone on his journey with food or money, by arranging for traveling companions, means of travel, etc. It means to send an apostle off with material sustenance (Ac 15:3; Ro 15:24; 1Co 16:6,11; 2Co 1:16; Tit 3:13; 3Jn 5-8). The same case can be made for the word welcome (Php 2:29; 3Jn 10). To welcome a church planter was to provide temporary lodging for him and to meet his physical needs. New Testament church planters were given lump sums to get them to their destinations. Once there, they would evangelize the area, establish churches, train them in the basics and move on. En route they might be welcomed at existing churches and then be sent along again.

1 Corinthians 9:1-14 states that apostles/church planters have the right to earn their living from the gospel. Paul was versatile enough to be able to supply his own needs when church funds were lacking. Others in the early church who received gifts were full time evangelists and qualified elders. A material debt is owed to those who sow spiritual blessings into our lives.

It is disturbing to contrast New Testament giving objectives with where ministry money often goes today. A Memphis newspaper reported in the mid-1980s that a local Baptist church's downtown building complex had 330,000 square feet of inside space, 1,400 parking spaces, 221 classrooms, and an auditorium that held 2,700 people. Their average *monthly* utility bill, even back then, was $25,000.00! Their pipe organ was valued at $800,000.[2] How did Paul and the other apostles *ever* get along without such ministerial tools? There is not much justification in the New Testament for such expenditures. Instead, New Testament pattern is to give to people, not property.

TITHING

"The Bible teaches it; I believe it; tithing." Such are the words chanted weekly by the congregation of a large church I used to attend. Some pastor-teachers have emphatically declared that unless God's people tithe, they are robbing God (Mal 3:8-10)! One mega-church has its members cite the "Tither's Creed." They repeat, "The tithe is the Lord's. In truth we learned it. In faith we believe it. In joy we give it. The tithe!"

Of course, the Bible does teach tithing. The same Mosaic Law that requires tithing also teaches God's people not to eat shrimp or oysters. The real question is whether such Old Covenant laws are still binding under the New Covenant. Is the law of Moses identical to the law of Christ?

By way of contrast, the Old Testament tithe was compulsory, not voluntary. Its purpose was to financially support a theocratic government. It was like our federal income tax. It was part and parcel of the whole Levitical system with its priests and temple (2Ch 24:6, 9). Unlike Israel, the church is not under a theocracy, but rather human, secular governments. Unlike Israel, the church has no special class of priests, but rather all in the church are priests. Unlike the Mosaic Covenant, the New Covenant has no elaborate temple to build and upkeep. Instead, the church met in the homes of its members, and believers themselves (both individually and corporately), make up God's temple (living stones in a spiritual temple). Just as there is no more temple, no more separate priestly class, no more theocracy, no more holy land, no more restrictive diet (oysters, shrimp), so also there is no more tithing. Tithing is never commanded in the New Covenant. There has been a change of law (Heb 7:12), the former regulation has been set aside (Heb 7:18), and the New Covenant made the first one obsolete (Heb 8:13).

Some brothers still feel compelled to tithe since the practice of tithing actually precedes the Old Covenant. For instance, Abraham tithed to Melchizedek, and since the Old Covenant was not initiated until several hundred years after that event, tithing is seen as an ongoing practice that transcends any one covenant. This argument seems plausible at first. However, once it is realized that this is an isolated (not an ongoing) event in the life of Abraham (the same can be said for Jacob's tithe), and that Abraham also offered animal sacrifices and circumcised the males of his household (both of which are now considered obsolete religious practices by all Christians), the strength of that argument wanes. At best, one should conclude that we only have to tithe once in our entire lives!

The Ministry of Giving

Other people's conscience are bound based on Jesus' statement that "you give a tenth of your spices . . . but you have neglected the more important matters of the law . . . you should have practiced the latter, without neglecting the former" (Mt 23:23). The key to correctly applying this lies with the word law (Mt 23:23). Jesus was speaking to the teachers of the law and to the Pharisees – men who lived prior to the initiation of the New Covenant. The law is that of the Mosaic Covenant, not the New Covenant. The Israelis of Jesus' day were indeed required to tithe (and, by the way, to make animal sacrifices). We of the New Covenant are under no such requirement since that first covenant and its law has passed away. *Viva* the law of Christ!

Of course, there is nothing wrong with tithing if that is what God has led you to do. As was pointed out above, Abraham and Jacob both tithed voluntarily before the law was given. They serve as good examples to follow! Just don't feel obligated to tithe. The key is that our giving is to be according to how we have purposed in our hearts to give. Did Jesus die on the cross so that we could give *less* than ten percent?!

REAPING & SOWING

Without dispute the New Covenant extols the virtue of generosity. In Matthew 6:19-21, Jesus taught us to store up treasures in heaven. In Matthew 19:21, Jesus told the rich young ruler that by giving to the poor, he could have treasure in heaven. 1 Timothy 6:18-19 exhorts us to be "generous and willing to share . . . lay up treasure . . . as a firm foundation for the coming age." We are to share with others, "for with such sacrifices God is pleased" (Heb 13:16). Based on your present giving habits, how much treasure do you have laid up in heaven?

But how much should we give? The answer depends on how much we want to reap later, how much we want to be blessed, and how much treasure we want in heaven. Scripture says to remember this: "whoever sows sparingly will also reap sparingly, and whoever sows generously will also reap generously. Each man should give what he has decided in his heart to give, not reluctantly or under compulsion, for God loves a cheerful giver" (2Co 9:6-7). According to the New Covenant, each man should give "what he has decided in his heart to give." That's all there is to it! Tithing, as required by Moses, is not a New Covenant practice. Notice that the text declares our giving is not to be done "reluctantly or under compulsion" (2Co 9:7). If some teacher says you must tithe, else you are robbing God, is that not placing you under compulsion? Yet do not use your freedom as a cover for stinginess. Give generously. Give cheerfully. Give frequently.

The Ministry of Giving

Give whatever you have purposed in your heart to give. Consider that perhaps it may not be the best use of your giving resources for them to be spent on special church sanctuaries, janitorial fees, landscaping, fancy throne-like furniture for pastors to sit in, or $800,000 pipe organs. Primarily, God intended for His people to give to help the needy and to support church workers (missionaries, church planters, apostles, evangelists, qualified elders, etc.). Pray about how much, and to whom, you should give.

— Steve Atkerson

NOTES

[1] "Where Church Revenues Go," *The Atlanta Journal And Constitution* (Atlanta, GA: April 19, 1992).

[2] John Belfuss, "Mississippi Boulevard OK's Bellevue Purchase," *The Commercial Appeal* (Memphis, TN), A-1.

The Ministry of Giving

1. Which group of believers is better able to fund ministers and assist the poor, a thousand believers organized in a single traditional church, or a thousand believers divided up to 50 house churches with mostly bi-vocational leaders? Explain your answer.

2. Since there is no building complex to support, no budget to meet, and no offering plate passed each week, what are house church believers supposed to do with do their tithes and offerings?

3. Only a few causes warranted a collection by the churches of the New Testament. What were they?

4. What euphemism is conveyed in the words that reference sending or receiving a church worker?

5. What giving principle should be derived from 1 Corinthians 9:1-14?

6. Evaluate this slogan, "The Bible teaches it, I believe it, tithing."

7. According to Jesus, how can we store up treasure in heaven (Mt 6:19-21)? See also 1Ti 6:18-19.

8. What does 2 Corinthians 9:6-7 indicate about how much we should give?

9. Based on your present giving habits, how much treasure do you have laid up in heaven?

Note: NTRF also offers a teacher's resource to help lead a discussion of New Testament church life. Request *The Practice of The Early Church: A Theological Workbook (Leader's Guide)* from www.NTRF.org.

Part III
CHURCH MATTERS

15

THE CITY CHURCH

The word church (*ekklesia*) was used various ways in the New Testament. Most of these usages fall into two categories. One is what theologians have called the catholic (or universal) church. The other is the local church. The universal church is made up of all believers who have ever lived, throughout time and all over the world. The local church is made up of living believers in one specific locale. Some teach that the proper expression of the local church is something called the city church. What is a city church? How does the city church relate to the house church? To answer this, we need to first understand the universal (catholic) church.

I. ONE CATHOLIC CHURCH

1. *The universal church is a biblical reality.* There are statements in Scripture that cannot refer to any one particular local church, but rather to the total, collective number of God's people, throughout all time and in all places (in heaven or still on earth), who belong to Jesus. For instance, Jesus said in Matthew 16:18, "Upon this rock I will build my church and the gates of hell shall not prevail against it" (KJV). It is a fact that some local churches have gone out of existence. This promise of the church's perpetuity was not made to any specific local church, but rather to the church as a whole.

The reality of the catholic church is also reflected in Romans 12:5, "in Christ we who are many form one body" (NIV). Further, Ephesians 1:22 states that God the Father gave Christ as "head over all things to the church" (NASV). Colossians 1:18 reinforces this idea in stating that Jesus is "head of the body, the church." Christ is the Head and the church universal is His body. Thus, there is but one universal church, one body of Christ. (Because of past abuses of the universal church concept, some prefer to refer to such examples as generic uses of the word church.)

2. *The universal church consists of the totality of all believers.* It is all those whose names are listed in the Lamb's Book of Life; all who are enrolled in heaven (Heb 12:22-23). Death separates the saints below from the saints above, and yet we are one company, one church.

3. *The universal church has never yet held a plenary meeting.* Many of its members have already passed into glory, many have not been born yet, and those living on earth today are scattered to the four winds. This gathering will occur at some point in the future, after time as we know it has ceased. This gathering is alluded to in various hymns: "Oh with that yonder sacred throng we at his feet may fall" or "When the role is called up yonder I'll be there." By all accounts it will be an out of this world experience.

4. *The universal church has no external earthly organization.* There is no biblical evidence that the followers of Christ, after the dispersion of the original church at Jerusalem, ever acted together as one externally organized society. Thus, in the sense of having no over-arching, human, earthly organization, it is invisible.

The universal church could be compared to the names listed in a phone book. Many names are listed in a directory. They all have one thing in common: telephones. They are the *Who's Who* of the dialing world. Yet those people listed do not all act together in any organized way. So it is with the universal church on earth. Each believer is listed in the Lamb's Book of Life. Each has Christ. Yet they are not organized together outwardly in any earthly way.

5. *The bond of the universal church is the internal bond of love.* This supernatural love has practical expression: Paul had a burden for the needs of the local Jerusalem church and took up an offering from throughout the Roman world to assist them. If one part of the body suffers, the whole body suffers. We feel keenly the mistreatment of our Chinese brothers and sisters because they are in the same family; we are in the same church. Romans 12:5 reminds us that "In Christ we who are many form one body, and each member belongs to all the others." 1 Corinthians 12 reveals each one is a part of the body of Christ and that "if one part suffers, every part suffers with it" (12:26-27).

6. *The universal church has recognizable, supernaturally gifted ministers.* Ephesians 4:11-12 says that Christ "gave some as apostles, and some as prophets, and some as evangelists, and some as pastors and teachers, for the equipping of the saints for the work of service, to the building up of the body of Christ" (NASV). Such gifted people can certainly be found as members of local, organized churches, but their gifting is from the Holy Spirit and their calling often is to the church universal, not necessarily just one local church. Such men minister locally but often have a burden globally. Examples include Paul, Barnabas, and Apollos. As John Wesley said, "I look upon all the world as my parish."[1] Such ministers think globally and act locally!

In sum, the universal church is the whole company of those who are saved by Christ. It is the collective set of all the redeemed in Christ, the entire household of faith. The universal church is made up of the citizens of the New Jerusalem. The existence of the universal church is expressed thusly in the Nicene Creed: "We believe in one holy catholic and apostolic Church."

II. Many Local Churches

Even though there is clearly only one church universal, the New Testament also makes mention of multiple churches (plural) throughout various regions (Ga 1:2, Re 1:4) or to distinct churches in different cities (Ac 13:1, 1Th 1:1). If there were groups of believers meeting in two different places, the Bible refers to them as two separate churches. This leads us to another use of the word church, the local church. The local church is a subset of the church universal.

Jesus said that if a brother is caught in sin, and refuses to repent, one of the steps in the restoration process is to "tell it to the church" (Mt 18:17). It was the local church, not the universal church, to which Jesus made reference. It is the local church that has the authority to expel sinful members, conduct regular meetings, have recognized elders, and be organized. None of this is true of the universal church.

Donald Guthrie wrote that "the initial idea of the church was of local communities of believers meeting together in one place . . . the importance of the community idea in the New Testament cannot be over-stressed."[2] According to the *New Bible Dictionary*, "An ekklesia was a meeting or an assembly . . . church is not a synonym for 'people of God'; it is rather an activity of the 'people of God.'"[3] Similarly, someone once quipped that birds fly, fish swim, and churches meet. The idea is, "If it don't meet, it ain't a local church!"

What is the proper expression of the local church? Is it the house church or the city church?

1 The City-Wide Local Church. Some hold that the proper expression of the local church is the organized city church, made up of multiple home fellowships networked together and that all meet together corporately. City church advocates argue that there is rightly only one organized church per city. It is further argued that this one city church should hold regular meetings for all the believers in that one town to attend.

Ultimately, any so-called house "churches" would really be more like neighborhood fellowship groups, or semiautonomous cell churches, all in submission to the mother (city) church. In practice, it would not be far different from a big Baptist church that has its members divided up into scores of Sunday School classes. Under the ideal city church scheme, no subset fellowship in any city is supposed to be autonomous, not any house church, not any of the Baptist churches, not the Presbyterian Church, not the Pentecostal assemblies. All are supposed to be united together under the larger organized umbrella of the one city church. City church meetings are said to be the proper venue for 1 Corinthians 14 participatory gatherings, not house churches. City church gatherings would seem to be the correct forum to celebrate the Lord's Supper. Only the city church would have the proper jurisdiction for disciplining a brother or sister. If the organized city church theory is correct, it leaves the individual house "church" with absolutely no scriptural direction whatsoever as to *what* it is supposed to do when assembled, or *why* it should even exist.

On what do they base their belief in the organized city church? One basis for the city church model are those instances in the New Testament where only one church is mentioned in a particular city. For instance, Revelation 1:4 refers to the "churches" (plural) in the province of Asia, and then deals with "the church" (singular) in each of seven cities in that province (2:1, 8, 12, 18, etc.). Adding fuel to the city-wide church fire is the fact that the New Testament never specifically refers to "churches" (plural) within the same city. The situation in Corinth could be presented as a prime example of the city church model.

THE CASE IN CORINTH

a. The Greeting. The salutation contained in 1 Corinthians 1:2 mentions "the church of God in Corinth." This greeting suggests that there was only one church in Corinth, not many churches. The city church theory holds that there is only supposed to be one church in any city, and it is to be an organized entity with its own government and leaders and meetings.

b. Church Discipline. In 1 Corinthians 5:4-5, Paul dealt with the immoral brother who needed discipline. He wrote, "When you are assembled in the name of our Lord Jesus and I am with you in spirit, and the power of our Lord Jesus is present, hand this man over to Satan" (NIV). Paul clearly wrote as if there was an assembling together of the whole church there in Corinth, of all the believers together in the same place.

c. The Lord's Supper. 1 Corinthians 11b reveals that there were abuses of the Lord's Supper in Corinth. There were deep class divisions. The rich evidently preferred not to eat with the poor, so they plotted to arrive early at the place of meeting. By the time that the poor finally got there, perhaps after work, the rich had already dined. No food was left. The nature of this abuse of the Lord's Supper could not have happened unless they all, rich and poor, were together in the same church, meeting in the same location. They clearly were not meeting in different places in Corinth for the Lord's Supper. The rich avoided the poor by eating at a different time, not in a different place.

d. The Participatory Meeting. The setting of the participatory meeting also implies a city church meeting. For instance, 1 Corinthians 14:23 states that "if the whole church comes together and everyone speaks in tongues, and some who do not understand or some unbelievers come in, will they not say that you are out of your mind?" (NIV). The KJV is even clearer: "If therefore the whole church be come together into one place."

e. Elders of the City. Advocates of the city church feel that it is the city church as a whole that is to have elders, not necessarily each house church. Indeed, how can the typical house church realistically produce multiple elders? Going beyond the Corinthian example, advocates of the city church would point to Titus 1:5, "For this reason I left you in Crete, that you might set in order what remains, and appoint elders in every city as I directed you" (NASV). They see in this a mandate for a presbytery of city church elders, not house church elders. Some are even calling for the rise of a ruling bishop and apostolic fathers to guide the city church.

2. The Local House Church. Others argue that the organized house church is the proper biblical expression of the local church, not any city-wide church. There is the church universal on one hand and then the local house church on the other hand. There is the macro church and a micro church, but no metro church.

How can the various house church texts be reconciled to championed city church texts? Arguably, any occurrences of the word church, apart from references to the universal church, refer to a group of believers who actually did all manage to meet together in one place for regular church assemblies. Certainly starting out fresh in a new city there would have been only one meeting place, but as the number of believers grew, so would the number of meeting places, and thus the number of churches within the same city. It was never intended for there to be only one house church meeting per city in perpetuity.

In other words, if the New Testament writers spoke of the church (singular) in a particular city, it was simply because there only happened to be a single fellowship, one meeting place, at that time in history, in that city. According to Mark Galli, the editor of Christian History magazine, "In A.D. 100, Christians numbered only about 7,000, a mere .0034 percent of the Roman Empire."[4] It is not surprising that there would have been only one congregation per city in those days. Yet over time, each initial church plant was expected to eventually multiply meeting places and so become multiple organized churches in that city rather than remaining only one house church.

How big was the church at Corinth? However big it was, all its members were evidently able to assemble together in one place to hold a plenary participatory meeting, all celebrate the Lord's Supper with each other, and corporately practice church discipline. Yet it was still only one single house church. In his letter to the Romans, written from Corinth, Paul wrote, "Gaius, host to me and to the whole church, greets you" (Ro 16:23, NASV). It seems to have been a very large house church, but a house church nonetheless, because Gaius was able to host the entire church in Corinth.

What is the evidence for the house church as the proper expression of the local church? It is a fact that, with the exception perhaps of Solomon's portico, *every* time the New Testament states clearly where a local church regularly met, it was in a private home. As we look out into church history, we see that the early believers continued to meet in private dwellings for the next two hundred years (for as long as the United States has been a nation). Where would this supposed city-wide church have met, if for centuries the primary venue for church meetings was someone's living room?

G. F. Snyder, in *Church Life Before Constantine*, wrote that "the New Testament Church began as a small group house church . . . and it remained so until the middle or end of the third century. There are no evidences of larger places of meeting before 300."[5] Those early house churches did grow, and rather than find ever larger places to hold their meetings, they instead started new house churches within the same city. This fact seems to be at odds with the theory of city church as an organized entity. The house churches referred to in the New Testament seem to be genuine, *bona fide* churches in their own right, not mere cell groups, not just home fellowships.

Those who advocate city church hold that churches ideally ought only to divide because of distance, as defined by city limits (geography). Those who hold to the house church as the correct model for the local church recognize division by geography as true in principle, but see city limits as the wrong boundary. They advocate a different separating factor: the boundaries of a home's den, of living room floor space, of geography in the sense of square feet rather than square miles. If all the believers can't all meet into one home, it is time to start a new church. The size of the average living room is the limit.

How are these house church references related to the occasional biblical statements about the church (singular) in a city? Is it really possible that the Bible speaks of "the church" in a certain city simply because there was only one assembly in that city at that time? If there had been several congregations, would it have been more proper to refer to the churches of that city rather than to the church of that city? Consider the case in Rome.

THE CASE IN ROME

Most New Testament epistles do *not* contain a greeting to "the" church in a certain city. In greeting the believers in Rome, for instance, Paul wrote "to all who are beloved of God in Rome, called as saints" (Ro 1:7, NASV). He did not greet "the" church in Rome as such. In fact, the New Testament never refers to "the" church in Rome. Could this be because there was more than one congregation in Rome?

Aquila & Priscilla (Prisca) were a Jewish couple living in Rome. Paul had never been to Rome when he wrote his letter to the believers in Rome, but he knew this couple from back when they had lived in Corinth and Ephesus. Thus, Paul greeted them in his letter when he wrote to the saints in Rome. He wrote, "Greet Prisca and Aquila, my fellow workers in Christ Jesus . . . also greet the church that is in their house" (Ro 16:3-5, NASV).

What is the difference between "all the saints in Rome" (Ro 1:7) and "the church that is in their house" (Ro 16:3-5)? The church that met in the home of Prisca and Aquila was especially singled out for greeting as a separate church, a subset of "all the saints in Rome." Paul would not have had to specify *which* church he was greeting unless there was more than one church in Rome. "Greet the church that is in **their** house" (emphasis mine) as opposed to the churches in *other* people's houses in Rome.

There evidently were considerable numbers of believers in Rome, many more than in Corinth, and they met in more than one place each Lord's Day. For instance, in Romans 16:14 there is a greeting expressed to "Asyncritus, Phlegon, Hermes, Patrobas, Hermas and the brothers with them." Who were the brothers who were "with" them? Likely, the rest of a different church that met with them.

The City Church

Consider also Romans 16:15, "Greet Philologus, Julia, Nereus and his sister, and Olympas and all the saints with them." Who were the saints who were "with" them? This strongly suggests that these saints were with them in yet another church in Rome, distinct from the 'brothers' who met with Asyncritus *et al*, and also separate from the church that met in the home of Priscilla and Aquila.

A good case can be made that there were at least three separate meeting places for believers in Rome, constituting at least three separate churches. Consider also that Paul only greeted by name those he already knew. Doubtless many other house churches were functioning in Rome that Paul had no personal acquaintance with when he wrote.

THE JERUSALEM EXAMPLE: METRO OR MICRO?

Let us apply all this to the Jerusalem church. The Jerusalem church is one of the few examples where the Bible does refer to only one church in a city (Ac 8:1). Arguably, this is simply because the believers there did all meet together in one place. The church in Jerusalem was indeed a single organized entity. For instance, Acts 2:1 records that "they were all together in one place" (NASV). Acts 6:1-2a states that "the twelve summoned the congregation of the disciples" (NASV).

Unlike Corinth, the Jerusalem church was not a house church at all (though they did eat together in various homes, Ac 2:46). At Pentecost some three thousand (Ac 2:41) were added to the original one hundred and twenty believers (Ac 1:15). Then, Acts 4:4 tell us that "many who heard the message believed, and the number of men grew to about five thousand." Luke further informs us, "The number of disciples in Jerusalem increased rapidly, and a large number of priests became obedient to the faith" (Ac 6:7). The Jerusalem church was a huge church even by today's standards. It was a *mega* church!

Where did so many people meet together? Acts 5:12 gives us the answer: "all the believers used to meet together in Solomon's Colonnade." Solomon's Colonnade was a huge assembly area, a roof supported by columns at regular intervals, with open sides. It was a portico, or veranda. This was prior to the persecution that later came upon the Jerusalem church and prevented such massive gatherings.

Should we copy the Jerusalem example in our churches today? (If so, it would run parallel to the house church concept). The answer is both yes and no. Under similar circumstances, yes. But their circumstances were unique, and not typical of our circumstances, so practically, normally and effectively, no. Too often the modern church has let this exception become the rule. This situation at Jerusalem was unique for several reasons.

First, the Jerusalem church was the very first church and was in its infancy. It was in the incubator stage. As Harvey Bluedorn pointed out, "There were many things yet to develop. This was a whole new construction project, and we must not confuse the scaffolding and building equipment with the building itself."[6]

Second, the Jerusalem church was composed solely of newly converted Jews. As such, they held a deep attachment to the things of the old covenant, including worship in the temple. Again quoting Bluedorn, "The church in Jerusalem was composed only of circumcised Jews who had lived their whole lives under the law and around the temple. They were culturally committed to a way of living under an administrative law which was jurisdictionally about to pass out of existence. They must presently begin the transition of peeling off the immature externally-conforming old covenant culture and at the very same time bringing forward the mature internally-transforming new covenant culture. There were many converted priests who were still zealously attached to the law, hence weak in conscience, hence hindered from maturing in the gospel. Many cultural accommodations were made in Jerusalem which we would not likely even consider today."[7]

Third, the church in Jerusalem was instantly confronted with an immense number of converts. Thousands were converted. Many of the converts were religious pilgrims, temporary visitors, who traveled to Jerusalem to observe Passover and Pentecost. Josephus recorded that the population of the city would swell to many times its normal size. Luke put it this way: "Now there were staying in Jerusalem God-fearing Jews from every nation under heaven . . . Parthians, Medes and Elamites; residents of Mesopotamia, Judea and Cappadocia, Pontus and Asia, Phrygia and Pamphylia, Egypt and the parts of Libya near Cyrene; visitors from Rome (both Jews and converts to Judaism); Cretans and Arabs" (Ac 2:5-11). Eventually these new converts needed to return home. In the interim however, these large numbers needed to be discipled, instructed and grounded in the faith. How does one handle three thousand Jews from many nations suddenly converted in Jerusalem (Ac 2:5-11, 41), and not long after that several thousand more local residents (Ac 4:4)? There were only twelve specially trained and designated apostles!

In order to quickly teach so many new converts, the church had to have big meetings. Thus, "they devoted themselves to the apostles teaching" (Ac 2:42) and met daily in the temple courts (Ac 2:46). This was also the era of their voluntary communalism (Ac 4:32-35), a unique giving in response to this unique training need. It was not repeated as a pattern in the other churches that later came into existence. The norm is micro churches, not mega churches, and the private ownership of property, not communalism.

Just imagine: Thousands of new believers with literally nowhere on earth to get training except right there in Jerusalem. The time available to train them was running out. Eventually they had to go home. Extra ordinary situations call for extra ordinary actions: mass meetings & communalism. If all the Mormons in Salt Lake City were suddenly born again and brought into a true saving faith in the Lord Jesus, that too would be a unique situation calling for an extra ordinary response by the true church.

These big meetings in the temple courts did not last long, because not only did the pilgrims eventually leave, but even the local residents later left, too, being forced out. Luke records that "a great persecution arose against the church in Jerusalem; and they were all scattered throughout the regions of Judea and Samaria" (Ac 8:1).

Years later, what was left of the Jerusalem church had yet another plenary meeting. This is recorded in Acts 15, the Jerusalem Council: "The whole assembly became silent as they listened to Barnabas and Paul telling about the miraculous signs and wonders God had done among the Gentiles through them" (Ac 15:12). Luke records that "the apostles and elders, with the whole church, decided . . ." (Ac 15:22). This was a greatly truncated church, not thousands of people as before.

(As a side note, the Jerusalem Council itself was also a fairly unique event in that the very nature of the gospel message was being decided. The issue was: "Is faith in Jesus enough, or must people also be circumcised?" The original apostles were still in Jerusalem, and they were the standard, the norm, for doctrine. The false gospel of circumcision needed to be condemned and the true gospel stated and defended. The Twelve were the men who could do just that. They were handpicked and trained by Jesus to represent Him on earth in a special way that no one else has been qualified to do since. It is not that the church in Jerusalem had authority over the other churches. Rather, from the apostles, in conjunction with the Jerusalem church, went forth an authoritative letter condemning the requirement of circumcision.)

THE CHURCH OF JUDEA, GALILEE AND SAMARIA?

The normal biblical pattern is to refer to churches (plural) within a region (Ac 15:41, 1Co 16:1, 16:19, 2Co 8:1, Ga 1:2). Accordingly, in Acts

9:31, the KJV reads, "Then had the churches rest throughout all Judaea and Galilee and Samaria." However, the NIV renders this same text with the word church in the singular: "Then the church throughout Judea, Galilee and Samaria enjoyed a time of peace." Which is the right reading, church or churches?

Differing underlying Greek texts account for the difference. If "church" (singular) is the correct reading, then this would be the *only* reference in the whole Bible to a regional church. Yet even if this is the correct reading, it arguably would have been used specifically with reference to the scattered church from Jerusalem. The Jerusalem church was the only church in the entire world. That original church was persecuted so fiercely that "all except the apostles" were scattered (Acts 8:1). Where did the church go? Throughout Judea and Samara (Ac 8:1). Thus, "the church" throughout Judea, Galilee and Samaria (9:31) likely refers to the scattered church of Jerusalem. Further evidence that Acts 9:31 refers to the scattered Jerusalem church is found in Galatians 1:22. Written years after the Jerusalem church was scattered, Galatians 1:22 reverts back to the normal usage and refers to the "churches" (plural) of Judea. This suggests that functioning, local, indigenous churches arose in Judea during the years following the scattering. Refugees from the Jerusalem church started new churches in the areas to which they fled.

Yet it is also possible that Luke referred to all the believers in those regions abstractly. In similar fashion we might say, "The church in China is being persecuted." There is no one organized church in China with which all believers are involved; it is an abstract reality. Both the church in China and Judea are abstract subsets of the one the universal church. The Bible does not speak of an organized regional church, no more than it does an organized universal church. There are examples of organized local churches (plural) within a region (like Galatians 1:2), but no instance of any organized regional church. There is no biblical basis for having a church whose earthly organization or authority extends beyond that of its local congregation. There is not a Biblical basis for an organized global church (like the Roman Catholic Church claims to be) nor even a regionally organized church (like the Church of Scotland or the Church of England or the Russian Orthodox Church).

Thus, the difference in Greek manuscripts underlying Acts 9:31 might allow for the consideration of a possible alternative way to view city church: one abstract church in each city made up of many organized local house churches. Granting that each house church is to be the correct expression of the local church, believers should still view themselves as a part of the greater church in their city. The city church should exist in our minds as a abstract reality, but with no intended earthly organization or authority. Our attitude should be that there is indeed one church per city, and that we are an integral part of it. Yet the house church is the proper unit of organization of the local church, not the city church.

In summation, the universal church is an abstract reality; the regional church is an abstract reality; and the city-wide church is an abstract reality. None of the three has any biblically modeled organization, meetings, or authority. Applied practically, a belief in the abstract city church means cooperating with other true churches in joint ventures (benevolence, prayer or evangelism), just like Paul took up a offering from the universal church to help the local church in Jerusalem. Abstract city church means being cemented together in the bond of love with all the believers in your city. Abstract city church means being accepting of all the believers in your town, regardless whether they are Baptist or Methodist or Presbyterian or whatever. It also allows for the elders of every town to cooperate together in a loose sort of presbytery.

CITY CHURCH CONSTERNATIONS

1. Where would the city-wide church of large city hold a plenary session? There are more people just in London than in the whole of other European countries. There have been believers in London since Roman times, and the number of Christians there now is doubtless huge. Even Watchman Nee, avid propagator of the city church, admitted that cities like London would have to be broken down into smaller units for something like borough church or postal code church. Yet if the city church really is the scriptural norm, what authority do we have to tamper with that and break London up into smaller units?

2. It has been two thousand years since the New Testament was written. Many former churches have ceased to be churches and have instead become synagogues of Satan. Other churches are full of unregenerate members; so-called brothers who live in open, known sin and yet are not put out of the fellowship. Some congregations have homosexual pastors. Others have elders who deny the Trinity, the virgin birth or Christ's propitiatory work on the cross. Are we to join ourselves with such so-called brothers in an effort to have a city-wide church? No doubt city church advocates would respond by saying that only true believers would be involved in the city church. But who is to make that determination? The potential for strife, resentment and division is great. One group of believers in Atlanta who hold to the city church idea constructed a large building with a sign out front that blares, "The Church in Atlanta Meets Here." How arrogant and cult-like that sign must appear to the thousands of other believers in metro Atlanta who do not gather there for church on Sunday.

Ironically, city church advocates face the same type of problem as did the Magisterial Reformers: separating true believers from unbelievers within state sponsored churches. They came up with the *Ecclesiola in Ecclesia*, the little church of wheat within a larger church of tares. History suggests that such attempts at inward reform are rarely successful.[8]

3. In a single, huge, city-wide church, how can God's people be protected against primadonnas, wolves in sheep's clothing, or false doctrine? Though a church of any size faces this problem, with the city church scenario one would likely end up with problems similar to what occurred in the Roman Catholic Church. When the top went bad, the whole structure below it went bad. With decentralized house churches, when one goes bad, the others are more isolated from the error.

4. Some are already abusing the city church idea as an excuse to flit around from house church to house church, Sunday by Sunday, spiritual gypsies accountable to no one. Considering themselves to be members of the church at large, they have no use for the mundane realities of "one anothering" with the same group of believers every week. Others have creatively turned the city church concept into an excuse to do whatever they want to do. To them, city church is essentially church without definition.

5. Church meetings are to be centered around the Lord's Supper as a full fellowship meal, followed by the participatory meeting. One of the things families do is eat together. Church is to be like a family and is to eat together. This is best done in a homelike setting with few enough people that you can actually get to know each of them and maintain relationships. If too many people are present, intimacy is lost.

While in seminary, I was on the part time staff of a church with over 14,000 members. We had Wednesday evening suppers at the church building in a huge hall with rows and rows of tables. Despite the fact that I was a staff member, I didn't know 90% of people there! The fellowship meal was very much like going to a restaurant. It was largely impersonal and institutional. How would a city-wide Lord's Supper celebration be any different?

6. Another ingredient of the Lord's Day church gathering is the participatory meeting (1Co 14), which is not supposed to be a "one man show" or "service" as such. Smaller assemblies better facilitate participatory meetings. Bigger assemblies are more suited to the lecture approach. If each of the brothers is realistically to be allowed to speak at the meetings (1Co 14:23), necessity would require a smaller, rather than a larger, meeting. If every week you come to the meeting with something you believe the Lord would have you to share and yet week after week you go home without having had the chance to share because so many others are there who are sharing, your meeting may be getting too big. How could a city-wide church realistically hold 1 Corinthians 14 meetings, with hundreds or even thousands of people present?

7. James 5:16 instructs, "confess your sins to one another, and pray for one another" (NASV). Galatians 6:1-2 requires that "if someone is caught in a sin, you who are spiritual should restore him gently. But watch yourself, or you also may be tempted. Carry each other's burdens, and in this way you will fulfill the law of Christ" (NIV). There was intimacy in the early church, and they made themselves accountable through these relationships. In a huge church you can easily get lost in the crowd. If you are not there, you are not missed. Your contribution to the church is like one more liter of water flowing under London Bridge. If you are in sin, you can more easily get away with it because no one knows what is going on in your life. A large church is too impersonal. Jesus clearly taught that we are to be a company of people who practice holiness and obedience. The process Jesus outlined for dealing with the disobedient is found in Matthew 18. This process works well in a smaller group where all know each other (house churches), but is increasingly impractical as one local church increases in size (city-wide church).

8. The New Testament is full of "one another" commands, all of which presuppose close relationships: "be devoted to one another in brotherly love, give preference to one another in honor, be of the same mind toward one another, love one another, accept one another, admonish one another, care for one another, serve one another, bear one another's burdens, bear with one another in love, submit to one another out of reverence for Christ, comfort one another, be kind to one another, encourage one another daily, let us consider how to stimulate one another to love and good deeds" (Ro 12:10, 12:16, 13:8, 15:7, 15:14, 1Co 12:25, Ga 5:13, 6:2, Ep 4:2, 4:32, 5:21, 1Th 4:18. Heb 3:13, 10:24). It is the local house church, not the city-wide church, that is the best venue for this.

9. If the apostles clearly taught or patterned something, there should be no contest regarding what we do. If the apostles were not definite, then there is freedom. The danger of city church lies in making obligatory an artificial structure that the New Testament knows nothing about.

SUMMARY

The city church is, at most, an abstract subset of the universal church. The proper expression of the organized local church is the house church, not the city church. City church is an attitude more than an entity. A philosophical belief in the city church should result in an attitude of cooperation with other churches in evangelism, benevolence, prayer, worship and training, of love for all the brethren, of interest in believers outside of our own fellowship. City church thinking helps us to overcome divisions and to create oneness with other believers in our town.

Those initially adopting the ideas in this book will naturally focus much of their time and attention on starting and maintaining their first house church. Yet our thoughts must not stop after that first church has been successfully established. One isolated house church, all alone, can soon become ingrown, monastic and unhealthy. The truth of the existence of the universal church means that we really do need to think globally and act locally. Correspondingly, a philosophical acceptance of the city church dictates that we also think metrolly and act locally. The city church theory, at the very least, suggests that we not be content with one house church, but rather focus our sights on a city full of autonomous, yet cooperating, local house churches.

Steve Atkerson

NOTES

[1] John Wesley, *Journal of John Wesley* (Chicago, IL: Moody Press, 1951).

[2] Donald Guthrie, *New Testament Theology* (Downers Grove, IL: Inter-Varsity Press, 1988), 788.

[3] D.W.B. Robinson, "Church," *New Bible Dictionary*, J.D. Douglas, editor. 2nd ed., (Wheaton, IL: Tyndale House Publishers, 1982), 205.

4 Mark Galli, "Adventures in Time Travel," Discipleship Journal (Colorado Springs, CO: NavPress, Issue #106 July/August 1998).

[5] G. F. Snyder, in *Church Life Before Constantine* (Macon, GA: Mercer University Press, 1991), 166.

[6] Harvey Bluedorn, personal correspondence,

[7] Ibid.

[8] Martin Llyod Jones, "Approaches to the Reformation of the Church," Puritan and Westminster Conference in 1965.

The City Church

1. Into what two broad categories of usage does the word "church" fall within the New Testament writings?
2. What scripture texts could be cited to prove the existence of the universal church?
3. How do theologians define the universal church?
4. What is the local church?
5. How is the local church different from the universal church?
6. What are the various views of the so-called city church?
7. How is the city church different from the house church?
8. What is the evidence for the house church as the proper expression of the local church?
9. Does autonomy lie with the city church or the house church? How so?
10. How can the various house church texts be reconciled to the various city church texts as the correct basis for the local church?
11. Evaluate the argument that the Bible speaks of "the church" in a certain city simply because there was only one assembly in that city at that time.
12. What is the difference between "all the saints in Rome" (Ro 1:7) and "the church that is in their house" (Ro 16:3-5)?
13. Should we copy the Jerusalem example in our churches today? Why?
14. What is unexpected about the statement that "the church throughout Judea, Galilee and Samaria enjoyed a time of peace" (Acts 9:31, NIV)?
15. Where would an organized, city-wide church of a large metropolitan city hold a plenary session?
16. How can we avoid joining ourselves with so-called brothers (theological liberals, the immoral, heretics) in an effort to have a city-wide church?
17. In a single, huge, organized city-wide church, how can God's people be protected against primadonnas, wolves in sheep's clothing, or false doctrine?
18. How could an organized city-wide church realistically hold 1 Corinthians 14 participatory meetings, with hundreds or even thousands of people present?
19. Is the proper expression of the local church: the city or the house? Why?

Note: NTRF also offers a teacher's resource to help lead a discussion of New Testament church life. Request *The Practice of The Early Church: A Theological Workbook (Leader's Guide)* from www.NTRF.org.

TRUTH PRACTICED — CHURCH DISCIPLINE

THE MOTIVATION OF DISCIPLINE

One of the many characteristics and actions of our Savior is His desire to see all of His children walk in truth. His love for us is demonstrated in many ways. He gave Himself, He saved us, He changed us, He empowers us, He lives in us, He guides us, directs us, teaches us and yes, He disciplines us. All is motivated by His love for His children. Consider the declaration of Revelation 3:19, "Those whom I love I rebuke and discipline. So be earnest, and repent."

This love-motivated discipline is the Father's desire for His children to know the truth and to walk in it. This love is a recognition that the Father knows best and that He wants the best for His children. It is the recognition that we see through a glass darkly and that we make sinful decisions and selfish decisions that bring sometimes horrible consequences to our lives. Since the Father sent the Son to bring us life, and that life more abundantly, we need correction and direction and discipline, which He lovingly provides.

The Father's love expressed in discipline is explained in Hebrews 12:4-11: "'My son, do not make light of the Lord's discipline, and do not lose heart when he rebukes you, because the Lord disciplines those he loves, and he punishes everyone he accepts as a son.' Endure hardship as discipline; God is treating you as sons. For what son is not disciplined by his father? If you are not disciplined (and everyone undergoes discipline), then you are illegitimate children and not true sons. Moreover, we have all had human fathers who disciplined us and we respected them for it. How much more should we submit to the Father of our spirits and live! Our fathers disciplined us for a little while as they thought best; but God disciplines us for our good, that we may share in his holiness. No discipline seems pleasant at the time, but painful. Later on, however, it produces a harvest of righteousness and peace for those who have been trained by it."

The *Evangelical Dictionary of Biblical Theology* states that "the notion of the discipline of God, and eventually the concept of the community and its leaders effecting God's discipline, derives from the notion of domestic discipline (Deut 21:18-21; Prov 22:15; 23:13). God is portrayed as a father who guides his child . . . The notion of discipline as familial chastisement remains in the New Testament (Eph 6:4; 2 Tim 2:25; Heb 12:5-11)."[1]

PERSONAL AND PRIVATE DISCIPLINE

How does the Father discipline us? His disciplines take a variety of ways and methods, but usually include a combination of both the Word and His Spirit. In a very private and personal way, through the Word and the conviction of the Spirit of God, He lovingly points out our sins and brings us to the truth. As we zealously repent, He delights in changing our minds and hearts and empowering us to overcome those areas that have defeated us in the past. How does the Word discipline us? 2 Timothy 3:16 declares, "All Scripture is God-breathed and is useful for teaching, rebuking, correcting and training in righteousness, so that the man of God may be thoroughly equipped for every good work." As we read and study His Word, and we are made aware of His commandments, we are given the opportunity to repent and do things His way. Proverbs 6:23 states: "For these commands are a lamp, this teaching is a light, and the corrections of discipline are the way to life." Most Godly discipline takes place during devotions while in the Word and in prayer. Privately and personally, the Father shows us His way and gives us the power to do it!

The Word works in conjunction with the Holy Spirit to convince us of the rightness of the Lord's ways. For instance, Jesus promised in Acts 1:8 that "you will receive power when the Holy Spirit comes on you; and you will be my witnesses in Jerusalem, and in all Judea and Samaria, and to the ends of the earth." When we are saved, the Holy Spirit comes to live in us: "Do you not know that your body is a temple of the Holy Spirit, who is in you, whom you have received from God?" (1Co 6:19). We have responsibility to guard what the Lord has given us through the Spirit. 2 Timothy 1:14 commands, "Guard the good deposit that was entrusted to you — guard it with the help of the Holy Spirit who lives in us." One of the tools we have to help us guard what the Lord has given us is the spirit of discipline. For instance, Paul reminded that "God did not give us a spirit of timidity, but a spirit of power, of love and of self-discipline" (2Ti 1:7).

All discipline is hard and difficult: "No discipline seems pleasant at the time, but painful. Later on, however, it produces a harvest of righteousness and peace for those who have been trained by it" (Heb 12:11). In contrast, according to Proverbs 12:1, "Whoever loves discipline loves knowledge, but he who hates correction is stupid." Our choice is clear; we can accept the discipline of the Lord and enjoy the peaceful fruits of righteousness or we can behave foolishly and reject His discipline.

PUBLIC CHURCH DISCIPLINE

What happens when a brother or sister refuses the conviction of the Spirit and the clear teaching of the Word? When a believer openly embraces and practices a behavior clearly forbidden by the Word? 1 Corinthians 12 teaches in detail that we are members of one body. Not only do we learn how the body functions and all the gifts in the body, we also learn that when one member of the body is sin sick, it affects the whole body. Verse 26 states, "If one part suffers, every part suffers with it; if one part is honored, every part rejoices with it." When our brother sins and does not repent it affects the whole body and the whole body suffers because of it. Remember, "Now you are the body of Christ, and each one of you is a part of it" (12:27). Consequently, we have a family responsibility to help our sinning brother. Motivated by love of the brother, we are commanded to confront the bother and the sin issue in order to restore the brother and guard the family that meets locally.

Although there are many scriptures that deal with this issue, the two main ones are found in Matthew 18 and Galatians 6. These passages are included for easy reference since they will be referred to often:

"If your brother sins against you, go and show him his fault, just between the two of you. If he listens to you, you have won your brother over. But if he will not listen, take one or two others along, so that 'every matter may be established by the testimony of two or three witnesses.' If he refuses to listen to them, tell it to the church; and if he refuses to listen even to the church, treat him as you would a pagan or a tax collector. I tell you the truth, whatever you bind on earth will be bound in heaven, and whatever you loose on earth will be loosed in heaven. Again, I tell you that if two of you on earth agree about anything you ask for, it will be done for you by my Father in heaven. For where two or three come together in my name, there am I with them" — Matthew 18:15-20

"Brothers, if someone is caught in a sin, you who are spiritual should restore him gently. But watch yourself, or you also may be tempted. Carry each other's burdens, and in this way you will fulfill the law of Christ." — Galatians 6:1-2

Truth Practiced — Church Discipline

THE FIRST STEP

The discovery process is always left up to the Lord. There is never to be a standing investigatory committee or an oversight group that is responsible for ferreting out the sin in one another's lives. As we walk out our lives in Christ, as we grow in intimacy and fellowship, we will naturally become more aware of what is going on in other's lives. As we walk out our life in Christ and we discover anyone in a trespass or if we see a brother sinning, we are then called to act on behalf of the brother. It is important to note that all of us, not just the elders and leaders, are called to this body ministry. If you are the one who sees a brother in trespass, you are responsible for going to the brother and confronting him. Don't go to the elders; go to the offending brother. The only qualification given for the person confronting is that he be a brother and that he be spiritual, indwelt by the Spirit of the Living God.

If the Lord has chosen you to be used in this fashion, the first step is to pray and check your motivation. Are we motivated by love of the brother? Are we operating in a spirit of gentleness? Are we trying to restore the brother? Are we being careful in case we are tempted in a like manner? Obviously, there is much to be prayed about and considered before we take the first step of talking privately with the sinning brother.

Having prepared yourself through prayer and self examination, the next step is to go privately to the sinning brother, "showing him his fault *in private*" (italics mine). I am convinced that this is the Lord's choice method. It springs from the fact that most discipline is personal and private and provides a bridge between personal and public discipline. Jesus was specific in using the words "in private." How wonderful that the Lord even cares if we get embarrassed and deliberately and specifically tried to protect us from the further embarrassment of public notice. What opportunity for quick and private repentance. When successful, this first step of public discipline brings the sinner to repentance, edifies the body and usually strengthens the relationship between the one confronting and the brother being confronted.

Time must be allowed for the Holy Spirit to convict and convince. Most people's initial reaction is not their final reaction. Give the brother some room to prayerfully consider what you have brought to his attention. Do not put a timetable on the work of the Holy Spirit but continue to make yourself available to him for prayer and counsel. Don't expect an initial first response to be immediate repentance. It is a privilege to observe the Holy Spirit working in a brother's life. A good rule of thumb is to give the brother as much time as you would want someone to give you.

If the brother listens to you, you have won the brother. The matter is finished and no further confrontation is necessary. Careful consideration must be given to the fruits of repentance to make sure that the brother is sincere and that he is taking biblical steps to remove himself from the occasion of temptation. Continued prayer and counsel may be necessary to help the brother. Both should be offered until both the confronting brother and the sinning brother are convinced that victory has been achieved.

THE SECOND STEP

What do we do if the brother refuses to listen and refuses to repent? Jesus said, "if he will not listen, take one or two others along, so that 'every matter may be established by the testimony of two or three witnesses.'" There has been much written on the second step in public church discipline. Some suggest that the two or more witnesses be witness to the original trespass. Others believe that the two or more witnesses are there to witness the brothers as they confront the sin issue and to determine the attitude and responses of the two men involved in the confrontation. This step definitely takes the process out of the private arena into the public. It is a dramatic escalation of the process and is designed to bring public pressure on the bother to quit sinning and repent.

With two or three witnesses, we are to go to the sinning brother. Who should these witnesses be? I don't believe they have to be witnesses to the act of sin but are there to be witnesses to the confrontation. The witnesses should also be spiritual men who are well grounded in the word and who will not be tempted in the area of sin. They should also have a relationship with both parties. They are there to observe the process and to offer counsel to both the confronter and the person being confronted. Because these confrontations sometimes get emotional and fiery, the witnesses can also act as overseers to make sure that there is a spirit of gentleness. While the person who is confronting the bother in sin, the two or three witnesses are to help keep the goal of restoration in mind and to keep the conversation going in the right direction. The person being confronted sometimes tries to change the focus by obfuscating, attacking the person or persons who are confronting him, offering excuses for the continued behavior or outright denial of the charges. The witnesses are to help both parties to remain calm, to keep the conversation focused on restoration, to make sure that the motivation of love of the brother is clearly communicated as the motive for the confrontation and to move the conversation towards a decision.

The Third Step

If, after being confronted privately and with two/three witnesses, there is no fruit of repentance, the original confronter and the witnesses are to tell it to the church. This is not the church universal but the local church, the local group who meets in fellowship. The telling should include the nature of the sin, the steps that have already been taken and the results of the previous conversations. The first telling might be at a men's meeting so that each man can discern what is going on and decide what, if anything, to tell his own wife and children. Since the telling includes a description of the sin involved, consideration should be given to immature believers and children. Remember that the Scripture, in Galatians, teaches that the ones doing the confronting be spiritual (mature) and have a spirit of gentleness. The goal of restoration must be adhered to even more arduously in the very public disclosures as the possibility for wrong thinking and action increases with the number of brothers and sisters involved. Great care must be given to avoid tale bearing and gossip and exaggeration and wrong attitudes. The goal is restoration, not crucifixion of the brother. All members of the local body are now involved in confronting and helping the brother.

There are only two groups of people in the world; those who are saved and are in the church and those who are outside of the church. Jesus was speaking to his disciples at the time of Matthew 18 and the church did not yet exist. When Jesus said that the unrepentant brother was to be understood as a Gentile, He was telling His Jewish audience that the sinning brother was to be treated as if he were not part of the covenant family, an outsider, apart from the grace of God. One of the best examples of this is found in the Corinthian letters where Paul tells the Corinthians to put the brother out who was in sexual sin with his stepmother and in the second letter he tells the Corinthians to take him back in to the fellowship of the church. As with all the other steps, this last and final step is to bring repentance and restoration.

Summary

The good shepherd always goes after the lost sheep. The wonder of the gospel is that provision is made for the sinning brother who can not find his own way to repentance can, in fact, rely upon the good graces of a loving fellowship to be used in helping him be restored to full fellowship. These clear scriptural instructions are the how to steps for that restoration to take place. Consider the following principles:

1. *The motivation for all discipline is the love of the Father.*
2. *Most discipline is private and personal.*
3. *Most discipline is accomplished through study and prayer of the Word and the active work of the Holy Spirit in a believer's life.*
4. *The practice of sin is a family issue and sometimes must be dealt with by other members of the church family for the sake of the brother and the family.*
5. *God Himself is the one who exposes and brings all things to light.*
6. *All mature spiritual members of the body are called to this body ministry.*
7. *Before confronting, prayer and self examination are required.*
8. *Be careful to protect the sinning brother's privacy by going to him in private.*
9. *If the brother rejects the counsel, go to him with two or three witnesses.*
10. *"If he refuses to listen to them, tell it to the church."*
11. *"If he refuses to listen even to the church, let him be to you as a Gentile and as a tax collector."*

— Mike Indest

NOTES
[1] Walter Elwell, *Evangelical Dictionary of Biblical Theology* (Grand Rapids, MI: Baker Publishing Group, 1996).

Truth Practiced — Church Discipline

1. According to Hebrews 12:4-11 and Revelation 3:19, what is an integral part of God's love for us?
2. According to Proverbs 12:1, what choice faces every believer?
3. How does God the Father use the Word and the Spirit to discipline us?
4. What should happen when a brother or sister refuses the conviction of the Spirit and the clear teaching of the Word (Mt 18, Ga 6)?
5. What are the steps of the church discipline process (Mt 18:15-17)?
6. What questions regarding motive should someone ask himself before taking the first step in the discipline process?
7. What is the purpose of taking along several witnesses in the second step of the discipline process?
8. What type of Christians should you take along with you as witnesses (Ga 6)?
9. What does it mean to deal with someone as a Gentile or tax collector?
10. What is the ideal goal during each step of the discipline process? See also James 5:19-20.
11. What different examples did Jesus use in Matthew 18:1-9 to show the seriousness of causing someone else to sin?
12. What application should Matthew 18:10-14 hold for us?
13. What function does Matthew 18:18-20 serve in relation to Matthew 18:15-17?
14. Jesus felt the need to caution us about forgiveness (Mt 18:21-35). Why would a church have a hard time forgiving a repentant brother? See 2 Corinthians 2:5-11.
15. Why is it that most churches today utterly ignore Matthew 18:15ff? See 1 Corinthians 5.
16. What should you do if you find yourself in a church that refuses to obey Matthew 18:15ff?

Note: NTRF also offers a teacher's resource to help lead a discussion of New Testament church life. Request *The Practice of The Early Church: A Theological Workbook (Leader's Guide)* from www.NTRF.org.

17

CHURCH FAMILIES

Malachi 4:4-6 foretells of God's family plan for Israel (and later the church). It shows what God expected of Israeli families – hearts turned toward each other. This turn of heart in family matters parallels the New Covenant change of heart in Jeremiah 31 where God says He will put His law into our hearts. Four hundred years later, the angel who appeared to Zechariah and announced the birth of John the Baptist quoted Malachi 4 to explain John's purpose and ministry. In Luke 1:13-17, the angel describes John as the one who will "turn many of the sons of Israel to the Lord their God" and as the one who will "turn the hearts of the fathers to their children and the disobedient to the wisdom of the righteous - to make ready a people prepared for the Lord." The angel's style and arrangement of these two descriptions make them corollaries. He arranged everything around verse 17a so that the facts about John's ministry would be obvious. John, as the forerunner, preached the message of turning toward the Lord, which in turn would restore the hearts of fathers to the hearts of their children.

One of the good works accompanying salvation will be a change in family attitudes and actions. The father will practice godly headship of the family; the mother will be the submissive support her husband needs as he strains to obey the Lord. The children will obey their father and mother. The family will love each other, will be kind to one another, and will be best friends with each other. In short, the family will be the model of the Godhead and Christianity upon the earth.

Children are not left out of this equation. We don't just "do our best and hope that they turn out all right." Look at Luke 1:17 again. The angel quoted only part of Malachi 4:6. He substituted "the attitude of the disobedient to that of the righteous" for "the hearts of the children to the fathers." The angel thus tells us what it means to have the "hearts of the children turned toward their fathers." The turning of the children's hearts (as expressed in Malachi) means that they will obey their parents (as expressed in Luke). When salvation genuinely reaches the parents, the children will eventually change from being disobedient to being righteous. This change, however, is not without great effort on the part of the parents. They will strive for godliness in their children. Part of the turning is repenting of the worldly way of rearing children. Parents who do strive for godliness in their children will be rewarded with their children's hearts turned toward them in obedience.

CHURCH LEADERSHIP

All this has great impact upon church leadership. Both the elder and the deacon "must manage his own family well and see that his children obey him with proper respect" (1Ti 3:4; 5; 12) and have children who "believe and are not open to the charge of being wild and disobedient" (Tit 1:6). Marriage and children are requirements for being an elder. But that requirement does not hold true for the traveling apostle – neither Paul nor Timothy were married, and they are not called elders. The apostle Peter, on the other hand, was married and calls himself an elder in 1 Peter 5:1-3.

The elder must have children whose hearts are turned toward their parents. The elder who is too busy with his own or church concerns (as "good" as they may be) fails to understand the absolute priority of rearing his children in a way pleasing to God. Indications are that he himself has not turned to the Lord if his own heart is not turned to his children (Lk 1:13-17). Who else sees him twenty-four hours a day at his best and his worst? If he does not live out his Christianity before his children, who is he to export it to others?

EVANGELISM

You might think that with the above emphasis upon children, they ought to be the objects of the church's evangelistic efforts. But who were the objects of the apostles' evangelism? The book of Acts shows us that the apostles evangelized the heads of households, not children. Cornelius, Lydia, and the Philippian jailer all came to Christ because of the apostles' efforts. Amazingly, their whole households came with them. Is this only a cultural phenomenon of that century? I don't think so. If we aim our evangelism at the fathers (or single mothers) we will, by the New Testament example, get the children. The man whose heart truly turns to the Lord will turn toward his children, and they too will likely come to Christ.

CHURCH DISCIPLINE

Family matters relate directly to church discipline. The man who follows God will discipline his children (Ep 6:4, NASB). He will hold his children accountable for their actions and train them to obey him and his wife (see Pr 1:8; 2:1; 3:1; 4:1; 5:1; etc.).

Modern churches do not discipline the disobedient members because we have forgotten the biblical reasons and methods for disciplining our own children. As we have raised generations of children without biblical discipline, we have also raised the same generations to expect that no one can hold them accountable for their actions, least of all a church whose only requirements of them are their money and a few hours a week of their time. Children who have been raised to expect those in authority over them to provide needed discipline will not run from the church which seeks to discipline them for their good. In fact, children who have been raised in the discipline and instruction of the Lord will need very little church discipline as adults. We would be amazed at the transformation of our churches (and our society) over a generation if we would discipline our children to respond to God-given authority and not reject their father's discipline (Pr 3:11,12; and Heb 12:5-6) and, subsequently, the church's discipline.

Church Meetings

I am convinced that children of all ages should be with the parents in the house church meeting. If we take Ephesians 6:4 at face value, it is the father who is to train his children, not another adult teacher. The father who teaches his children the things of the Lord six days a week will not need someone else to do it on Sundays. A father who also disciplines his children will have them under control. His control will allow the children to be with the parents in the house church meeting. Remember that we are not training our children to remain children, but to be adults. They need to see how adults meet as a church and learn by participating as well. In our church, the families sit together. When necessary, the parents correct their children in our meetings or remove them for discipline, which some Sundays is often! But that is part of maturing as a church and as families. It is something we have taught to, and expect from, our parents and children. Children can do far more than we sometimes require. If they need to nap, they sleep in Dad's or Mom's lap, or in the chair or on one of our beds. Often the children play with quiet toys, read, or color (sometimes on paper, and then sometimes on the floor!). It's just like family.

God's way of communicating truth to the next generation has not changed. God intends truth to be taught and learned by children in a family setting. Neither the church nor society has this direct responsibility; fathers and mothers do. The sooner we learn this lesson in the body of Christ, the sooner we will put aside all the worldly ways of teaching and training children and have generations of godly men and women in the church who can turn the world upside down once again.

CHRISTIAN MINISTRY

Paul's concept of ministry was derived partially from family life. Paul drew upon a godly family as he illustrates his own apostolic ministry to the Thessalonians in 1 Thessalonians 2:5-12. He used the nursing mother, and then the father, as examples. As an apostle, Paul could have been paid for his work among them as he preached the Gospel and taught them discipleship. However, he worked hard among them day and night so they would not think him greedy. A nursing mother who cares for her children day and night provided the perfect example of Paul's service. Her emotional ties to her children propel her in her ministry of love and devotion. She nurtures her children in contrast with the man's primary role. Women are to be the nurturer in the home, and their emphasis on relationships gives impetus to Paul's ministry. Paul's tender care, and his willingness to sacrifice his time and energy for their welfare, imitated the godly mother caring for her children.

On the other hand, Paul also looked to the godly father who was very concerned with the righteousness of his children and apparently, their reputation. Paul convincingly wrote that the father directing the moral development of the children proved to be the perfect example for the apostle exhorting, encouraging, and imploring the new Christians at Thessalonica to walk worthy of God. This goes back again to the father's responsibility to his children; teaching them righteousness and training them to that standard. However, the father who loves his children and wants God's blessing upon them does not impose legalism upon the household. That breeds rebellion. Christians do not earn a right standing before God, nor keep it, by what they do. It means that through the relationship we have with our children, we fathers urge as strongly as possible our children's obedient walk with God. Paul capitalized on his observations of godly men who concern themselves with their children's conduct.

The passive father will raise sons who are themselves passive and liable to be dominated by women. His daughters will tend to be domineering in all areas of family, church, and society. The emotionless mother will produce children who cannot relate to people. All this can be prevented by involved fathers and mothers who see to the well-being of their children and teach them the proper roles of men and women in the family, church, and society. It seems to me that Paul took the outstanding characteristics of the mother and father and applied them to his ministry:

the emotional ties which caused sacrifice by the mother and the desire for children worthy of the family name which caused much involvement by the father. We must do the same.

CONCLUSION

A church is a family. Paul names it the "household of God," calls salvation "adoption as sons," describes us as "heirs," tells Timothy to "entreat an elder as a father," calls Christians "brother" and "sister," and uses a childhood name for father (*abba*) to address the heavenly Father. All of these descriptions point to the relationships we have to God and to one another.

A family is people relating to one another. Church relationships, good and bad, overwhelm the New Testament reader if he looks for them. The good church nurtures and builds those relationships and does not substitute an endless parade of activities for them. People desire healthy relationships more than anything else. However, house church members must be prepared to get close, very close. Think of it as porcupines snuggling up to get warm in the winter. The closer they get, the more quills they feel. When they draw back, they get cold. It is better to feel the quills!

The house church model best resembles a family because it meets where people live. The family who hosts a church meeting and the members who go there draw themselves together as a unit. The atmosphere is real, not surreal. The conversation does not compete with the organ prelude, the relationships with the clothes and cars, or the truth with hypocrisy.

The church which meets in a home also best contributes to a family's spirituality and best enables a father as the head of the family to encourage their well-being. A house church allows the free time to teach one's family what it means to be a Christian in the kingdom of Christ and God. Indeed, it does not just allow; it places upon a father that responsibility because there is no one else designated to do it. One cannot delegate this duty to a Sunday School teacher, Bible study leader, youth minister, or minister – there are none of those in a house church. The weekly teaching does not substitute for the father's teaching, but complements it.

— Tim Melvin

Tim teaches a wonderful weekend seminar on biblical child training. Contact him through NTRF about coming to your church to present it! — Editor

Church Families

1. The angel, in Luke 1:13-17, applied Malachi 4:4-6 to John the Baptist's ministry. What import does this have for new covenant family life?
2. Which of the qualifications for church leadership (1 Ti 3:4; 5; 12) touch on family life? Why is this so important for a potential church leader?
3. Why were the heads of households the objects of the apostles' evangelism?
4. How do family matters relate directly to church discipline (or the lack thereof)?
5. Why should children of all ages should be with their parents in the house church meeting?
6. How did Paul draw upon a godly family to illustrate his own apostolic ministry to the Thessalonians, in 1 Thessalonians 2:5-12?
7. What type of children will a passive father raise?
8. Why did the author compare church life to porcupines snuggling up to get warm in the winter?

Note: NTRF also offers a teacher's resource to help lead a discussion of New Testament church life. Request *The Practice of The Early Church: A Theological Workbook (Leader's Guide)* from www.NTRF.org.

18
DIVINE ORDER

All of us hate confusion. Ask any parents if they prefer confusion and openly promote chaos in their homes. Ask a librarian if the best way to run a library is to just throw all the books in a warehouse and look through the entire jumble every time a book is needed. What would our fellowship meetings be like if everybody spoke at once and if there were three teachings going on at the same time? What would our highways look like without lights, signs, an understood agreement that we all drive on the right side of the road, speed limits, and so on? The world in which we live could not function without order.

The questions is, whose order will we follow . . . man's or God's? This is the question we face in every decision we make as we allow the Holy Spirit to form Himself in us. Certainly we all know the Scriptures that teach us to deny self and to put others first and esteem others more highly than ourselves. We remember with joy that we are being conformed to the image of His Son, Jesus the Christ. Yet still try to order our worlds according to the latest wisdom of man.

T. Austin-Sparks wisely observed: "To those who have a knowledge of the Bible it is evident that the whole of the Scriptures open up along the four lines that we have indicated; namely that

1. God is a God of order;

2. Satan is the prince of a world under divine judgment, and the nature of that judgment is confusion;

3. Christ, in Person and work, is the embodiment of divine order;

4. The church is the elect vessel in which, and through which, that divine order is to be manifested and administered in the ages to come."[1]

There is a discernible pattern of divine order in all that the Lord does. Starting in eternity past, we can discern divine order in the Trinity. As the Lord created the world and His institutions, we can observe this divine order being duplicated in the family, in government, and in the church.

Divine Order

For instance, Holy Writ declares that "The head of every man is Christ, and the head of the woman is man, and the head of Christ is God" (1Co 11:3), and that "God is not a God of confusion but of peace, as in all the churches of the saints" (1Co 14:33).

THE TRINITY

Consider the Trinity and, in particular, the relationship between the Father and the Son. The Father and the Son are equal in attributes and essence. A quick review of the names of Christ (God, Son of God, Lord, King of Kings and Lord of Lords), His attributes (omnipotent, omniscient, omnipresent, immutable, life and truth) and His works (creates, sustains, forgives sins, raises the dead, judges, sends the Holy Spirit) all convince us that Jesus is God. In addition, the direct statements of Jesus in John 10:30, 14:9, 17:21ff, and Matthew 28:19 all convince us of the deity of our Savior. But is it possible to be equal and submitted? What does 1 Corinthians 11:3 mean where it is declared that "the head of Christ is God"? Here is divine order in its purest form and practice. While fully God, Jesus "who, although He existed in the form of God, did not regard equality with God a thing to be grasped, but emptied Himself, taking the form of a bond-servant, and being made in the likeness of men. Being found in appearance as a man, He humbled Himself by becoming obedient to the point of death, even death on a cross" (Phlp 2:6-8).

Listen to the confession of Christ as He explains His submission to His Father:

John 6:38 — "I have come down from heaven not to do my will but to do the will of him who sent Me."

John 4:34 — "My food is to do the will of him who sent me and to finish his work."

John 5:30 — "I can of mine own self do nothing: as I hear, I judge: and my judgment is just; because I seek not mine own will, but the will of the Father which hath sent me."

Matthew 6:10 — "Thy kingdom come. Thy will be done in earth, as it is in heaven."

Matthew 26:39 — "My Father, if it is possible, may this cup be taken from me. Yet not as I will, but as you will."

Equal but submitted! That is how divine order works in the Trinity. It is this divine order that is stamped on all of His creation. The family, government and the church all have explicit instructions as to their function and practice. All of these commands are grounded in the demonstrated order that exists within the workings of the Trinity. They are not

222

arbitrary commands of a capricious God nor are they limited by culture or time. God created the family, government and the church to look like and to work like the Trinity and to enjoy the blessings of divine order in all that we do.

THE FAMILY

Next in the order of creation is the family. There is no other institution on earth that more closely resembles the Trinity in its order and function. Make no mistake, all of the comparisons between the covenant of marriage and God's covenant of salvation found in Ephesians and Colossians are a reflection of His love and His desire to share that love with us. But we must order our marriages according to *His* plan, not ours. In the same way that the Trinity operates in divine order, the Lord expects us to live our marriages the same way.

A husband and wife are equal in attributes and essence. Galatians 3:28 reveals that "There is neither Jew nor Greek, slave nor free, male nor female, for you are all one in Christ Jesus." Like the Father and the Son, a husband and wife are equal in attributes and essence. But in order for the family to function biblically, God has clearly and unequivocally stated the divine plan. The husband is definitely the head of the wife: "the head of the woman is man" (1Co 11:3). As the head, he is commanded to love his wife just like Christ loved the church and gave Himself for her. He is to love her like he loves his own body and to nourish and care for her. The wife is to submit to her husband in everything (just like within the Trinity: equal, but submitted). And, the children are to obey. Simply stated, the plan for divine order in the family is: Husbands love, wives submit, children obey.

Notice how closely this resembles the order that exists between the Father and the Son. Since we are predestined to be conformed to the image of His Son, see how divine order works to our benefit, how much better the Lord's plans are than men's. Consider the utter chaos and confusion that exists in all those who choose to order their family life according to man's wisdom instead of God's wisdom. Some chafe under God's order, arguing from a cultural point of view that these directives are out of date or were only for the time in which it is written and that we live in a more enlightened time or culture. How superfluous! God's plan for the family is nothing more than what He and His Son have enjoyed for time eternity, and it works!

Notice the order in the divine order. The Son submits to the Father. Man submits to the Son. The wife submits to the husband. The children obey the parents. Not under compulsion but willingly, humbly, and with joy as we walk out God's plans for us.

THE GOVERNMENT

Next in order of creation in time is government. The main passages stating the divine order in government are Romans 13:1ff, Titus 3:1ff, and 1 Peter 2:14ff. From these, three principles can be discerned:

Principle #1 — "For there is no authority except that which God has established. The authorities that exist have been established by God" (Ro 13:1).

Principle #2 — "Everyone must submit himself to the governing authorities" (Ro 13:1).

Principle #3 — "Consequently, he who rebels against the authority is rebelling against what God has instituted, and those who do so will bring judgment on themselves" (Ro 13:2).

It takes faith to submit to God; it takes faith for a wife to submit to her husband; it takes faith to submit to governing authorities. We sometimes forget that history is "His" "story" and that the Lord is working His will at all times. Peter, in 1 Peter 2:13, urged: "Submit yourselves for the Lord's sake to every authority instituted among men: whether to the king, as the supreme authority, or to governors, who are sent by him to punish those who do wrong and to commend those who do right. For it is God's will that by doing good you should silence the ignorant talk of foolish men."

In order to build faith, we need to remember that the Lord:
•"Takes off the shackles put on by kings and ties a loincloth around their waist" (Job 12:18).
•"Judges: He brings one down, He exalts another" (Ps 75:6-7).
•"Changes times and seasons; He sets up kings and deposes them. He gives wisdom to the wise and knowledge to the discerning" (Da 2:21).
•"Is sovereign over the kingdoms of men and gives them to anyone he wishes and sets over them the lowliest of men" (Dan 4:17, 32).

Government is the minister or servant of God. He established governing authorities to be ministers of wrath, to punish those who do unrighteousness. Our submission includes obeying the laws (Titus 3:1) and the financing of those laws through the payment of taxes (Ro 13:7). It is the same pattern in the Trinity and in the family . . . divine order!

THE CHURCH

The Word is full of commands concerning our gathering together to worship. Emphasis is placed on the public demonstration of divine order as we join together to celebrate the Lord's supper, to pray, to exhort, to sing and to enjoy fellowship. But do our assemblies reflect the divine order or do they reflect the best man can do?

Who is the head of the church? Paul writes "He is the head of the body, the church; He is the beginning and the firstborn from among the dead, so that in everything He might have the supremacy" (Col 1:18); "God placed all things under his feet and appointed Him to be head over everything for the church" (Ep 1:22); "Instead, speaking the truth in love, we will in all things grow up into Him who is the Head, that is, Christ" (Ep 4:15); and "The head of every man is Christ, and the head of the woman is man, and the head of Christ is God." (1Co 11:3). Not a pastor or elder, not a denomination nor a general superintendent, not a bishop or an apostle but *Christ*, is the head of His church.

In the same way that Jesus submitted to His Father, in the same way that the wife is to submit to the husband, in the same way that children are to obey their parents, in the same way that we are to submit to the governing authorities, the church is to submit to Him in all things. The public expression of our fellowship is to be an example of this submission in all that we do.

How do elders factor into this equation? Elders are supposed to be examples of the divine order at work. Notice the qualifications for elders and their job descriptions. 1 Timothy 3:1-7 and Titus 1:7-9 describe these men as men who are the heads of their houses, who have their houses in order (divine), whose wives and children are functioning in that order. 1 Peter 5:1-5 states that these elders are to lead by example, not by compulsion, providing oversight by their own faithful example of submission as well as their family's example of faithful submission. They are not to lord it over the fellowship, but following the example of the Lord, they are to lead exemplary lives of submission.

All of the commands of 1 Corinthians are the how to's of expressing divine order publicly: Don't get drunk, don't eat all of the food before others arrive, head coverings, women be silent, male leadership, the instructions concerning the gifts, and most importantly the instructions concerning the Lord's supper. All are for the purpose of expressing the divine order. Like all of the Lord's commands, they are not subject to cultural or time considerations but are the continuing expressions of His own submission.

EQUAL BUT SUBMITTED

The Father and the Son and the Holy Ghost from eternity past lived in perfect society. We were created to fellowship with the Father. Sin broke that fellowship and instead of perfection our world became filled with chaos and death. In submission to His Father, the Son died so that we might again have fellowship with His Father. We are predestined to be conformed to His image. As a result, the Father created the family to work just like the Trinity. One head, the husband. God then created governing authorities and calls us again to submit to them. On the day of Pentecost, His church was born. The church is to operate just like the family and just like the Trinity. Divine order: In the Trinity, in the family, in government and in the church.

— Mike Indest

PART TWO: AN EXAMPLE OF DIVINE ORDER IN THE CHURCH

Correctly applying 1 Corinthians 14:33b-35 is a challenge, especially for those involved with a church that has participatory meetings. The text reads: "As in all the congregations of the saints, women should remain silent in the churches. They are not allowed to speak, but must be in submission, as the Law says. If they want to inquire about something, they should ask their own husbands at home; for it is disgraceful for a woman to speak in the church" (1Co 14:33-35).

Since this passage must be applied on a weekly basis, it is something that needs to be dealt with seriously and honestly. Before attempting to explain what this passage means, a few general, preliminary observations about the text should first be made.

First, it was intended for all congregations everywhere. Specifically with regard to women's silence, Paul made an appeal in 1 Corinthians 14:33b to a condition that was already true in "all the congregations of the saints." This suggests that, whatever Paul wanted of the women, it was a universal practice. Further, he stated that the women should be silent in the "churches" (plural, 14:34). Since the Bible generally speaks philosophically of there being only one church per city, the use of the word "churches" in the plural arguably referred to all other city-churches in existence at that time.

Second, this passage is not simply Paul's uninspired opinion. Perhaps in anticipation of opposition to this instruction about the role of women during the participatory phase of the church gathering, Paul buttressed his command with the reminder: "If anybody thinks he is a prophet or spiritually gifted, let him acknowledge that what I am writing to you is the Lord's command" (14:37). Then he warned, "If he ignores this, he himself will be ignored" (14:38). Thus, whatever this passage means, it is not merely Paul's opinion. It is the Lord's command. We dare not ignore it.

Third, the word silent is from *sigao* and means the absence of all noise, whether made by speaking or by anything else. It is insightful to note how *sigao* is used other places in 1 Corinthians 14. Tongue speakers were instructed to keep quiet (*sigao*, 14:28) if there was no interpreter present, and prophets were to stop (*sigao*, 14:30) if a revelation came to someone else. No statement to the church was to be made by either a tongues speaker or a prophet under certain circumstances. Thus, whatever the correct application for women, there are times when a sister is not to address the gathered church. The core command is that women remain silent (14:34) during participatory church meetings.

Fourth, the context surrounding this passage concerns order during the participatory phase of the weekly Lord's Day church gathering (1Co 14:40). The main reason the church gathers weekly is in order to be edified (1Co 14:4-5, 12, 26, Heb 10:24-25). The primary method to achieve this edification is through the fellowship of the Lord's Supper as an actual meal (see 1 Corinthians 11b). Like any large dinner event, it is a time when many conversations take place simultaneously and where no one person is singled out. Both men and women talk freely, relax, and fellowship at the same time over the meal. In the early church, as the fellowship feast finally drew to a close, the second phase of the meeting began. This second phase is described in 1 Corinthians 14. This is the time for teaching, singing, testimony, etc. The over-arching rule for this part of the meeting is that only one person at a time should address the congregation. All others are to listen quietly. Speaking is to be "one at a time" (14:27) and "in turn" (14:31). Thus, whatever this passage about silence means, it specifically concerns silence with respect to being the only one publicly speaking to the assembly. Logically, it would therefore not apply to congregational singing, corporate responses, or whispered private conversations, and certainly not to fellowship during the Lord's Supper (1Co 11:17-35).

Fifth, the requirement for women to be silent with respect to speaking publicly to the gathered congregation is not a matter of ability, gifting, or spirituality. Rather, it is a matter of divine order, obedience, and of putting others first for the sake of the advancement of the kingdom. For instance, a brother coming to the meeting prepared to speak in a tongue is required to hold back on the use his gift if no interpreter is present. A prophet may have a burning word that is genuinely from the Lord, but if another revelation comes to someone else, that first brother is to end his prophetic utterance. Similarly, Christian sisters are called upon to be silent in certain limited settings.

TWO VIEWS

Among the authors of this book, two views prevail as to the exact meaning of the words in this passage. One is the silent in judgment view, which holds that a woman may indeed speak to the gathered church, except to verbally judge a prophecy that has been given. According to this view, a woman is to be silent only with respect to judging prophecy during the interactive phase of the church gathering. The other view is the silent in public speaking view, which understands the Bible to teach that there is never a time when a sister should address the 1 Corinthians 14 plenary assembly.

The silent in judgment view is quite popular with the church at large today. Historically, however, the silent in public speaking view has been the most commonly held position. What all the authors of this book *do* agree upon is that God created men and women with divinely designed differences. Each gender is uniquely suited to the Lord's respective ministry and calling. We stand as one in support of God ordained roles for both men and women.

THE SILENT IN JUDGMENT VIEW

With those favoring the silent in judgment view, 1 Corinthians 14:33b-35 (remain silent) is taken to apply to the judging of the various prophecies mentioned in 14:29-33a. In 14:29a, Paul commanded that two or three prophets should speak; he then regulated the prophecy in 14:30-33a. Then, in 14:29b, Paul ordered that the prophecies be carefully judged. He next regulated the judgment in 14:30b-35. Thus, just as tongue speakers were to be silent under certain circumstances (14:28 - i.e., only with regard to speaking in tongues when there was no interpreter present), and just as the prophets were to be silent under certain circumstances (14:30 - i.e., only with regard to prophecy when another prophet received a revelation), so women were to remain silent under certain circumstances (14:33b-35 - i.e., only with regard to the judging of prophecies).

For women to judge prophecy in the church would be to assume an authoritative posture and, hence, would be to violate the requirement to be in submission found elsewhere in the Scriptures (1Ti 2:11-13). Notice how Paul links the silence of women in this passage to submission (14:34), indicating that this silence is in regard to exercising authority. Accordingly, women are not authorized to quiz, question, or interrogate the prophets as to their orthodoxy. To do so would place them in a position of authority over the prophets. Instead, they should ask their own husbands at home, after the meeting, as to why certain prophecies might have gone unchallenged (14:35).

Also, those holding to the silent in judgment view regard 1 Corinthians 11 (about women prophesying) as occurring in a plenary, interactive church meeting. This is because the instructions immediately following this passage, 11:17-34 (concerning the Lord's Supper), clearly do deal with a corporate church meeting. Thus, in 1 Corinthians 11:2, the Corinthians were praised for what they did rightly in their meetings, and in 1 Corinthians 11:7 they were chided for what they did wrongly in their meetings. The seeming contradiction that is thus created between 1 Corinthians 11:2-16 (women praying and prophesying) and 1 Corinthians 14:33b-35 (women not speaking) is resolved by understanding the silence in 1 Corinthians 14:33b-35 to be conditional. Women may speak if their statements are "in submission" (14:34). If, however, their utterances would entail passing judgment upon prophecies spoken in the meeting, then under this condition the women must be silent. Thus the sisters only have to be silent sometimes, but not always.

THE SILENT IN PUBLIC SPEAKING VIEW

In support of the silent in public speaking view, notice the seeming absoluteness of 1 Corinthians 14:33b-35. The injunction seems crystal clear. As has already been shown, the Greek behind silent (*sigao*) genuinely means mute. This is in contrast to another word Paul could have used (*hesuchia*) which usually means "silent" in the sense of tranquil, calm, or settled down, but not necessarily mute (see its use in 2Th 3:12; 1Ti 2:2, 11-12). Moreover, as if to anticipate that someone might misunderstand the meaning of "women should remain silent in the churches," Paul added the clarification that women "are not allowed to speak" (14:34). He did not limit it by specifying that they are not allowed to speak in tongues nor speak a prophecy nor speak in judgment nor speak a teaching. No qualifier was added. Evidently, the women are not to speak anything to the gathered assembly. In fact, they are not even to ask a question in church (14:35), because "it is disgraceful for a woman to speak in the church." The original footnotes in the Geneva Bible of 1599 put it this way: "Women are commanded to be silent in public assemblies, and they are commanded to ask of their husbands at home."

Gordon Fee, in the *New International Commentary on the New Testament: The First Epistle To The Corinthians*, observed that: "Despite protests to the contrary, the 'rule' itself is expressed absolutely.

That is, it is given without any form of qualification. Given the unqualified nature of the further prohibition that 'the women' are not permitted to speak, it is very difficult to interpret this as meaning anything else than all forms of speaking out in public . . . the plain sense of the sentence is an absolute prohibition of all speaking in the assembly."[2]

According to *The Expositor's Bible Commentary*, "women were not to speak in public worship (33b-36) . . . The command seems absolute: Women are not to do any public speaking in the church."[3] Further, B.B. Warfield wrote that "precisely what the apostle is doing is forbidding women to speak at all in the church . . . It would be impossible for the apostle to speak more directly or more emphatically than he has done here. He requires women to be silent at the church meetings; for that is what "in the churches" means, there were no church buildings then."[4]

Southern Baptist theologian John Broadus, commenting on 1 Corinthians 14:33-34 and 1 Timothy 2:11-15, stated, "Now it does not need to be urged that these two passages from the Apostle Paul do definitely and strongly forbid that women shall speak in mixed public assemblies. No one can afford to question that such is the most obvious meaning of the apostle's commands."[5]

An examination of first-century cultural norms would also suggest that Paul truly intended for women to be silent in public speaking. In Jewish synagogues, women were not allowed to speak publicly. Also, the secular Greek biographer, Plutarch, wrote that the voice of modest women ought to be kept from the public, and that they should feel as much shame over being heard as over being stripped.[6] Plutarch's comments seem to reflect the common Greek/Roman sentiment of the day. Thus, if Paul had intended for women to be allowed to speak in church, would he then not have had to write extensively to convince his readers of such a counter-cultural practice? However, no such argument can be found in the New Testament. Instead, there is the command for silence; a command not based on the culture of Paul's day, but upon the universal practice of all the churches and upon the Hebrew Scriptures ("as the Law says", 14:34). Paul certainly did assert the equality of the sexes in Galatians 3:28 (in contrast with first-century culture), but he still maintained the subordination of wives to their husbands (1Co 11, 14:34, Ep 5:22ff, Co 3:18) and that leadership in the church should be male (1Ti 2:11-13, 1Ti 3, Tit 1).

What is the purpose for women being silent during 1 Corinthians 14 participatory meetings? According to the text, their silence is a form of submission: "They are not allowed to speak, but must be in submission, as the Law says." Old Testament Law obviously does not deal with women being silent in church meetings, but it does teach the submission of women to their husbands and it models male leadership in both religion and society. In a church situation where the whole church has come together in one place to be edified through teaching, praise, worship, testimony, etc., the men are called upon to be the primary servant leaders. The women are to practice a dynamic silence that encourages the men to speak out and practice their leadership.

The silence in public speaking view harmonizes the statements about women prophesying in 1 Corinthians 11 with 1 Corinthians 14 by noting that nowhere does the text specifically state that the prophesying of 1 Corinthians 11 has a plenary meeting of the church in view. The prayer and prophecy of 1 Corinthians 11 is thus understood to occur at a setting other than that of the plenary church assembly. The presence of the word churches in 11:16 is taken to refer not to church *meetings*, but to the consensus of the *totality of Christians* living in various geographic locations.

What of the clear statements in 1 Corinthians 14:26 that everyone can speak in the meeting or that all can prophesy? In many contexts the word brothers refers to both men and women. Other times, it refers only to believing men (as in 1Co 7:29, 9:5). It is a fluid term. Some argue that throughout the letter to the Corinthians, brothers refers to both men and women. Is this the case also in 1 Corinthians 14? Sailing into chapter 14, having begun in chapter 1, the flow would seem to indicate so. The readers, throughout 1 Corinthians 14, are addressed as either brothers or you (second person pronoun). However, there is a significant and unexpected pronoun shift from you to they (third person pronoun) in the paragraph concerning women (14:33b-35). Rather than writing, "women . . .you", the text states, "women . . . they." Why did Paul not write directly to the sisters, if they were included in the term brothers?

This pronoun shift can be easily accounted for if the word brothers throughout 1 Corinthians 14 actually refers primarily to the men. The women would thus be referred to in 3rd person, since they are written about, rather than directly addressed. So, when it is stated that all, anyone, or each one of the brothers can participate in the interactive meeting (14:26), it may be specifically the men who are referred to. The women ("they") are not to make comments designed for the whole church to hear. Interestingly, the *Textus Receptus* adds the word your before women in 14:34, further evidence that the term brothers throughout 1 Corinthians 14 specifically referred to the men and not the women. Since Paul had no hesitation about addressing women directly in other of his letters (for instance Euodia and Syntyche in Php 4:2), the fact that he did not here, in 1 Corinthians 14, makes the case above all the more compelling. Gordon Fee, in his commentary on this passage, observed, "all the previous directions given by the apostle, including the inclusive 'each one' of v. 26 and the 'all' of v. 31, were not to be understood as including women." (p. 706).

CONCLUSION

The women's silence is both an object lesson and an application of the order that is to exist in the home and the church. It encourages the men to take the lead in the meeting, to be responsible for what goes on, to verbally participate, to improve in the articulation of their thoughts, to learn to be leaders, etc. One wife joyously observed that the quieter she was in the participatory church meeting, the more her passive husband spoke up and took the lead (compare 1Pe 3:1-2).

Sometimes those who explain away those passages of Scripture that limit women's roles in ministry fail to see the overall picture of God's family order, set at creation, that encompasses both the Old Covenant and the New. The church is primarily made up of families. For church order to contradict the order of the family (Ep 5) would be disorder and chaos. The Lord created and gifted men and women with complimentary ministry roles. Truly understanding God's order in both the family and the church causes us to realize that these limiting passages are not so much restrictive as protective. They protect women from the burden of leadership and of having to function as men. They also encourage men to be servant leaders. And, He is presenting to us a picture of Christ and His bride, the church, which is submissive to Christ as Head.

This is a serious issue with far reaching consequences regardless of how it is applied. We all have to do something about this passage at least on a weekly basis. My purpose in writing has been to offer a biblical alternative to the prevailing approaches that are common today, and not to attack those who hold views contrary to mine. For those reading this who have not made a decision on how to apply 1 Corinthians 14:33b-35, please realize that we cannot simply stick our heads in the sand and pretend it does not exist. As Paul warned, "If he ignores this, he himself will be ignored" (14:38).

— Steve Atkerson

NOTES

[1] T. Austin Sparks, *The Collected Writings of T. Austin Sparks*, Vol. 2, (www.austin-sparks.net), 70.

[2] Gordon Fee, *The New International Commentary on the New Testament, The First Epistle to The Corinthians* (Grand Rapids, MI: W. B. Eerdmans Publishing Co., 1987), 706-707.

[3] Frank E. Gaebelein, editor, *The Expositor's Bible Commentary*, Vol. 10 (Grand Rapids, MI: Zondervan, 1998), 275-276.

[4] B.B. Warfield, "Women Speaking in the Church" (The Presbyterian, Oct. 30, 1919), 8-9.

[5] John Broadus, "Should Women Speak In Mixed Public Assemblies?" (Louisville, KY: Baptist Book Concern pamphlet, 1880).

[6] Fritz Reinecker & Cleon Rogers, *Linguistic Key to the Greek New Testament* (Grand Rapids, MI: Zondervan, 1980), 438.

(For fuller treatments of this challenging subject, see the Articles section at www.ntrf.org)

Divine Order

1. Why is order so important?
2. What did T. Austin Sparks say about order and chaos?
3. How does the Trinity illustrate divine order?
4. What is the biblical order for the family, and how is it similar to that of the Trinity?
5. What is God's order as it relates to government?
6. What are the various out workings of divine order for the church?
7. Why is the divine order expressed in 1 Corinthians 14:33b-35 particularly relevant to churches with participatory meetings?
8. What evidence is there that 1 Corinthians 14:33b-35 is applicable to all churches everywhere?
9. Why should 1 Corinthians 14:33b-35 not be viewed as merely Paul's opinion?
10. What does the Greek word *sigao* ("silent") mean?
11. How does the context dictate that the silence is only with respect to being the only one speaking to the gathered assembly?
12. What other speakers are told to hold back and be silent in the gathering?
13. Explain the silent in judgment view.
14. Explain the silent in church view.
15. What did Gordon Fee say about the unqualified nature of 1 Corinthians 14:33b-35?
16. Does the "Law" (1Co 14:34) teach silence, submission, or both? See Genesis 2:20-24, 3:16.
17. What would be the purpose for women not addressing the 1 Corinthians 14 participatory meeting?
18. What of the statement in 1 Corinthians 14:26 that everyone can speak in the meeting or that all can prophesy?
19. Explain the significance of the use of the pronoun "they" (rather than "you") in 1 Corinthians 14:33b-35.
20. How would 1 Corinthians 14:33b-35 apply to the Lord's Supper portion of a church gathering (1 Co 11:17ff)?
21. How should 1 Corinthians 14:38 motivate each church to take the time to honestly deal with 1 Corinthians 14:33b-35?

GROWING PAINS — GETTING TOO BIG

PART ONE

In the most common scriptural sense of the term, the church can never get too big. As long as the Lord leaves His people on this earth, it will always be His intent for the church to grow. And even in the sense of the true local church (all the truly redeemed ones in a locality) it is always God's intent for us to welcome growth as a blessing (try a Bible search on "multiply" for a sense of God's heart on numerical growth).

But what about a given congregation of saints meeting together regularly? Is it possible for such a gathering to become too large? In today's church paradigm, that hardly seems conceivable. After all, the goal is numerical growth, isn't it? Isn't growth evidence of spiritual health, of fulfilling the great commission? The bigger a church is, the more effective it must be, right? The more people that are in one church, the more varied and specialized its programs can become, meeting more specific needs. Such assumptions as these are common, but do they really reflect God's desire for His house?

The growing number of Christians involved with house churches sense a longing for intimacy in fellowship with other believers around the Lord. And many have experienced the increasingly impersonal characteristics of program-centered churches, especially as they become larger (or endeavor to seem larger than they are). Many have sensed the disconnect of being disenfranchised by the increasingly professional production that many churches aspire to provide in their services.

As for me and my house, I find compelling the scriptural arguments favoring churches meeting exclusively in private homes. Paul's insistence (in 1Co 4:16-17; 11:1-2, 16; 14:33; Ep 2:20; Php 3:17; 4:9; 2Th 2:15; 3:6-9; 1Ti 1:16; 1Ti 3:14-15; 2Ti 1:13) that the churches follow the apostolic pattern (and his own example) are persuasive arguments against the notion that where churches meet is not a matter of scriptural mandate.

Gathering around the Lord in an authentic way is so exciting, interesting, and enjoyable that numerical growth will likely result, in time, as saints mature corporately in their proficiency in letting the Holy Spirit lead their feasts/gatherings. What should churches do when they grow to the point that they can no longer fit in a typical private home? How many is too big?

Growing Pains — Getting Too Big

Jesus used an analogy (a parable - Mt 9:17; Mk 2:22; Lk 5:37-39) contrasting new and old wine and wineskins in defending His disciples' lack of fasting. Clearly the wine is more important than the wineskin, but the wrong wineskin can be detrimental to the benefit of the wine. The function is more important than the form, but the wrong form can inhibit the intended function.

It is always risky (and thus sometimes questionable) to speculate on God's purposes for His acts. Yet He calls us to learn His ways (Ps 25:4; 51:13; 95:10). Let me cautiously propose why the New Testament church was so consistently portrayed as gathering in homes. I suspect a key is to be found in Paul's explicit description of a church gathering in which all things are to be done "decently and in order" (1Co 14:40).

Throughout 1 Corinthians 14, Paul contrasts practices that are disorderly and confusing with those that are orderly and edifying. Interestingly, Paul's definition of orderliness is significantly different from what many of us would find comfortable, at least in a formal meeting (which may be a key to understanding the problem). Paul cautions against such confusing practices as speaking out in languages other people don't understand, having more than one person speaking at a time, having women lead, and other things focusing on one's own enjoyment rather than the benefit of the whole group. But then he contrasts these with descriptions of orderly, edifying corporate experiences.

For example, after portraying an inappropriate situation in which "an unbeliever or uninformed person" (presumably an uninformed believer) comes in where "the whole church comes together in one place, and all speak in tongues" and concludes "that you are all out of your mind" (1Co 14:23), Paul then describes the appropriate alternative. Interestingly, the better practice is not sitting still and listening to experts expound on Scripture. Instead, Paul says (1Co 14:24-25) that "if *all* prophesy," this "unbeliever or uninformed person" will be "convinced by *all*" and "judged by *all*." The final outcome is that "falling on his face" [this is orderly?] he will worship God and report that God is truly among you."

The incredible thing is that this prophetic participation by all is what Paul means by "decently and in order." He goes on to argue (verse 26) that when the brothers come together each one brings something to be done for edification. These things might include a psalm, a teaching, a tongue, a revelation, or an interpretation. Note that this list includes things that could be planned ahead, but also things that couldn't likely be previously prepared.

236

A little later he says (verse 30) that if someone is speaking and "anything is revealed to another who sits by," the first speaker is to welcome the interruption and let the second brother speak. He continues with the phenomenal contention (verse 31) that "you can *all* prophesy one by one." At first glance this seems to contradict his directive two verses earlier to "Let two or three prophets speak and let the others judge." If only two or three can prophesy, yet he says "all" can prophesy, one possible interpretation is that there should only be two or three brothers present. Although I doubt this is the correct interpretation of the passage, it would certainly point to relatively small gatherings.

Actually, I suspect the correct interpretation is that the prophecies were to be voiced conversationally, among two or three brothers, with those listening discerning whether or not they are hearing the voice of the Shepherd (Jn 10:3-5, 16, 27). This still sounds like a fairly intimate conversation, with some participating and the others leaning forward (inclining their hearts) as they listen with their ears and their spirits.

Even in the next section, where Paul addresses the women's dynamic silence (exerting unspoken pressure on the men to lead out), there is a sense of the interactive context of the gathering when he says (verse 35), "if they want to learn something, let them ask their own husbands at home." Apparently the men were to be free to interact during the gathering, asking questions. It is clear that the church gathering envisioned by the apostle was interactively participatory, personally intimate, and spontaneously led by the Holy Spirit, yet orderly in the sense that each person was to consider the good of the group rather than simply his own edification (considerate). A congregation is too large if all cannot participate intimately.

An interesting thing about private homes is that they are seldom large enough to facilitate gatherings of more than just a few families. I think we are wise, and cooperating with the Lord's ways, when we choose to design our homes to facilitate groups of saints to meet there. But is it possible the Lord ordained that churches gather house to house in order to keep the numbers relatively small? If so, we might be undermining His intent when we seek for larger facilities.

If I could build a house with a living room that could facilitate gatherings of 200 people, would that be an aide to the church? Or might I possibly be compromising the Lord's design to keep groups somewhat smaller? I doubt the Lord is pleased to have us set numerical limits. Yet it appears to me there is a general principle we should anticipate regarding the size of congregations gathering together intimately.

Growing Pains — Getting Too Big

In 1993, for the fourth time, our family began meeting together with a couple of other families as a church. Over the years the size of the group has grown, and sometimes diminished. At one point some of us felt we had reached a size that was too large for a home. I suggested that we consider finding some larger hall in which to meet, but the Lord used several of the other brothers to keep us from going down that path. It appears the Lord's provision for us at that time was to have the size of the group diminish. Over a relatively short period of time several of the families moved to other regions, thus relieving the pressure of dealing with the question of what to do if the congregation becomes too numerous to fit in a home.

Recently the Lord has once again brought growth to the circle of saints we're walking among. There are currently five participating families living in our community of Springfield, California, whose geographic proximity allows a frequency of contact encouraging us to walk together in relative intimacy (although we all recognize a longing for the Lord to work more in bonding our hearts together around Him). Two other families are currently in the process of moving here. Another two families living about a half-hour away have expressed a desire (and realistic intentions) to move here. Two other participating families live within a half hour of Springville, and another two families live nearly an hour and two hours away, but have attended the weekly meetings for years. Finally, there are several other families who visit the weekly gatherings fairly often. (Those living further away are hindered from much of the "exhorting one another daily" experience of Hebrews 3:13, as a result of geographic limitations.)

We clearly are at a point where not all who want to gather with us can participate in a single meeting in a private home. If all the families who have identified as part of the congregation were present in one place, at one time, there would be ninety people. If any of the regular or infrequent visitors were present, that would be even more.

We want to hear the Lord's direction regarding what we should do regarding this situation. We could try to plan a response, but the likelihood of resolving on an approach that He doesn't find pleasure in is very high. Solomon said (twice, Pr 14:12 & 16:25), "There is a way that seems right to a man, But its end is the way of death." Yet the Lord is apparently pleased to have us ponder His ways revealed in Scripture, and anticipate what He will likely lead. Let's consider some possible approaches, that might (or might not) eventually be what the Lord leads.

Although I seriously doubt the Lord would have us find a larger meeting place to accommodate everyone, that is a possibility that others have felt is pleasing to the Lord. It is certainly a possibility, though a doubtful one.

We could simply do nothing. This could be of the Lord as we "Stand still and see the salvation of the LORD" (2Ch 20:17). It's quite possible the Lord would provide a solution without asking any of us to change what we have been doing at all. Or He might call us to bear the crowding with joy. Most of us have heard stories of congregations in third world countries where lots of folks gather in a very confined space. But as things are now, few of the families are willing to open their homes for gatherings, knowing there is no way everyone will fit. It seems to me the incentive to avoid hospitality is something we should seek the Lord to eliminate.

Another possibility (however remote) is that the Lord would lead us to limit the number of folks who are welcome to gather with us. We could do as some home school support groups do and simply have a closed group, requiring any others who are interested in walking in the way the Lord is leading us, to find others to gather with. As doubtful as this option is to me, I want to leave the door open to whatever the Lord leads.

An option that has been discussed among many in the house church movement is the obvious possibility of multiplying by splitting a large group in two. This could be done based on geography, or it could be done based on some other method (casting lots, number or ages of family members, common interests, convictions, theology, etc.). It seems to me that distinguishing one church from another on the basis of anything other than geography is the kind of factiousness that Paul addressed in the first several chapters of 1 Corinthians. Choosing to fellowship only with folks who are similar to myself is a tacit acceptance of divisions in the body. If I must conclude that someone is truly a member of the body of Christ, I must also welcome fellowship with that person.

A couple of the families we gather with, who live quite a ways from many of the rest of us, have expressed fear that they might sometime be asked to split off and form a distinct group. Interestingly, if all the non-Springville families were to gather together, distinct from the Springville families (including those definitely moving here), the two groups would have exactly the same number of families. This is certainly a possibility the Lord could lead. However, my sense is that such an arbitrary division smacks of human manipulation rather than listening to the leading of the Holy Spirit.

Growing Pains — Getting Too Big

Yet in Scripture geographic distinctions in the church were the one legitimate basis for unique church identity. The church in Antioch was one with the church in Jerusalem, but there was a sense in which they were distinct churches. There is only one body of Christ, made up of all believers of all time throughout the world. But there are distinct churches (plural) based on geography (not on human loyalties, distinctive practices, or unique theological positions). While we must admit that the modern church is splintered, the solution is to see the church from Jesus' perspective. There is thus only one church in Springville, California, and all the Christians in Springville are part of the church in Springville. Even all the Christians in the church of Springville can't possibly (and, I believe, shouldn't) meet regularly in one place. If we don't meet in one place because there are too many of us, how do we decide who meets where?

Another possibility is scheduling meetings at different times, and welcoming folks to participate in the meetings that best fit their schedule and preferences. Certainly this is an approach that is considered a no-brainer for institutional churches that outgrow their sanctuary. We could have an early service and a late service. (I'm almost gagging as I write this.) Folks could choose which love feast they want to participate in. They might alternate participation, and even occasionally enjoy both feasts. Perhaps several of the brothers who sense a special calling to provide oversight to the congregation could particularly make it a point to participate in both groups.

These are exciting times, as we find the Lord leading us in paths that are distinct from the traditions that have been set over the centuries. May we humble ourselves before the Lord, acknowledging that we can't figure out the best approaches, and that we are utterly dependent upon the Holy Spirit's leading, in order to truly be a pleasure to our Bridegroom.

— Jonathan Lindvall

PART TWO

When the authors of this book argue that the New Testament pattern is for each local church to be smaller rather than bigger, we don't mean small in the sense of three or four people. We mean small in the sense of scores of people versus hundreds or thousands of people. Having too few people in a church can be just as problematic as having too many. What scriptural evidence is there as to the numbers involved in a New Testament house church?

There was a single house church at Corinth. In his letter to the Romans, written from Corinth, Paul wrote, "Gaius, host to me and to the whole church, greets you" Ro 16:23, NASV). Gaius hosted the entire church of Corinth in his home. Further, the salutation contained in 1 Corinthians 1:2 greets "the church of God in Corinth," which suggests that there was only one house church in Corinth.

1 Corinthians 11b reveals that there were abuses of the Lord's Supper in Corinth. There were deep class divisions. The rich refused to eat with the poor, so they plotted to arrive early at the place of meeting. By the time the poor finally got there, perhaps after work, the rich had already dined and no food was left. The nature of this abuse of the Lord's Supper could not have happened unless they all, rich and poor, were together in the same church, meeting in the same location. They clearly were not meeting in different places in Corinth for the Lord's Supper. The rich avoided the poor by arriving at a different time, not different a place.

In 1 Corinthians 5:4-5, Paul dealt with the immoral brother who needed discipline. He wrote, "When you are assembled in the name of our Lord Jesus and I am with you in spirit, and the power of our Lord Jesus is present, hand this man over to Satan" (NIV). Paul clearly wrote as if all the believers at Corinth came together in the same place.

The Lord Jesus outlined the church discipline process in Matthew 18. Count the numbers of people who were potentially involved: the sinner, offended brother, then the two or three witnesses. That is four people. After that, the whole church is get involved. Presumably the number of people in the rest of the church is not merely one more person (a fifth person); presumably there are at least as many in the church as have already been involved in the discipline process (at least four more). That would mean that Jesus envisioned a typical church to contain *at least* 8 adults. Most likely many more remained in the church than had been involved in the initial steps of the discipline process. At that time in history when Jesus spoke this, the synagogue system evidently required there to be ten Jewish men in a place before a synagogue could be formed. If that general principle carried over to churches, ten men plus their wives equates to a score of people. Add in children and you've got a packed house!

Yet another indicator that at Corinth there was only one congregation meeting in one place can be found in 1 Corinthians 14.23, "if the whole church comes together and everyone speaks in tongues, and some who do not understand or some unbelievers come in, will they not say that you are out of your mind?" (NIV). The KJV is even clearer: "If therefore the whole church be come together into one place . . ."

An examination of the various gifts present in the Corinthian assembly suggests scores of people were in that one church. Three tongues speakers plus interpreter and three prophets are mentioned in 1 Corinthians 14:27-32, totalling seven people. Add in just one person with a hymn and another with a word of instruction (14:26) and the total rises to nine. Factor in the women (who didn't speak, 14:33b-35) and the number of adults present easily reaches eighteen. Around twelve different spiritual gifts are mentioned in 1 Corinthians 12:7-31 with the implication that all were operative in Corinth. This was a healthy sized house church!

How big was the house church at Corinth? It clearly was not a mater of "us four and no more." There were dozens of people in that one house church, not hundreds of people, not thousands of people, and not just one or two families. When we envision the size of the typical New Testament home church, we should envision a packed house with scores of believers present. Correspondingly, in our churches today we need to think small in a really big way! Many people involved with house churches would not be content in a conventional church with hundreds or thousands of people. They also should not be content in a house church with a very few people. The church is to be vibrant and growing, reaching new people with the gospel. The norm is for there to be dozens of people.

You may be wondering how a home could accommodate so many people for church. It is interesting that the New Testament often indicates that the church regularly met in the same person's home. For instance, Paul sent greetings to the church that met in the home of Priscilla and Aquila (Ro 16:3-4), to the church that met in Nympha's house (Co 4:15), and to the church that met in Philemon's home (Phlm 1-2). These fellowships did not rotate around from house to house. This may be because those people owned homes large enough to host the meetings of the whole church. If the norm is for a house church to have scores of people in it, and some member's houses are too small to serve that many folks, the church may not be able to hold its meetings in that home. Early church history reveals that the church met in the homes of its wealthier members, presumably because they had houses better able to accommodate larger numbers of people.

It can reasonably be expected that a body of believers that walks with the Lord and radiates light into a dark community will attract new members. As a house church grows numerically, space will be at a premium. Historically, believers have solved this problem (and it is a good problem to have) by erecting bigger and bigger buildings to hold more people. However, the New Testament pattern is *not* to build special buildings in order to accommodate more people than can fit into a typical living room. Yet there is no New Testament pattern for a house church dividing, either. The apostolic witness is silent about how the early church accommodated growth. Unless some other existing New Testament pattern is violated, this ultimately is a matter of freedom in the Lord.

People resist dividing (and understandable so) because the prospect of lost relationships is just too painful. Others justifiably fear that a lack of qualified leaders in the new group may result in disaster. Another concern is that in a new, pioneering work, those on the fringes may leave the church (pioneers can have a rough life). Yet another reason to resist dividing is the concern that the new church may make decisions that are contrary to the earlier decisions of the original church that may lead to conflict. All these can be valid concerns.

Poor reasons to divide include: hosting a large number of people is just too much trouble to prepare for; there are too many wild kids to keep up with; and minor theological differences make it easier to leave than to work out or tolerate. Motives are important. Why do you want to divide? Are your motives selfish or to greater serve the body of Christ?

On the other hand, it may be time to consider a new work when so many folks regularly attend the 1 Corinthians 14 meeting that it becomes difficult for everyone who so desires to participate. Another indicator that it is time to start a new church is when so many are in attendance that the host home simply cannot accommodate them all (no place to sit). Also, an ever larger group will necessarily result in some loss of intimacy and accountability (a network of only so many friends can be maintained). Having a smaller church will also encourage the more timid to speak up and begin to learn how to be servant-leaders themselves (increased on-the-job training).

Ultimately, it becomes a capacity issue. If a church wants to be used of God to be more and more of a blessing to others, new people must somehow be welcomed and accommodated. To start with, there must be room for them to get into the meeting! The only long-term biblical solution for this is to begin a new church. Ideally, the new church will have qualified leaders in it, maintain close contact with the founding church, have gifted teachers present, musicians, have folks willing to host the church in their home, be a good mix of young and old, etc. But, that is the ideal. Not all of these are necessary. The main

243

requirement is for some type of mature leadership and oversight to be present, either through an apostle or from the mother church. (It must be emphasized that no one should be pressured, forced or ordered into doing anything regarding where they participate in church. Church government is to be by consensus, not command. There should not be an arbitrary nor contrived nor pressured assignment of who goes where, or when.)

In most well established churches there are usually those who are truly **committed**, those who come out of **convenience** but who don't really believe in following New Testament patterns, those who live nearby and form the **core community**, those who **commute** in from long distances, those who are **celibate** (singles), and also those who function as **coaches** (elders). This mix should be taken into consideration by the leadership when pondering the birthing of a new church out of an existing church.

In sum, a church has several options once its seating capacity is reached:

1. Remain the same and cease to grow numerically. In this scenario, newcomers will eventually be resented and seen as problems. Sensing this, visitors will either not come back a second time or soon leave for a more welcoming fellowship. Surely this is not God's way! The kingdom, like the yeast hidden in the bread dough, is bound to grow and spread. Let us work with God, not against Him.

2. Erect ever bigger buildings to house more people. This is the most commonly chosen option historically, but it violates the New Testament pattern. The problem is that too many people present in a single church begin to hinder the purpose for even having a church meeting in the first place. Size is not necessarily an indication of strength (blubber is not muscle). 1 Corinthians 14 meetings become impossible (which is how worship services got started). The Lord's Supper as a full meal can still be carried out, but it becomes difficult, if not impossible, to speak with everyone during the course of the meal since so many are present. Intimacy is lost, and accountability begins to suffer. Dealing with the various issues that people have grows problematic. The church becomes more like a business than a family.

3. Divide the church somewhat evenly, splitting strengths and weaknesses as evenly as possible, as folks are led by the Spirit (and not coerced).

4. Send out smaller parties (subsets) from the main group to start new works. For example, two thirds stay, one third goes out. The subset forming the new church will have a God-given burden to do so; no arm twisting would ever be in order.

At the end of the day, one must ask, "What is the mind of the Lord on this? What is God's will for our church?" Let's stay tuned to His frequency and see what He has to say!

— Steve Atkerson

Discussion Questions

1. Is it possible for a single gathering to become too large?
2. What are the drawbacks to large or program-centered churches?
3. What should churches do when they grow to the point that they can no longer fit in a typical private home? How many is too big?
4. What cautious proposals did the author offer as to why the New Testament church was so consistently portrayed as gathering in homes?
5. If you could build a house with a living room that could facilitate gatherings of 200 people, would that be an aide to the church? Why?
6. What options did the author give to solving the good problem of having too many people than could squeeze into a living room?
7. What scriptural evidence is there as to the numbers involved in a New Testament house church?
8. Did New Testament churches rotate from house to house, or always meet in the same home? Explain.
9. Why did people resist leaving an existing church to start a new one?
10. What are the indicators that it is time to consider starting a new church?
11. What factors should be taken into considered when studying the planting of a new fellowship?

Note: NTRF offers a teacher's resource to help lead a discussion of New Testament church life. Request *The Practice of The Early Church: A Theological Workbook (Leader's Guide)* from www.NTRF.org.

CHURCH TRADITIONS

It is amazing to realize, though nevertheless a fact, that Jesus' conflict with Israel's religious leaders was *not* over the Mosaic Law. Jesus kept the Old Covenant to the letter. Apart from one attempt to trip Him up using the occasion of a woman caught in adultery, those who sought to do battle against Him did so for other reasons. What made them so angry with Jesus wasn't that He went against anything in the Old Testament Scriptures, but rather that He challenged and went against something called the tradition of the elders.

We read in Mark's Gospel, "Now when the Pharisees and some of the scribes who had come from Jerusalem gathered around him, they noticed that some of his disciples were eating with defiled hands, that is, without washing them. (For the Pharisees, and all the Jews, do not eat unless they thoroughly wash their hands, thus observing the tradition of the elders; and they do not eat anything from the market unless they wash it; and there are also many other traditions that they observe, the washing of cups, pots, and bronze kettles.) So the Pharisees and the scribes asked him, 'Why do your disciples not live according to the tradition of the elders, but eat with defiled hands?'" (Mk 7:1-5). So what, precisely, is going on here? The answer is that whereas in *theory* Israel considered the Old Testament scriptures to be its final authority in matters of both faith and practice, the *reality* was somewhat different. The Jews actually paid far more heed to a system of teaching and practice known as "the tradition of the elders" or "the Oral Law."

Pharisaic Judaism taught that when Moses was on Mount Sinai he was given not one, but two laws by God. The written law, or Mosaic Law, was recorded in the pages of the Old Testament. However, a second, secret law was said to have been passed on purely orally down through the generations. This secret law allegedly only came to public light in the years preceding the time of Jesus. When the inevitable conflict between these two laws and what they taught came about, Israel had to eventually decide which one was their actual final authority. After all, you may claim to have two things equally as your final authority (in this case the Old Testament and the Oral Law), but you can really only have one, and it is that which you obey if contradictions between the two emerge. Incredibly, Israel went with the Oral Law, and relegated the Mosaic Law, and thereby the Old Testament scriptures, to second place. Indeed, the Pharisees taught that it was more punishable to act against the tradition of the elders than the Old Testament scriptures.

What we must understand is that, at the time of Jesus, the nation of Israel lived under the authority of a system of teachings and practices which, in vitally important ways, went against other teachings and practices laid down in the Old Testament. They did this whilst claiming to have been led to do so by God Himself, under the pretext that this Oral Law had supposedly been given to Moses by Him. A system of completely man-made and merely humanly originated teachings and practices had therefore usurped and replaced the revealed truth of the written Word of God, yet under the claim that, even though they contradicted the Old Testament Scriptures, such traditions and teachings had nevertheless come from the Lord God of Israel Himself.

However, if we ask what the Lord God of Israel thought about this (supposedly) inspired Oral Law, then all we have to do is to look at Jesus' responses to it: "He said to them, 'Isaiah prophesied rightly about you hypocrites, as it is written, 'This people honors me with their lips, but their hearts are far from me; in vain do they worship me, teaching human precepts as doctrines.' You abandon the commandment of God and hold to human tradition'" (Mk 7:6-8).

Hypocrisy! That was the Lord's clear and unwavering verdict on such traditions as were causing His people to go against the inspired traditions as revealed in the Word of God. To hold to merely humanly originated practice, whatever it may be, as opposed to biblical practice is, according to the Lord Jesus Christ, to "abandon the commandment of God."

I think you'll agree that this is pretty heavy duty stuff, and I can imagine the kind of responses even now being elicited from my readers: "Amen brother! That's terrible what Israel did!" "Imagine that! Israel going against the Mosaic Law in favor of their own man made teachings and practices and traditions. No wonder God judged them!" "What? Abandoning the commandment of God by holding to merely human tradition? Unthinkable!" *But I have to tell you that, for virtually two millennia, we Christians have been doing exactly the same thing.*

It is incredible beyond words to realize that when it comes to our experience of church life, by which I mean the traditions, or established practice, which the vast majority of Christians unquestioningly follow, virtually all of it is based on a system of practices which, just like Israel's tradition of the elders, has nothing whatsoever to do with the Word of God. Far from being what we see revealed in the pages of the New

Testament, it rather originated from, and was implemented by, men who came on the scene after the Apostles of Jesus were dead and therefore after the writing of the New Testament was completed.

Many church traditions are not just different from what we see in Scripture, in the sense of being merely variations. They are actually the complete opposite of what we see in the New Testament. Far from being mere developments whereby biblical practices are applied in slightly different ways, they are rather practices which are actually at complete variance with what the New Testament teaches. They are practices that cause those adhering to them to go directly against what we see revealed in the Word of God, the very thing Jesus so unwaveringly and blatantly condemned.

I am going to make some simple observations now which no Bible commentator, scholar or historian worth his salt would challenge. They pertain to the way in which churches in New Testament times were set up and organized according to the traditions passed on by the Apostles of Jesus, and as revealed in their writings — the very New Testament itself. I am simply going to describe what it was like when a group of believers met together as a church, as revealed in the pages of Scripture. And let me emphasize this point: revealed so clearly that, as already mentioned, no scholar would challenge it.

Let's go back in time to the midway point of the first century and take a glimpse at what church was like in New Testament times. The immediate thing to say is that, when you went to the coming together of any church, you would have found yourself going to someone's house. Numbers would therefore be small, and you would be part of a small and intimate group of people who knew you, and who you knew, very well. Extended family would be the idea that best summed it up. The general tenor of the gathering would, at all points, have been that of intimate informality. When you thus came together with your brothers and sisters, the following two things would have happened.

First, though this is not meant to imply any set chronological order, there would be a time of sharing together during which all were free to take part as they felt the Lord was leading. From worshipful singing to prayer and intercession. From bringing a teaching, to declaring a prophesy. From sharing a burden to speaking a word of knowledge or wisdom — all would be free to take part. No one led the proceedings from the front. Indeed, being in someone's lounge with everyone sitting face to face around the room, as opposed to being in rows merely looking at the back of someone's neck, there is no front to lead from. All is of a spontaneous, free, unstructured and Spirit-led nature. The atmosphere is that of worshipful, reverent and informal joy.

Then second, everyone present would have eaten a meal together. In fact, you would eat the main meal of the day together. Part of this meal would have been a loaf of bread and a cup of wine that everyone shared in common, this reminding the assembled church that Jesus is the guest of honor and that, though an ordinary shared meal, this was also a very special shared meal: the Lord's Supper and Table. This, the covenant meal of individual believers gathered as a corporate church, would have bound you all together as an extended family of God in whatever area you were located.

There is something else you would most likely notice as well, and it is that any leadership such as existed is a very low-key affair indeed, and far more of a back seat thing rather than anything up front or high profile. Further, it would be seen purely as functional and would not in any way be thought of as being positional with official titles and the like. Moreover, it would also have been plural. Any idea of one man being in charge of a church would have been a completely foreign thought to those gathered. These men would have all originated from that same church. They were home grown guys — indigenous local lads who everyone in the church knew extremely well. As for designation (for there were no official titles) these men were variously called elders, overseers or bishops (depending on which translation of the Bible you read) and pastors or shepherds (again, depending on translation), each being synonymous terms for the same people. Those with various other ministries (apostles, prophets, teachers, etc.) might sometimes pass through in order to help out here and there, and as invited, but they would eventually move on to other places. The only ongoing leadership in the church would have been these local home grown older brothers. They ensured that the format was always that of open and spontaneous free participation, and leading from the front was the last thing they wanted to do for the simple reason that they had been taught by the Apostles that such was not the Lord's will.

That is what church gatherings were like whilst the teachings and traditions of the Apostles, as revealed to us in the pages of the New Testament, held sway. Further, and do please underline this in red ink, I repeat what I wrote earlier: no Bible commentator, scholar or historian worth his salt would question this description in any significant way. I have simply laid out what, as simple matters of fact, is to be seen in the New Testament. Scripture reveals only one prescribed way in which believers were taught to come together as churches and to do things. So how do we do things today when we come together as churches? (In fact, how have believers been doing it for pretty much the whole of church history?) As pointed out earlier, we don't just do things differently, we do things virtually exactly the opposite!

For a start, we meet in large numbers in public buildings. Let me ask: Is that merely a variation on meeting in small numbers in private homes? No, it is the exact opposite!

Second, we have services which are led from the front by (usually) professional paid leaders, which positively ensures that all are not free to partake as the Spirit leads. Tell me, is that merely a variation on an open and completely participatory gathering without leadership from the front and with all free to take part? No, it is the exact opposite!

Third, after the main service (and we have just seen that the New Testament churches didn't have anything that even vaguely resembled worship services) we tack on another one — a ritual with bread and wine. Again I ask, is that merely a variation on having a meal together? No, it's a totally different thing altogether! It is something that would have been completely alien to the Apostles who taught the churches to share a meal together. Indeed, the very Lord's Supper! (The Greek word employed in scripture, *deipnon*, means the main meal of the day towards evening.)

Last, though there are other things I could have included but space doesn't allow, how do we go about conducting leadership? What does it look like in our churches as opposed to the churches back then? Well, we bring in hierarchical and positional leadership from the outside in the shape of an individual with an official title of some kind. That is, we usually go for variations on the theme of having one man at the top — and virtually always a paid professional brought in from the outside as well. Compare that with non-positional, plural, homegrown brothers who aren't professionally salaried, and again I ask: Is that merely a variation of some kind? Is it just tinkering at the edges and moving things round a little? No, it is the complete opposite of the way the church did things as taught by the Apostles of Jesus. Where did they get their ideas from? From the Lord Himself!

We need to be aware too that it is irrelevant as to which church we are talking about here. Whether Catholic or Presbyterian, Anglican or Baptist; whether Pentecostal or Methodist; whether Episcopalian or Free Evangelical, when it comes to church practice all are similarly based on the same traditions and teachings of men who appeared after the canon of scripture was closed, and who taught practices that go against the revealed Word of God. All the aforementioned churches are based in buildings, with religious services and bread and wine rituals, and all likewise practice leadership that flies in the face of what we see revealed in Scripture. In other words, though different from each other in matters of detail, all are nevertheless exactly the same as each other regarding the point of church practice and do the opposite of what Scripture patterns.

The Early Church Fathers (as history has named the men who took on the leadership of the Christian churches in the years and generations after the Apostles died) did much good and were greatly used by God. But in the things we are looking at here they erred badly. I, and many others, are now asking that we reject and renounce the false practices which they introduced (though not the biblically sound things they did and taught), and that we therefore reject too the heritage of the completely unbiblical church life and experience they have subsequently bequeathed to us. As I have already made clear, no one who knows their biblical stuff would challenge my description of New Testament church life and practice in contrast to the way in which the Fathers changed things. However, what I am further maintaining, and here is where the debate is raging, is that they were wrong to teach what they taught concerning church life and practice, and that we have likewise been wrong through the centuries to have continued with it all.

Israel disobeyed the Old Testament at various points because of their beloved, yet totally wrong and unbiblical, tradition of the elders. The Christian Church has done exactly the same thing, only with the tradition of the Early Church Fathers. In England we call that a double-whammy, and it's time we started to put it right. What are we going to go with? The traditions of man? Or the traditions of the Divine? I leave you, dear reader, to decide for yourself!

Addendum – Although this is the last chapter, we wish it weren't! We have posted that which should be the last chapter in the articles section of www.NTRF.org. It's called "Practical Considerations for Starting a House Church" and is the compilation of over twenty years of house church experience.

DISCUSSION QUESTIONS

1. If opposition to Jesus from the religious leaders was not over His obedience to Mosaic law, then why did they oppose Him?
2. What was the tradition of the elders?
3. How did Jesus' response to the Oral Law show what God really thought of it?
4. What is the source of much present day church practice?
5. When does historical church tradition become hurtful rather than helpful?
6. What were the basics of New Testament church practice, as generally agreed upon by scholars?
7. At what points is the typical modern church different in practice from what the early church practiced?
8. Where did the original apostles get their ideas of what church should be like?
9. What ambivalent evaluation did the author express concerning the early church fathers?
10. Since there is no substantial controversy within scholarly circles regarding the practice of the early church, where does the controversy come in?
11. Every true church desires to be biblical in its theology. Why is it important is it to be thoroughly biblical in church practice also?
12. Is your church following the traditions of the early church fathers, or the traditions of the apostles? Explain.

Note: NTRF also offers a teacher's resource to help lead a discussion of New Testament church life. Request *The Practice of The Early Church: A Theological Workbook (Leader's Guide)* from www.NTRF.org.

CONCLUSION

What if you've read this book and are sold on the basics of New Testament church life? Now what? One option is to remain within your present church and seek to reform it gradually toward the traditions of the apostles. Alternatively, if you are gifted in leadership, you might seek your present church's blessing to send you out to start a new church. Work with the existing church, not against it. Since our position regarding adherence to New Testament patterns is so far in the minority, it is not fitting to sharply rebuke the historical church for its neglect of them. It is much like Paul's instruction to Timothy not to harshly rebuke an older man, but rather to appeal to him as a father (1Ti 5:1). Throughout history, God has raised up those who call the church to repentance, obedience, action, or accountability. Many and determined the guardians of the *status quo*. As any past reformer would advise, expect opposition when you take a stand for truth. Be glad and rejoice! Great will be your reward in heaven (Mt 5:12).

To some of those reading this we caution: *Don't try this at home.* Starting a church, even a house church, is a serious matter. It is not something to toy around with. Some people speak of the house church model. The house church is not a model — its the real thing. Many of God's people are not supernaturally gifted in leadership. If this describes you, then our advice is not to try to start a house church alone. You and your family would be far better off to stay where you already are in fellowship. Be a Puritan. Satan would love nothing more than to make you discontent, isolate you off by yourself, and make you ineffective in kingdom service. It is the old divide and conquer scheme (2Co 2:11). Someone involved with a new church plant needs to be father figure, mature in the faith, and with clear leadership inclinations, in order for the church to hold together and succeed in the long term.

If you are inclined to plant a new church, it is important to realize that in order to have any real hope for success in achieving New Testament church life, at least two things are necessary from core church families. First, there must be an absolute, resolute and unshakable love for Jesus that is expressed in an absolute, resolute and unshakable commitment to obey all His commands. God's Word must be held up as the inerrant authority governing all that is said, thought, or done. We must love Jesus enough to bring our churches into compliance with everything Jesus commanded. Second, the core group must possess an undying love for each other. We must love the brethren enough to put up with their faults, shortcomings and shortsightedness. Reformers must be patient, long suffering and understanding of others in the fellowship. Unless there is a total commitment to both the Lord and His people, any church is in serious trouble (see John 14:15, 21-24, 15:9-17).

Many people are driven to consider house church out of sheer desperation. They've tried everything else, or they've been mauled by the system, and so they finally consider the ways of the apostles. We sincerely believe that the ways of the apostles are to be preferred. Yet the reality is that no matter how one structures the church, it still contains people. As Pogo said, "we have met the enemy, and they is us." Recreating the practice of the early church is not an escape from either reality or people. First century believers were far from perfect. Nearly all the letters in the New Testament were written in response to people problems in the early church. Following clear New Testament patterns will, on the one hand, help us avoid many situations that God never intended for His people to deal with. On the other hand, it will put us in a better position to genuinely help people become true disciples.

A word should also be said about expectations. Though house churches are the norm many places in the world, you should not labor under any illusion that it will quickly become popular in the West. Western Christianity is so associated with church buildings that the typical Christian will give about as much consideration to the idea of house church as he would another piece of junk mail in his post office box. From a numerical and percentages point of view, house church simply does not "work" in the West at present. Should the Holy Spirit convict you that adhering to apostolic traditions is what He wants you to do, don't worry about what others do or don't do. You must please the Lord, not anyone else (Jn 6:66-69).

After the Hebrews had been in Babylonian captivity for seventy years, God providentially raised up a pagan ruler who was inclined to grant the Jews freedom to return to their Promised Land. Few, however, found it convenient to return home. Babylon was simply too comfortable and Jerusalem too devastated. Only a minority, led by Nehemiah, Ezra, and Zerubbabel, ventured forth to rebuild that which had been lost. A similar choice is facing you. Will you remain at ease with the indifferent, or will you help reform the church?

— Steve Atkerson
12/20/07

DISCUSSION QUESTIONS

1. If a person is persuaded that it would be honoring to the Lord to follow New Testament church life patterns, but finds himself in a church that does not follow those patterns, what are his options?

2. Why is it not fitting to harshly rebuke an established church for failing to follow the traditions of the apostles?

3. Why should some people not try to start their own house church?

4. To have any real hope for success in experiencing New Testament church life, what two things are necessary from core church families?

5. Why is merely recreating the practice of the early church not a panacea to all our problems?

6. Why is it important to realize that, although you may be excited about house churches, most of your friends probably never will be?

7. What would the Lord Jesus have you to do as a result of having studied the practice of the early church?

Note: NTRF also offers a teacher's resource to help lead a discussion of New Testament church life. Request *The Practice of The Early Church: A Theological Workbook (Leader's Guide)* from www.NTRF.org.

ABOUT *NTRF*

The New Testament Reformation Fellowship is part of a growing body of believers who have come to see the importance of following New Testament church patterns. We have taken to heart the evangelical belief that the Bible is our final authority, not only in matters of faith, but also in matters of practice. We see theological significance in the distinctive traditions of the apostolic church.

Our emphasis on reformation does not reflect a belief on our part that the true church somehow ceased to exist after the time of the apostles. God has always guided and preserved His elect throughout the years. We are deeply indebted to those who have gone before us and thankfully stand on their shoulders. The idea of reformation comes from our desire to reform today's church with New Testament practices (ortho*praxy*), just as New Testament theology (ortho*doxy*) was reaffirmed during the Reformation.

We seek to aid others in recapturing the intimacy, simplicity, accountability and dynamic of the first century church. Our goal is to provide resources and training in how the early church met together in community. We are glad to mail out our materials at no charge to those who can't help us with our expenses. Suggested donation amounts are listed for those who are able to co-labor with us through voluntary giving.

All materials produced by NTRF are consistent with the Doctrines of Grace, New Covenant Theology, the Chicago Statement on Biblical Inerrancy and the Danver's Statement on Biblical Manhood and Womanhood. The essential tenants of the faith to which we subscribe are identical to those found in the doctrinal statements of any sound evangelical institution. One of our favorite statements of faith is the First London Baptist Confession of 1646.

NTRF Publications

• *House Churches: Simple, Strategic, Scriptural* — An introductory book covering most topics related to New Testament church life: the Lord's Supper as an actual meal, participatory meetings, elder-led congregational consensus, home-based churches, the importance of following New Testament patterns, the ministry of elders, full-time workers, integrating church and family, church discipline, giving, etc. (It replaces both *Toward A House Church Theology* and *Ekklesia: To The Roots of Biblical House Church Life*, now out of print).

• *Radio Talk Show Broadcast: House Churches* — A recording of a radio call-in talk show about New Testament styled house churches. Great for introducing other believers to New Testament church life!

• *Searching for the New Testament Church* — A six session audio series that is both practical and theological in dealing with the main issues of New Testament church life (apostolic tradition, church government, church meetings, the Lord's Supper, house churches, etc.). A good resource for listening to while driving.

• *The Practice of The Early Church: A Theological Workbook* — A learner's workbook that will guide you to and through every major topic in the New Testament about church life. Covered are such issues as apostolic tradition, the Lord's Supper, interactive meetings, consensus governing, church discipline, home fellowships, women in ministry, baptism, the Lord's Day, elders, apostles, and giving. It is arranged in a Socratic (questioning) format.

• *The Practice of The Early Church: Leader's Guide* — A in-depth teacher's resource for use in conjunction with the learner's workbook (above). The Leader's Guide is designed to help someone lead a series of interactive discussions on what the Bible says about our Lord's church using the Workbook (above). The Leader's Guide contains Greek word studies, historical data, illustrations, the answers to the harder Workbook questions, suggested applications and other information for effectively leading a group study.

• *Equipping Manual* — A one year study course designed to help equip believers for effective service. It covers Christian basics: how to study the Bible, salvation, evangelism, the origin and authority of the Scriptures, the "big picture" of the Bible, how to teach interactively, etc. Designed for use by teachers in a group setting, it is not really suited for self-study.

• *House Church Weekend Workshops* — NTRF teams are available to conduct weekend workshops on God's design for His church. For more information, contact us through the web site www.NTRF.org.

• *Searching For Church, DVD* — Is a church without a building really a church? Join professional filmmaker Gary T. Smith as he travels from America to Europe, across Europe to the edge of Asia, and back to America in search of an answer to the question, What makes up a New Testament type of church? His journey (through both time and place) leads to discoveries that might surprise you. From ancient Israel to modern day America, you'll see and hear how the church got started, how it changed from its simple beginnings, and you'll find out what's happening to help it return to a simpler form of meeting.

• *The Lord's Supper: Rehearsal For the Marriage Banquet of the Lamb, DVD* — In China, the Lord's Supper is called the Holy Meal. The early church celebrated the Lord's Supper as an actual meal, a time of edifying fellowship, centered around one loaf and cup. This DVD presents the biblical basis for centering our church meetings around the Lord's Supper as a sacred, covenant feast. Run time: 94 minutes. Bonus: CD with PDF files of articles on the Lord's Supper, how to teach the material to others, helpful hints for hosting the Holy Meal, and an audio presentation on the Supper.

Many of our resources can be downloaded directly off the internet.

www.NTRF.org

Who doesn't like to receive a free gift? We have two gifts to tell
you about. The first is a copy of the book you are holding in your hand,
Ekklesia. If you have neither the means nor inclination to help us offset
our expenses in distributing this book, we are glad to send you your own
copy for free, *gratis*, no charge. Just write or e-mail us. Our interest is in
seeing the advance of God's kingdom, not in selling books! Of course if
you are able to assist us in the area of giving, it would be greatly appreciated and would help us to continue our ministry.

The second gift we would like to tell you about is of infinitely greater
worth that any free book offer. Yet it is from a book that we first learned
of this gift ourselves. The Bible is God's Word to believers. The focus of
the Bible is the person and work of God's Son, Jesus Christ. It is in the
Bible that we discover the free gift of God: "eternal life in Christ Jesus"
(Romans 6:23).

THE GOOD NEWS

In John 5:39 Jesus said, "The Scriptures bear witness of Me." Here,
He was referring to the Old Testament, Genesis through Malachi. When
Moses wrote the first five books of the Old Testament (Genesis—
Deuteronomy), Jesus noted, "He wrote about Me" (John 5:46). After
His resurrection, Jesus met two of His disciples and encouraged them
by saying, "All the things which are written about Me in the Law of
Moses and the Prophets and the Psalms must be fulfilled." When you
read the Old Testament, look for promises about Jesus Christ: He is the
Seed who crushes Satan's head; He is the Lamb of God; He is the
Prophet we must listen to; He is the Priest who offers Himself up to
God; He is the King who rules His people.

In the New Testament, the Gospel has come and commands us to
believe in Christ, the One God promised in the Old Testament and sent in
the fullness of time. What is the Gospel? The Gospel is the "Good News"
that through belief in the death, burial and resurrection of Christ we can
have forgiveness of sin and eternal life (1 Corinthians 15:3-4).

But why did Jesus have to come into this world? He came because
of our sin problem — we do things that displease God. But why are we
sinful? Because the first people God created, Adam and Eve, fell into sin

(they disobeyed God's revealed will), and as a result we are born as sinners, and experience the wages of our sin: death and eternal condemnation (Genesis 3:1-19; Romans 5:12; 3:23; John 3:18).

Because of our sinfulness, we are alienated from God. He is holy (without sin) and cannot allow wickedness in His presence. But Jesus was a very special person. He was both God and man. Because he was God, He never once sinned. He always pleased His heavenly Father, and gave His life as payment for His people's sin. Being both God and man, He could mediate between a holy God and a sinful people (1 Timothy 2:5). His shed blood provided an atonement (covering) so that sinners could be forgiven and justified. The third day after His crucifixion, Jesus was glorified and exalted forever when His Father raised Him from the dead. For forty days, He appeared alive to many witnesses and then ascended to heaven to take His place at the right hand of the Father where He is now ruling and reigning over His kingdom and making intercession for His people (Acts 1:9; Romans 8:34). Those who die in faith will be resurrected to everlasting life when Jesus returns in the fullness of His glory at the end of the present age. They will be joined by believers who are still alive and together will receive the kingdom promised to them. All who have not obeyed the gospel's call for repentance and belief in his name — whether dead or alive when He returns — will stand before His righteous court to be condemned to everlasting punishment. (2 Thessalonians 1:8-10).

After His resurrection, Jesus said that repentance from sin and forgiveness of sin must be proclaimed to all nations (Luke 24:47). When people look to Jesus by faith for the forgiveness of sins, they must also repent of their sins. Repentance means that a person has godly sorrow for his or her sins and turns from evil in order to practice righteousness (2 Corinthians 7:1). Paul captured this gospel truth when he noted of the Thessalonian believers, "You turned to God from idols to serve a living and true God, and to wait for His Son from heaven" (1 Thessalonians 1:9-10).

All who stop trusting in their works — in anything they do — to be right with God, and look by faith to Jesus Christ as their substitute are accepted by God. God no longer sees the sins of those who believe in Christ, but sees the perfect life and work of His Son (Romans 3:21; 5:18-19). The New Testament calls this "justification" — God accepting sinful people on the basis of Christ's finished work (Romans 4:1-8). In Luke 18, Jesus told the story of a tax-collector who was convicted of his sinfulness. He did not compare himself to others. He knew his best efforts could not satisfy God's righteous demands. Instead, he beat upon his breast and cried, "God be merciful to me, the sinner." Jesus said, "I tell you, this man went back to his home justified" (Luke 18:14).

In order to stand before God we must be holy. Since we are very unholy in His sight, we must look outside of ourselves to Jesus, Who alone is holy and perfect. We will all stand before God's judgment some day. We will either stand there in our sins and be condemned, or stand before Him clothed in the righteousness (perfection) of Christ.

All of us tend to think that God will accept us into His presence because of something we do. Perhaps we think that if our good deeds outweigh our bad deeds, He will accept us on Judgment Day. But it is only what Jesus did that God accepts. God only accepts people who are "in Christ." We can only come to God through His Son. Have you ceased from your own works and rested your soul in the work of Christ? Are you trusting in Christ's life, death, burial and resurrection as the only acceptable means to your salvation? May the Holy Spirit bring you to cry out, as did the tax-collector, "God be merciful to me the sinner, through your Son, Jesus Christ!"

BAPTISM

After His resurrection, Jesus said, "All authority has been given to Me in heaven and on earth. Go therefore and make disciples of all the nations, baptizing them in the name of the Father and the Son and the Holy Spirit, teaching them to observe all that I have commanded you; and lo, I am with you always, even to the end of the age" (Matthew 28:19-20).

If you have faith in Jesus for salvation, you have become His disciple. Jesus has commanded that His disciples be baptized with water. It was promised that after Jesus' resurrection, He would "baptize with the Holy Spirit" (Matthew 3:11). On the Day of Pentecost, the exalted Jesus poured out the Holy Spirit upon His people (Acts. 2:33). That day about 3,000 people believed in Jesus, and those who received the word of the Gospel were baptized with water (Acts 2:41).

When the Gospel extended beyond the Jews to the Gentile nations, "the gift of the Holy Spirit was poured out" upon them also, and Peter said, "Surely no one can refuse the water for these to be baptized who have received the Holy Spirit just like we did" (Acts 10:45, 47).

"Since we have a great high priest over the house of God, let us draw near with a sincere heart in full assurance of faith, having our hearts sprinkled clean from an evil conscience and our bodies washed with pure water" (Hebrews 10:21-22). If you are a believer now, you could be baptized by the person who first shared Jesus with you, or by someone in the group of believers with whom you are fellowshipping.

FOLLOWING JESUS CHRIST

Jesus said to all who had come to Him for salvation, "Take up your cross and follow Me" (Matthew 16:24). The apostle Paul asserted that Christ died so that all His people should no longer live for themselves, but for Him who died for them (2 Corinthians 5:15). If you have indeed come to Christ for salvation from your sins, you will desire to live a life that pleases Him and not yourself. Because He loved you first, you will love Him and love his people fervently and keep his commandments (1 John 4:7-11, 19-20).

Special thanks to Jon Zens for this explanation of forgiveness. It is taken from Salvation in Christ: A Handbook for Discipleship.

— *Editor*

ADDENDUM

HELPFUL HINTS FOR HOSTING THE LORD'S SUPPER

Although we may understand scripture and desire to practice hospitality, the idea of having 30 or so folks, many of whom are children, in our home for a full meal can be quite overwhelming! *Where do* they all eat? *How* do I set up the food for service? *What* do we have? *Who* fixes what? The questions just go on.

This little lagniappe chapter is neither ecclesiological nor theological in nature. It's a practical look at how to "do" the Lord's Supper, the fellowship meal that either opens or culminates our time as believers in the home church. It is written mainly to the women for, as we know, the burden of the details of the meal falls on us. These ideas are merely suggestions, answers to questions we encounter often, based on our own experiences. Each fellowship must work out the details as they go.

Hopefully these words will be helpful as you think through the logistics of implementing this wonderful time of encouragement in the easiest way for the host family and those participating. This article is a compilation of 15 years of my own experience home churching with many talented and creative hostesses. To them I dedicate this article.

Hosting the body for the meeting and the fellowship meal is a privilege. What a perfect opportunity to practice hospitality, a commandment in God's word. Peter writes: "Be hospitable to one another without complaint. "(I Peter 4:9). Paul exhorts in Romans 12: 10-13: "Be devoted to one another in brotherly love . . . contributing to the needs of the saints, practicing hospitality."

Hospitality is a command. Many women practice it with great ease and comfort, always willing to share. Those who are not as talented in this regard have to learn to be hospitable. As co-laborers in this fellowship meal, those who love hospitality must never condemn or criticize the one who is learning but instead, as an "older woman" in that field, come alongside and encourage. Philippians 2: 3-4 exhorts, "Do nothing out of selfish ambition or vain conceit, but in humility consider others better than yourselves. Each of you should look not only to your own interests, but also to the interests of others."

What Do We Eat?

First of all, the host family *does not* provide the entire meal. It's a joint effort between all families involved. Some churches decide on a menu from week to week and each cook knows what every other cook is bringing. This idea might be particularly helpful to insure a balanced meal if the group is small. Some groups prefer potluck or as we say "pot providence." Others plan theme meals such as Italian, Mexican, southern, breakfast, new recipe day, etc. Have fun with it; but however you plan it, each one should bring enough to feed her entire family as well as another.

The Lord's Supper is a feast of good and bountiful food with fellowship centered around Christ, a picture of the marriage banquet of the Lamb. It is a time to give and share liberally with our brothers and sisters in Christ. If you were having one more family over for dinner with your family, how much of one dish would you prepare? If church were canceled for some reason, could you satisfy your own family with what you prepared to take to the Lord's Supper? Most of our ladies bring a main dish and a side of either a vegetable, salad or fruit. Desserts in our group are considered to be optional and are brought as a third dish but never as the only dish by a family. We encourage the singles, especially the men who might not be so inclined to cook, to bring drinks, peanuts, cookies, chips and dip, or a prepared deli item such as potato salad or rotisserie chicken.

An example of a recent potluck meal provided by seven families in attendance was: pork roast, chicken and rice casserole, ground beef casserole, meatballs, tuna noodle casserole, two large salads, butter beans, green beans, squash, potato salad, fruit salad, and three desserts, water and tea. When serving time comes, our fellowship arranges the food and drink buffet style either on the kitchen counter top, dining room table or folding table.

How Do We bring It?

Confusion is minimized at the time of serving if your dish is ready when you arrive. Cook it before you come. Consider investing in a Pyrex Portables insulated hot/cold carrier that will keep your food at the temperature at which it was prepared. Many of the ladies in our fellowship have bought hot plates that can be plugged in to keep their dishes warm. Others bring crock pots. The oven can be put on "warm" and dishes stored there. Wool blankets or beach towels work well for hot/cold insulation during transport; and, of course, coolers in the summer months are great for icing down that cold dish.

The main point to remember for food safety is to keep hot foods hot at 150 degrees and cold foods cold at 40 degrees. Once the food is out for serving, it should sit out no longer than 2-3 hours before it is refrigerated. Dispose of any food left out longer than four hours.

WHAT SHOULD THE HOSTS DO TO BE READY?

The kitchen should be clean and tidy ready to receive dishes with plenty of counter top room and space in the refrigerator, serving utensils and an empty dishwasher. Everyone will be much more willing to help with preparation and, more importantly, cleanup, if they do not have to deal with your last night's or morning's dishes in the sink or dishwasher. If the oven is to be available for keeping hot foods at a safe temperature, then the hostess must also have her dish cooked by the time the guests arrive. A large empty trash can should be ready and in a convenient location. Rag towels and paper towels are a must for an occasional spill. Aluminum foil and plastic wrap should be on hand for help with after meal storage and transport home.

The host family in our church provides the one cup and one loaf. Some ladies bake their own bread; some use unleavened bread; and some buy uncut deli loaves. The one cup is either grape juice or wine. The host family also furnishes cups, plates, napkins and utensils. Each hostess decides if these items are to be disposable or to be washed and put away for use again. Some of our ladies throw everything away; some save the cups and utensils. Some use plastic washable plates. My neighbor uses stainless silverware she has collected from garage sales.

I have an odd assortment of mugs I put out for coffee and since each one is different, my guests know their mug from others sitting around. Other families use styrofoam cups. And by the way, brew the coffee *before* the guests start arriving. Ice can be stored in a cooler or ice bucket.

WHAT ABOUT THE REST OF THE HOUSE?

Your house does not need to be spotless, but neat and tidy does help. Remember, the church has gathered for the purpose of fellowship, not to see how well you cleaned. However, a few places do need a little extra attention.

Wipe down the bathrooms and check the toilet paper supply. We use paper towels for hands to cut down on germ spreading. If you do prefer bath linens, make sure plenty of clean ones are out. Check the soap dispenser for plenty of soap. Start the day with empty trash cans.

What About The Children And The Meal?

Sometimes, even though as much as we love them, the children can cause stress on the host family, especially if they do not have children or if there are many small children at the meeting. Parents, consider walking through the line helping your children prepare plates. Little ones often have eyes bigger than their stomachs and much food can go to waste. Many of us prefer to buy smaller than 12 or 16 ounce cups. Most folks tend to fill their cups full, often not drinking it all. Smaller cup makes less waste. It is better to go back for refills than to throw away unwanted drink.

A word about hygiene might be appropriate — there can *never* be enough hand washing among friends! Be sensitive to germs. All folks going through the serving line should wash before touching all those serving utensils. Several ladies in our group put out a pump jar of hand sanitizer right by the plates at the beginning of the line.

Parents, make sure you understand the expectations of the hostess. Some women are more particular than others, but in her home do as she does. I do not allow my own family to eat on the furniture, so I ask the kids to eat at special tables or on blankets laid out on the floor. I usually throw old bedspreads over my sofa and chairs as the rate for accidents and spills is much greater when everyone cannot sit around a table. If the carpet is a concern, have everyone remove their shoes and spread plastic tablecloths on the floor for the kids. If the weather permits, optional outside eating areas can be fun. Let everyone know if any parts of the house are off limits. If the bedrooms, upstairs, basement, etc., are not "open to the public", say so. Again, each hostess has different peculiarities (or maybe none at all)—teach your family what to do.

How Can I Be A Good Guest?

Being a good guest and member of the body also means letting the host family know if you are not coming. This courtesy helps the family in their preparation as far as putting out the right number of chairs and it helps all the families in the amount of food to prepare. If half the body is out a particular Sunday for various reasons, it affects how much other food needs or doesn't need to be brought.

If you are scheduled to host church and something comes up so that you can't, don't just announce, "Sorry guys, we can't do church this Sunday," dumping it into their laps to figure out. Love the body by taking the responsibility of finding another family with whom to swap and then let everyone else know about the changes.

The Lord's Supper is a great time of fellowship and a wonderful opportunity to practice the biblical command of hospitality. Share the experience of hosting among the families. As much fun as hosting can be, it is also nice to visit someone else's home. Just as the meeting is designed to be participatory, so should the hosting of the fellowship meal. Our body rotates regularly through the members as we draw up a two month calendar of the rotation. We swap around if our Sunday falls on a date that we cannot host.

There are circumstances that sometimes make it difficult for a family to host, such as health issues, size of home, limited parking, new baby, living too far from the rest of the church. In that case, share with a hosting family by contributing plastic and paper goods, occasionally bring the one loaf and one cup and making special efforts to help with clean up. We have one family that does not host due to the long commute to their home. This family gives generously of their food by bringing large roasts, big lasagnas, etc.

One house church sister in Washington State observed that, as a good guest, you can help watch for things that are falling through the cracks. Examples include individuals that look left out, coffee that needs refilling, trash that needs emptying, a spill that needs wiping, and children running where they should be walking and may need a friendly reminder. Even if it isn't your home, to help serve would really be a blessing to the hostess who has to keep everything under control.

The fellowship meal does wonders in cementing your church together. Hosting will even strengthen the bond as you learn to serve the body and commit yourself to it. There are many more wonderful ideas about hospitality waiting to be shared among you ladies. May the Lord richly bless your times together.

— Sandra Atkerson

Special thanks to Arietta Watson, my friend, neighbor and fellow church hostess, for the following checklist to use in preparation for hosting church.

Lord's Supper Items
· one loaf
· one cup
· coffee
· coffee cups
· creamer
· sugar
· coffee spoons
· sugar spoons
· drink cups
· utensils
· serving utensils
· napkins
· plates
· ice
· water

Bathroom Items
· toilet paper
· paper towels
· clean hand towels
· soap dispenser
· clean sink and counter
· clean toilet
· empty trash can

Other Items
· chairs
· table
· sweep entrances

Kitchen Items
· ice bucket or cooler
· paper towels
· dish soap
· hand soap
· hot plate
· refrigerator space
· dirty fork tray
· trash can with bag
· cloths or towels for spills
· aluminum foil
· plastic wrap
· empty dishwasher

Romans

1 Corinthians

MacArthur, John, 108
Macedonia, 168
maranatha, 38
Martin, R.P, 32, 38
martyr(s), 37
Martyr, Justin, 107
Mary Magdalene, 175
Mathison, Keith, 137
McGavran, Donald, 101, 103
McReynolds, Paul, 79
mega churches, 23, 118
Melchizedek, 185
Melvin, Tim, 219, 258
Methodist, 16, 202, 251
Miller, Hal, 144
Milikin, J, 55
mimatai, 17
ministers, see church leaders
missionaries, 88, 102, 145, 152-153, 159, 168, 170, 183, 187
misthos, 153-155, 160
Mormons, 200
Moscow, 146
Moses, 19, 33, 39, 147, 151-152, 154, 186, 247-248, 265
mosque, 102
music, 40, 53, 60, 65, 74, 103, 117, 165
musicians, 49, 56, 61, 243
Muslims, 102
Nadab, 39
Nee, Watchman, 20, 130, 145, 202
New Zealand, 50
Nicea, 140
Nicene Creed, 140, 193
Noah, 36, 37
oikodomé, 52
Oliver, Gerald, 99
Onesiphorus, 179
opsonion, 155
organization, 11, 17

orphans, 102, 107-108
orphanages, 183
orthodoxy, 76
overseers, see pastors
Packer, J.I, 99
paradosis, 18-19, 21
parliament, 80
parents, 23, 31, 42, 49, 61, 65, 68, 72, 79, 115-120, 122, 170, 176, 215, 217, 220-221, 224-225, 272
parousia, 37
participatory meetings, 11-22, 23, 41, 50-55, 57-60, 62-68, 75, 87, 93, 96-97, 121, 123, 131, 133-134, 137, 143, 194, 195-196, 203, 206, 226-230, 232, 234, 237, 250-251, 273
Passover feast, 31-33, 35, 42, 46, 99, 199
lamb, 32
pastor(s), 23, 27, 55, 57, 62, 71, 78, 87, 96, 101-103, 105, 108, 112, 119, 121, 123, 137, 142-145, 147, 150-151, 153, 155-159, 164, 172, 185, 187, 192, 202, 225, 250
patér, 171
patria, 171
Paul, 16-21, 35, 51-52, 55, 74, 105, 108, 130, 132-134, 145-146, 151-153, 155, 158-160, 168-169, 173-174, 176-179, 184, 192, 200, 216, 218-219, 226-227, 230, 236, 255, 266
peitho, 79
Pelikan, J., 36
Pentecost, 198-199, 226, 267
Pentecostal, 16, 43, 58, 194, 251
persecution, 83-84, 93, 104
Peter, 38, 75, 143, 157, 160, 175-176, 216, 267

Notes